"Written with tremendous conviction and power . . . Grossman means for us to see that the occupier and the occupied are brutalized alike by their unresolved quarrel. His theme is the despair of the defeated and the uneasy sleep of those who must police them."   —David Lehman, *Newsweek*

"His report opens our eyes . . . He shows that on both sides of the conflict there are thoughtful, sensitive, intelligent human beings. And he puts us readers directly in touch with them."
     —Christopher Lehmann-Haupt, *The New York Times*

"If there is one word for Grossman's faith, it is humanism. This word is in some dispute today; it is rare and awesome to come across the real thing."
     —Marshall Berman, *The Nation*

"*The Yellow Wind* is a novel contribution to the literature of the Israeli-Arab dispute because it navigates between the icebergs of political solutions, myth, and guilt, choosing to skate on the thin cover of experience. Grossman records the voices, images, and impressions flowing beneath the ice. . . . [He] is a filter, a prism, not only a camera or a tape recorder."
     —David Twersky, *The Partisan Review*

"[Grossman] saw what seems to me the essential point—that the story of the occupation is a story of honor and humiliation."
     —Avishai Margalit, *The New York Review of Books*

"Grossman has written a great and terrible book . . . brilliant and eloquent."
     —Michelle Bisson, *Seattle Post-Intelligencer*

"A portrait of a situation far more complex than the simplistic stereotypes fed us by government officials and the media—a portrait of an occupying force at once brutal and considerate, of a Palestinian people as much at odds with itself as with its enemy, and of intransigence and generosity of spirit on both sides."
     —Richard Caplan, *The Cleveland Plain Dealer*

"A penetrating, poignant, and highly personal report on life and animosity on the West Bank . . . A stunning account."
     —Peter I. Rose, *The Christian Science Monitor*

"Grossman's writing has the resonance of good poetry and the acuity of good journalism."   —Diane Winston, *Dallas Times Herald*

The Yellow Wind

By David Grossman

Novels

The Smile of the Lamb
See Under: LOVE
The Book of Intimate Grammar
The Zigzag Kid

Non-fiction

The Yellow Wind
Sleeping on a Wire

David Grossman

The Yellow Wind

Translated from the Hebrew

by Haim Watzman

Picador

Farrar, Straus and Giroux

New York

www.picadorusa.com

Picador® is a U.S. registered trademark and is used by Farrar, Straus and Giroux under license from Pan Books Limited.

For information on Picador USA Reading Group Guides, as well as ordering, please contact the Trade Marketing department at St. Martin's Press.
Phone: 1-800-221-7945 extension 763
Fax: 212-677-7456
E-mail: trademarketing@stmartins.com

Portions of this book first appeared in *The New Yorker* in a slightly different form.

Grateful acknowledgment is made to Harcourt Brace Jovanovich, Inc., and the Estate of the late Sonia Brownell Orwell and Secker and Warburg Limited for permission to reprint sections of "Shooting an Elephant" from *Shooting an Elephant and Other Essays* by George Orwell, copyright 1950 by Sonia Brownell Orwell; renewed 1978 by Sonia Pitt-Rivers.

Library of Congress Cataloging-in-Publication Data

Grossman, David.
　　[Zeman ha-tsahov. English]
　　The Yellow wind / David Grossman ; translated from the Hebrew by Haim Watzman.
　　　　p. cm.
　　ISBN 0-312-42098-6
　　1. West Bank—Description and travel. 2. Arab-Israeli conflict—1973–1993. 3. Grossman, David—Journeys—West Bank. I. Title.

DS110.W47 G7613 2002
956.95'3—dc21   2002067325

First published in the United States by Farrar, Straus and Giroux

D 30 29 28 27 26 25 24 23 22 21 20

Contents

Introduction

So many things have happened since *The Yellow Wind* was written, and so little has changed. There was the Intifada, the Madrid Peace Conference, Baruch Goldstein's massacre in Hebron, the Oslo process, the mutual recognition of the Palestinians and the Israelis, the handshake between Rabin and Arafat, the establishment of the Palestinian Authority, and the return of Arafat and his people to the occupied territories. Then there was Rabin's assassination, and the string of suicide attacks by the Islamic fundamentalist organizations, especially the one called Hamas, which brought the right in Israel back into power. There were the bloody events following the opening of the Western Wall tunnel, the Israeli army's evacuation of Hebron, the construction at Har Homa, and the slowdown of the peace process almost to a standstill.

So much has happened, and so little. Israel has withdrawn its army from most of the territories in which Palestinians live, and today only a small portion of the Palestinian population continues to be ruled by the occupying forces. Yet the occupation is still tangible and present in the life of every Palestinian. Almost anytime a Palestinian travels from one village to another, he or she must pass through an Israeli roadblock. Israel sets the water allowance of every Palestinian village, town, and city, blocking and renewing the flow at its own discretion. It also controls the import and export of merchandise to and from the territories. It grants, or withholds, as its own needs dictate, permits to work in Israel, which allow hundreds of thousands of Palestinians to eke out their livings. Israel continues to prevent Palestinians from building themselves homes, and when they do so, illegally, Israel destroys them (according to data from the B'tzelem civil rights organization, Israel has, in the last ten years, demolished more than 1,800 houses built without permits, leaving more than ten thousand Palestinians homeless). All this while Israel's own settlements, including those built illegally, expand through the construction of thousands of homes without permits, which are then retroactively legalized.

It would serve no purpose to enumerate all the points of friction. They are only symptoms of the main problem. After the brief, all too brief, interlude we all gained in the wake of that handshake at the White House, goodwill, mutual trust, and hope have faded. Miraculously, Israelis and Palestinians were finally given the chance to begin living normal lives. But, instead of looking to the great opportunity that lay before them, the opportunity to overcome the obstacles imposed by their natures and the fears their histories have etched in them, they have been all too quick to revert to the behavior of the past.

Arafat, returned from Tunis, had a hard time giving up his use of terror as a weapon in the political struggle. Hamas launched a series of murderous attacks on the streets of Tel Aviv and Jerusalem. These attacks caused many Israelis who had believed for a moment that there was a chance for peace to retreat into their old suspicions and fears, and into the despairing acceptance of the view that "the sword shall devour forever." Yitzhak Rabin, who guided the Oslo process, was murdered by a right-wing religious zealot, and Binyamin Netanyahu, who campaigned against the agreement and against the negotiations with Arafat, was elected prime minister.

It is hard to decipher Mr. Netanyahu's intentions, but by his deeds it would seem that he is trying to create a (surrealistic) situation in which Israel will rule the occupied territories while remaining deliberately unaware of the people who are being occupied. He declares that he will never establish a Palestinian state and grasps at every Palestinian violation of the terms of the Oslo agreements in order to delay and halt their implementation. He vigorously develops Israeli settlements, paves "Arab-evading" roads, tunnels, and bridges that pass under and over Palestinian settlements, and ensures that any Palestinian entity established in the future will be segmented by a crisscross of Israeli roads and roadblocks, and that an Israeli settlement will overlook every Arab one. It is hard to see how such a situation can promise tranquillity or security for either side.

At about the time of the signing of the Oslo agreement, a group of Israelis and Palestinians, mostly professionals—doctors, lawyers, psychologists, writers, and so on—began to organize. They attempted to create a new type of relations, relations deliberately not based on political agreement, in the hope that as these links multiplied, a connection would be forged between the peoples that would reduce stereotypes and fears, and foster what is most important in relations between peoples—personal ties.

For three years I particpated in such a group of Israeli and Palestinian writers. The first meeting was like a volcano of conflicting emotions—excitement, animosity, resentment, joy in what was shared, indignation at what was different, despair occasioned by deep misunderstandings. Waves of heat and cold swept over us; it was very important for each side that the other immediately recognize its isolation, its suffering, provide some sort of profound confirmation that it understood.

Only after a long time did we really begin to speak with one another, and listen, to stop being "representatives" of our peoples and be human beings, parents of children, women and men who were artists, whose dearest and most intimate inner spaces had been degraded by the occupation.

We held dozens of meetings, built personal and family friendships. The Israelis did all they could to relieve the distress of the occupation for their friends. The Palestinians incurred great risks in maintaining their contacts with the Israelis, in the face of hostile Palestinian public opinion.

I will never forget how, after one of the bus bombings in Jerusalem, one of my Palestinian friends called and offered to donate blood to the wounded. "It's the least I can do," he said.

But the years went by and the meetings grew fewer, whether because long periods of curfew and siege prevented the Palestinians from coming, or because of ever-growing despair, and we felt that anything we might do in our tiny group could hardly be of any consequence in the face of the waves of violence and hatred. Today, most of the members of the group are active advocates of peace among their own peoples, but our meetings no longer take place.

Precisely because the Israelis and the Palestinians were so close to beginning to realize some possibility of life together, today's reality seems like a fulfillment of the curse placed on both peoples—the curse of self-destruction, the curse of the fear of peace. Once again, it shows how much we, Palestinians and Israelis, are enslaved by the proficiencies we have been forced to develop in hundreds of years of conflict—our proficiency for war and our overly developed talent for enmity.

The heart cringes at the thought that we are doomed to endure another round of blood, worse than its predecessor, so we understand there is no choice other than the way of peace, the way we have barely tried. In the coming years—whether negotiations continue and reach the point of decision on the most charged issues, including the question of Jerusalem, or whether the process comes to a halt—the most fanatical, primal, cruel forces in each nation are likely to break loose.

This book attempts to depict those forces, as well as others that will determine our fate. So much has hap-

pened since it was written, but really so little. I dedicate
it to those who remember, still, what is really worth
fighting for; to those who know that today the real enemy is not the Palestinian or the Israeli but the extremist
and the fanatic on either side.

David Grossman

April 1998

The Yellow Wind

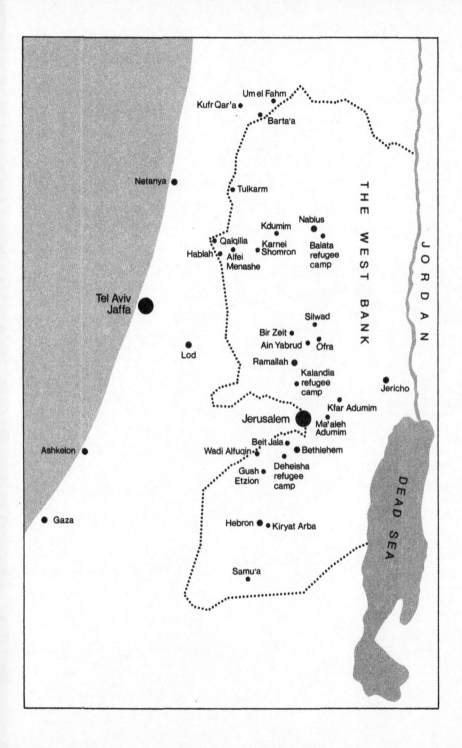

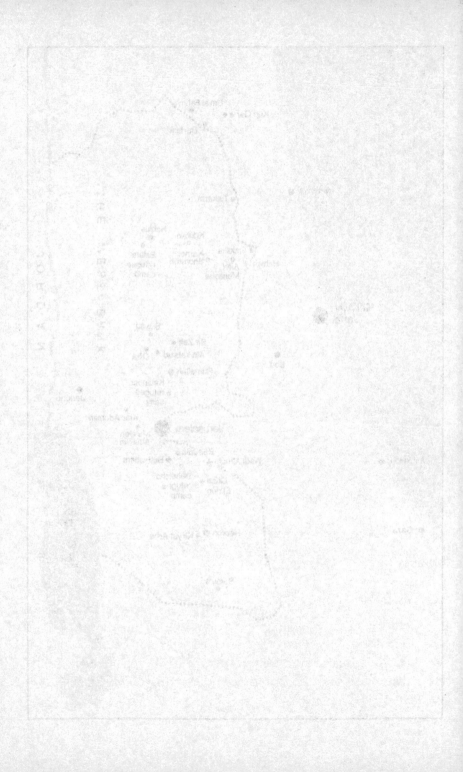

1

A Man Is Like
a Stalk of Wheat

On a day of turbid rain, at the end of March, I turn off the main road leading from my house in Jerusalem to Hebron, and enter the Deheisha refugee camp. Twelve thousand Palestinians live here in one of the highest population densities in the world; the houses are piled together, and the house of every extended family branches out in ugly cement growths, rooms and niches, rusty iron beams spread throughout as sinews, jutting like disconnected fingers.

In Deheisha, drinking water comes from wells. The only running water is the rainwater and sewage flowing down the paths between the houses. I soon give up picking my way between the puddles; there is something ridiculous—almost unfair—about preserving such refinement here, in the face of a few drops of filth.

Beside each house—a yard. They are small, fenced in with corrugated aluminum, and very clean. A large *jara* filled with springwater and covered with cloth stands in each yard. But every person here will tell you without hesitation that the water from the spring of his home village was sweeter. "In Ain Azrab"—she sighs (her name is Hadija, and she is very old)—"our water was so clear and healthy that a dying man once immersed himself, drank a few mouthfuls, and washed—and was healed on the spot." She cocks her head, drills me with an examining gaze, and mocks: "So, what do you think of that?"

I discover—with some bafflement, I admit—that she reminds me of my grandmother and her stories about Poland, from which she was expelled. About the river, about the fruit there. Time has marked both their faces with the same lines, of wisdom and irony, of great skepticism toward all people, both relatives and strangers.

"We had a field there. A vineyard. Now see what a flowering garden we have here," and she waves her brown, wrinkled hand over the tiny yard.

"But we made a garden," murmurs her daughter-in-law, a woman of wild, gypsy, unquiet beauty. "We made a garden in tin cans." She nods toward the top of the cinder-block fence, where several pickle cans bring forth red geraniums, in odd abundance, as if drawing their life from some far source of fruitfulness, of creation.

A strange life. Double and split. Everyone I spoke to in the camp is trained—almost from birth—to live this double life: they sit here, very much here, because deprivation imposes sobriety with cruel force, but they are also there. That is—among us. In the villages, in the cities. I ask a five-year-old boy where he is from, and he immediately answers, "Jaffa," which is today part of Tel Aviv. "Have you ever seen Jaffa?" "No, but my grandfather saw it." His father, apparently, was born here, but his grandfather came from Jaffa. "And is it beautiful, Jaffa?" "Yes. It has orchards and vineyards and the sea."

And farther down, where the path slopes, I meet a young girl sitting on a cement wall, reading an illustrated magazine. Where are you from? She is from Lod, not far from Ben-Gurion International Airport, forty years ago an Arab town. She is sixteen. She tells me, giggling, of the beauty of Lod. Of its houses, which were big as palaces. "And in every room a hand-painted carpet. And the land was wonderful, and the sky was always blue."

I remembered the wistful lines of Yehuda Halevy, "The taste of your sand—more pleasant to my mouth than honey," and Bialik, who sang to the land which "the spring eternally adorns," how wonderfully separation beautifies the beloved, and how strange it is, in the barrenness of the gray cement of Deheisha, to hear sentences so full of lyric beauty, words spoken in a language more exalted than the everyday, poetic but of established routine, like a prayer or an oath: "And the tomatoes there were red and big, and everything came to us from the earth, and the earth gave us and gave us more."

"Have you visited there, Lod?" "Of course not." "Aren't you curious to see it now?" "Only when we return."

This is how the others answer me also. The Palestinians, as is well known, are making use of the ancient Jewish strategy of exile and have removed themselves from history. They close their eyes against harsh reality, and stubbornly clamping down their eyelids, they fabricate their Promised Land. "Next year in Jerusalem," said the Jews in Latvia and in Cracow and in San'a, and the meaning was that they were not willing to compromise. Because they had no hope for any real change. He who has nothing to lose can demand everything; and until his Jerusalem becomes real, he will do nothing to bring it closer. And here also, again and again, that absolute demand: everything. Nablus and Hebron and Jaffa and Jerusalem. And in the meantime—nothing. In the meantime, abandoned physically and spiritually. In the meantime, a dream and a void.

It's all bolitics, the Palestinians say. Even those who can pronounce the "p" in "politics" will say "bolitics," as a sign of defiance, in which there is a sort of self-mocking; "bolitics," which means that whole game being played over our heads, kept out of our hands, crushing us for decades under all the occupations, sucking out of us life and the power to act, turning us into dust, it's all bolitics, the Turks and the British, and the son-of-a-whore Hussein who killed and slaughtered us without mercy, and now all of a sudden he makes himself out to be the protector of the Palestinians, and these Israelis, who are willing to bring down a government because of two terrorists they killed in a bus, and with the considered cruelty of an impeccably meticulous jurist they change our laws, one thousand two hundred new laws they issued, and deprive us of our land and of our tradition and of our honor, and construct for us here some kind of great enlightened prison, when all they really want is for us to escape from it, and then they won't let us return to it ever—and in their proud cunning, which we are completely unable to understand, they bind their strings to us, and we dance for them like marionettes.

"It's all bolitics," laughs the ironic woman, who reminds me slightly of my grandmother, and slightly of the cunning, old, loud Italian from *Catch-22*, the one who explains to proud American Nately why America will lose the war in the end, and poor Italy will not win, but survive. "The strongest weapon the Arabs in the occupied territories can deploy against us," a wise man once said, "is not to change." And it is true—when you walk through the Deheisha camp you feel as if that conception has internalized itself unconsciously here, seeped its way into the hearts of the people and become power, defiance: we will not change, we will not try to improve our lives. We will remain before you like a curse cast in cement.

She suddenly remembers: "There, in the village, in Ain Azrab, we baked bread over a straw fire. Not here. Because here we don't have livestock, and none of their leavings." She falls silent and hugs herself. Her forehead wrinkles repeatedly in a spasm of wonder. The brown, wrinkled fingers go, unconsciously, through the motions of kneading.

Everything happens elsewhere. Not now. In another place. In a splendid past or a longed-for future. The thing most present here is absence. Somehow one senses that people here have turned themselves voluntarily into doubles of the real people who once were, in another place. Into people who hold in their hands only one real asset: the ability to wait.

And I, as a Jew, can understand that well.

"When a person is exiled from his land," a Jewish-American author once said to the Palestinian writer from Ramallah, Raj'a Shehade, "he begins to think of it in symbols, like a person who needs pornography. And we, the Jews, have also become expert pornographers, and our longings for this land are woven of endless symbols." The author was speaking of the Jews of hundreds of years ago, but on the day I went to Deheisha the Knesset was storming in fierce debate over the symbolism of the name "Judea and Samaria," and Knesset member Geula Cohen demanded that this remain the only legal designation, and that the terms "West Bank" and "territories" in all their permutations not be used. "Judea and Samaria" really sounds more significant and symbolical, and there are many among us for whom the phrase activates a pleasant historical reflex, a sort of satisfying shiver reaching into the depths of the past, there spreading ripples of longing for other sleeping phrases as well— the Bashan, the Gilad, the Horan, all parts of the ancient Greater Israel and today parts of Syria and Jordan.

About half a million Palestinian refugees live today in the Gaza Strip. In the West Bank there are about 400,000. (We are speaking here only of refugees, and not of the entire Arab population under Israeli rule.) In Jordan there are about 850,000. In Lebanon, some 250,000. Syria also has about 250,000. A total of about two and a quarter million refugees. Even if the problem of the refugees living under Israeli rule is solved, the bitterness of their more than a million brothers in the Arab countries, living in no less appalling conditions, will remain. This is why the feeling of despair is so deep among all those who know this problem well. This is why the refugees allow themselves to become addicted to their dreams.

Raj'a Shehade, writer and lawyer, admits that he, too, was a pornographer of views in his youth. Of the view of Jaffa and the coastal plain, about which he has heard stories and legends. When he hikes today over the hills next to Ramallah, it happens that he forgets himself for a minute and he can enjoy the contact with the earth, smell the thyme, gaze upon an olive tree—and then he understands that he is looking at an olive tree, and before his eyes the tree transmutes, and becomes a symbol, the symbol of struggle, of loss, "and at that very same moment the tree is stolen from me," says Shehade, "and in its place is a void, filling up with pain and anger."

The void. The absence, which for decades has been filling with hatred.

A.N., whom I met another time, in Nablus, told me: "Of course I hate you. Maybe at the beginning I didn't hate and only feared. Afterwards, I began to hate." A.N., thirty years old, is a resident of the Balata refugee camp. He spent ten years of his life in jail (the Ashkelon and Nafha prisons) after being found guilty of belonging to the Popular Front for the Liberation of Palestine. ("I didn't actually take part in operations. They only taught me to shoot.") "Before I went to jail, I didn't even know I was a Palestinian. There they taught me who I am. Now I have opinions. Don't believe the ones who tell you that the Palestinians don't really hate you. Understand: the average Palestinian is not the fascist and hating type, but you and the life under your occupation push him into hatred. Look at me, for example. You took ten years of my life from me. You exiled my father in '68. He hadn't done anything. He wasn't even a PLO supporter. Maybe even the opposite. But you wanted to kick out anyone who had an opinion about anything. So that we would be here completely without leaders. Even without leaders who were a little bit for you. And my mother—for six years you did not allow her to go to visit him. And I—after prison, you don't let me build a house, or leave here to visit Jordan, nothing. And you constantly repeat: See what progress we have brought you. You forget that in twenty years everything has progressed. The whole world strides forward. True, you helped us a little, but you aren't willing to give us the most important thing. True, we progressed a little, but look how much you progressed during that time. We remained way behind, and if you check it out, maybe you'll see that we are even worse off in a relative sense than we were in '67." (The standard of living may be measured by personal consumption per capita and GNP per capita. I checked the facts with Dr. Meron Benvenisti, author of *The West Bank Data Project*. In his study, private consumption per capita in the West Bank is estimated at about 30 percent of that of Israel; GNP per capita in the West Bank is four times smaller than in Israel.)

"Then," the young man from Balata continued, restrained in his expression but transmitting cold, tight-lipped anger, "then you say under the Jordanians it was bad for you. Maybe so. But the Jordanians took only our national identity from us, and you took everything. National identity, and the identity of every one of us who fears you and depends on you for his livelihood, you took everything. You made us into living dead. And me, what remains for me? Only the hatred of you and thoughts of *siyassah* [politics]. That's another evil you brought upon us, that you made every man here, even the most ordinary fellah, into a politician."

I drink tea with three women in Deheisha. One hears the most penetrating things from the women. The men are more afraid of imprisonment and intimidation. It is the women who march at the head of the demonstrations, it is the women who shout, who scream out the bitterness in their hearts before the television cameras. Brown women, with sharp features, women bearing suffering. Hadijah is seventy-five years old, her mind sharp and her narrow body healthy. *"Allah yikhalik,"* I say to her, may God be with you, and she laughs to herself, a thin chuckle of bare gums, and says: "What is it to him?" and explains to me that a man is like a stalk of wheat: when he turns yellow, he bends.

She has lived in this house, a standard refugee house, for forty years. The United Nations Welfare and Relief Agency (UNWRA) built it, and the UN symbol can still be found on the walls and doors. At the head of each refugee camp in the West Bank and Gaza Strip stands an UNWRA-appointed director. He serves as middleman between the agency and the residents. He is himself a former refugee and lives in the camp. He has the authority to distribute food and welfare payments, to grant the right to live in the camp, and to recommend students for university admissions.

The house consists of two small rooms and does not have running water. The electricity is usually out. Today it is raining outside, and the house is almost completely dark. Hadijah and her elderly sister sit on a straw mat and examine the medicines the camp doctor has prescribed for the sister. She suffers from asthma. The teachers and doctors who work in the refugee camps come, in general, from outside, from the nearby cities. The simplest jobs, cleaning and sanitation and construction, are filled by the camp residents. In the house in which I now sit live five people. In the room in which we drink our tea there is one cabinet, a suitcase on top. Half open. As if waiting to move on. A few wooden chairs made by an untrained hand, a few shelves holding vegetables.

The young woman, tense, offers oranges and a paring knife. Another item of furniture found in every house here is the dowry chest of the woman of the house, made from the soft trunk of the Judas tree. Here she keeps her dowry, the bedsheets, the wedding dress, and perhaps some childish luxury, a toy, a pretty handkerchief—after all, she was no more than a girl when she was married.

"And if someone were to offer you today a dunam [one-quarter acre, the standard measure of land in countries once under Turkish rule] of land in a nice place, with light, in the open air?"

Yes, yes—she laughs—of course, but only on my own land. There.

She also declaims this, like the politicians, like those purveyors of her fate over all these years. She, at least, has the right to do so. I try to remember how many times Palestinian leaders missed opportunities to gain themselves a homeland: there was the partition proposal of '36 and the second proposal of '47, and maybe there were other chances. They—in their blindness—rejected them all. We drink silently. The men are at work. On the wall, two nails. They serve as a wardrobe. On one hangs the black 'igal (headband) of a kaffiyeh.

Whoever has served in the army in the "territories" knows how such rooms look from the inside during the night. Whoever has taken part in searches, in imposing curfews, in capturing a suspect at night, remembers. The violent entry into rooms like this one, where several people sleep, crowded, in unaired stench, three or four together under scratchy wool blankets, wearing their work clothes still in their sleep, as if ready at any moment to get up and go wherever they are told. They wake in confusion, squinting from the flashlight, children wail, sometimes a couple is making love, soldiers surround the house, some of them—shoes full of mud after tramping through the paths of the camp—walking over the sleep-warm blankets, some pounding on the tin roof above.

The old woman follows, it seems, my gaze to the bare cement walls, the heating lamp, the wool blankets rolled up on the floor. Suddenly she boils over: "Do we look like gypsies, do we? Miserable, are we? Ha? We are people of culture!" Her sister, the sick woman, nods rapidly, her sharp chin stabbing her sunken chest: "Yes, yes, people of culture!" They fall silent, wheezing. The young woman, of the wild, exotic presence, wants to say something and is silent. Her hand literally clamps her mouth closed. Within the arabesque filigree of manners and considered delicacy, of conversation and the protection of hospitality, the wires suddenly go taut. I am confused. The young woman tries to make amends. Change the subject. Is her mother-in-law willing to tell this Israeli here about, for instance, her childhood in Ain Azrab? No. Is she willing to recall the days when she worked the land? No, no. Salt on a wound. Would you be willing, *ya mama*, to sing the songs the fellahin, the winegrowers, the shepherds sang then? No. She only tightens her cracked lips stubbornly, her balding head shaking, but again, out of the conquering power of absence, her left foot begins to tap to a far-off rhythm, and her body moves silently forward and back, and as she traps my cautious gaze, she slaps her thigh with a trembling hand, and her nose reddens with rage: "Culture! You people don't know that we have culture! You can't understand this culture. It's not a culture of television!"

Suddenly she is completely emptied of her anger: once again her face takes on an expression of defeat, of knowing all, the ancient signs written on the faces of the old: "The world is hard, hard . . ." She nods her head in bitter sorrow, her eyes close themselves off from the small, dark room: "You can't understand. You can't understand anything. Ask, maybe, your grandmother to tell you."

2

I Want to

Shoot Jews

Again in Deheisha. It is a quiet day today. No demonstrations. No stone throwing. The army can be seen only from afar, riding along the road. A week later there would be riots and demonstrations and rocks would fly, and around Deheisha would rise a six-meter fence, to prevent stones from being thrown on every passing car. Deheisha would become invisible as far as the travelers along the road were concerned, and the fence would become, it seems, a new Palestinian symbol. The rainwater and the sewage still flow in rivulets along the paths. A man lays a heavy stone on a tin roof to prevent the wind from blowing it away. A group of young men build another room onto a house. They are building everywhere here. With determination and without any plan. "Why is Thekla's construction taking such a long time?" Marco Polo asked the hardworking builders in Italo Calvino's book *Invisible Cities*, and they answered him—without pausing for a moment from lifting pails and moving their long brushes up and down: "So that its destruction cannot begin." Do you fear that the minute you take down the scaffolding the city will begin to crumble and fall to pieces? And the residents of the invisible city answered hastily, in a whisper: "Not only the city."

The owner of the little grocery store is surprised at my entry, and rises in concern. The merchandise is scanty and old. For the most part it consists of cigarettes, soft drinks, and cans of pineapple displaying suntanned young women covered with dust. Why bother describing it? We are all acquainted with a store just like it. The store-owner's friend, Abu Hana, checks first to see if I am not from the *mukhabarat*, the intelligence service, and afterwards says that he will speak of anything except bolitics, since bolitics is a science in which it is very difficult to discover anything new, no?

Yes, it would seem.

It is better to remain silent, he says. Then he finds that he cannot hold back, and sounds a hurried whisper: "Napoleon, Bismarck, Hitler," he says. "None of them lasted. They were too strong. It's best to sit quietly and wait."

Wait for what?

I don't know. I'm no genius. What do I know?

And he smiles me a calculated, distancing smile.

I look him over. An Arab dressed in a kaffiyeh and enveloped in a neutral, purposeful expression, against the background of a strongly lined face, engraved by a harsh hand. The bank clerk who told me a week ago, in the voice of one making me party to a secret, "I most hate working on the tenth of the month, when all the *arabushim* get their pay," was thinking, no doubt, of this *arabush*. Or maybe she meant the other *arabushim*, who also wear a mask of ignorance and apathy, to the point that the mask has seeped into their skins.

And on the slope of the hill in Deheisha, I passed a group of small children racing upward. *Rowda*. An Arab kindergarten. Two teachers (Don't give our names, but you can quote) and thirty-five children from two to five years old. The Deheisha kindergarten.

I want to expand a little on this subject: the small children, nameless, with running noses, the ones we see along the roads, playing by the passing cars. These are the children who in '67 sold us figs for a *grush* and washed our parents' cars for ten *grush*. And afterwards they grew up a little and became the *shbab*, you know, the ones with the look of hate in their eyes, rioting in the streets and throwing stones at our soldiers, tying a lasso to the crown of a cypress tree, bending it to the ground, attaching a Palestinian flag to it, and freeing the tree—and you, the soldier, go cut down the moon; and afterwards they grew a little more, and from among them came the ones who make the Molotov cocktails and the bombs. They are the same children from '67. Nothing has changed in the refugee camps, and their future is etched on their faces like an ancient, fossilized record.

For now, they are little children in kindergarten. One group shouts and cheers, and after making a conscious effort—necessary, perhaps, for all strangers and for Jews and Israelis in particular—I begin to differentiate their faces, their voices, their smiles, their characters, and slowly also their beauty and delicacy, and this is not easy. It requires an investment of energy on my part, since I also have trained myself to look at Arabs with that same blurred vision which makes it easier for me (only for me?) to deal with their chiding, accusing, threatening presence, and during this month of encounters with them I must do exactly the opposite, enter the vortex of my greatest fear and repulsion, direct my gaze at the invisible Arabs, face this forgotten reality, and see how—as in the process of developing a picture—it emerges before me slowly, slowly from the emulsion in the darkroom of my fears and my sublimations.

The teachers? They giggle, they blush, they consult each other: yes. They would be happy to take me to see their kindergarten. We stride upward between the boulders and the puddles. In every direction, someone is busy building. Renovating. Painting. The families are large, and more and more must be built. "Where is the plan you are following, the blueprint?" Italo Calvino's Marco Polo asked the citizens of Thekla, and received no answer until night fell and the star-filled heavens were spread above. "There is the blueprint," they answered him.

And on the roof of one of those houses sits a boy, twelve years old perhaps, head shaved and eyes closed, and he plays devotedly on a comb wrapped in paper. Fiddler on the roof.

Between two buildings sits a cement structure, plastered white on the outside. Closed with an iron door on which is the UNWRA emblem. It looks like a public bomb shelter from the fifties. The young teacher opens the iron door, filled with holes, and I enter the Deheisha kindergarten.

First, one has to get used to the dimness. There is no electricity in the kindergarten. I stand in a long, narrow space, divided into two rooms. There is not one picture on the grayish walls; because of the dampness, the wall crumbles if you try to pound a nail into it. In the corner of the room, a metal table and two chairs. And one other piece of furniture: a thin reed mat.

The teacher tells the children to sit, and they do so, crowding onto the mat. They chatter with each other, as children do, until the teacher tells them to be quiet. From that moment on, they are totally silent, not making a sound during the entire conversation. In an Israeli kindergarten the children are unable to remain quiet for a single minute. They jump up from their places, run to the teacher, say what they have to say, argue. They are free children, and you can understand what this blessed, natural freedom is only when you see its opposite. "The children here are so quiet and disciplined," I said to the kindergarten teacher in Deheisha, and she answered with an Arabic proverb: "The gosling floats like the gander"—like father, like son.

"Where are you from?"

"From Zakaria. A village."

"Were you born there?"

She laughs. Really. Even her mother has no memories from there. Mother was five years old when they fled. It is Grandmother who preserves the family tradition. Grandmother, married at the age of seven to a twenty-year-old man. This is what happened: the Turkish Army was at the gates of the country, and the Arabs feared that the Turkish soldiers would take the girls. So they betrothed them while they were still in diapers. Grandfather himself went out to the Great War, and when he returned once on furlough his little wife called him a bad name. He became angry with her, lifted her up in his hands, and threw her far away. That's how little she was!

And the giggly kindergarten teacher bends over with laughter as she tells the story. Today that grandmother has four sons and a daughter in Deheisha. She has survived the Turks, the British, the Jordanians, and the Israelis—four occupations.

She is attractive, the ruddy-cheeked teacher, and looks the way our high-school girls once looked. That anarchist enthusiasm of youth. She is sharp and excitable, and is not afraid to say what is on her mind. She was born in Deheisha, and she supposes she will spend her whole life here. She is engaged to a young man from the camp. How do they enjoy themselves? There isn't much to do here, she answers, we go to friends, to relatives. Even after the wedding, the couple has no place to be alone.

"Where will you build your house?"

"In the camp, over my parents' house."

"And you don't want to leave here for a better place?"

"Only for my homeland. Even if they offer me a palace. Our parents made a mistake when they left their homes. We won't make that mistake."

"And you don't dream sometimes, only dream, that you might live in a better place?"

"Dreams?" She laughs. "I have a responsibility," she says, "to the suffering my parents endured, and to my own suffering."

"And because of responsibility to suffering you won't try to achieve even limited possible happiness?"

"I can't. I don't want to."

"And who will help you return to your village—Arafat?"

"Arafat? Arafat is bourgeois. He drives a Mercedes. He doesn't feel the suffering of the refugees. All the Fatah commanders have houses in Syria and the Gulf states. Arafat has no supporters here. Only we can represent ourselves."

"And if Arafat achieves a political settlement? There is talk now of an international conference, you know."

"Understand. We are against Arafat, because Arafat wants peace. We want a solution by force. What was taken by force will be returned by force. Only thus."

Only thus. I remember the similarity between the symbol of the Irgun and that of the PLO: here a fist grasping a rifle against a map of the land of Israel, and there two fists, holding rifles, against the very same map.

The young and enthusiastic kindergarten teacher was neither the first nor the last person I met during these weeks who voluntarily turned himself into an object, a play toy in the hands of those dealers in life and death, into an impersonal symbol. Into a collective noun. When I stand before such people, I have no idea where to begin unraveling this web of iron.

"And the children, what about them?" I ask.

"The children here know everything," she says, and her friend nods. "Some of the children here are the fourth generation in the camp. On any night the army may enter their house, right into the house, conduct a search, shout, turn over the blankets and slash at them with their bayonets, strip their fathers—here, Naji here—"

Naji is two and a half years old, short for his age, black eyes, curls.

"A month ago they took his father, and he doesn't know where he is, or if he will ever return."

"A little while ago," says the second teacher, somewhat heavy, blue-eyed, and delicately made up, always on the edge of a giggle or a blush, "a little while ago the military governor visited the kindergarten and asked if I teach the children bad things, against Israel and the Jews."

"And what did you say to him?"

"I said that I don't. But that his soldiers do."

"What do you mean?"

"What do I mean? I'll explain. When a child goes for a walk outside and sees a tree, he knows that the tree bears fruit and leaves, right? When he sees a soldier, he knows very well what that soldier does. Do you understand?"

"What do soldiers do?" I ask a girl of about four, called Naima, green-eyed, little gold earrings in her ears.

"Searches and beatings."

"Do you know who the Jews are?"

"The army."

"Are there other Jews?"

"No."

"What does your father do?"

"Sick."

"And your mother?"

"She works in Jerusalem for the Jews. Cleans their houses."

So she answers me, the new little Palestinian problem.

"And you"—a chubby boy, somewhat dreamy— "do you know who the Jews are?"

"Yes. They took my sister."

"Where to?"

"To Farah."

(Both his sisters are there, in jail, the teachers explain.)

"What did your sisters do?"

"They did *not* throw stones," he says angrily.

Suddenly a little boy gets up, holding a short yellow plastic stick in his hand, and shoots me.

"Why are you shooting me?"

He runs to the teacher, peeks at me from behind her arm, and laughs. He is two years old.

"Who do you want to shoot?" the teachers ask, smiling, like two mothers taking pride in a smart child.

"Jews."

Their lips make out the answer with him.

"Now tell him why," they encourage the little one.

"Because the Jews took my uncle," he says. "At night they came in and stole him from the bed, so now I sleep with my mother all the time."

"Is this the answer, to bring up another generation and another in hatred? To teach them that this hatred justifies the refusal to work toward a solution? Couldn't you try, maybe, another way?"

"There is no other way," they answer, both of them, each in her own way, in a whisper or with self-assurance, but the same words.

I stand and listen and try to be neutral. To understand. Not to judge. And also not to be like an American or French correspondent, completely severed from the whole complex of events, and quick to pass judgment. But I also stand here as a reserve soldier in the Israeli Army, and as a human being, rising up against this education in blind hatred, and against such tremendous energy being expended for the preservation of malice, instead of being spent in an effort to get out of this barrenness, this ugliness in which this kindergarten lies, these little children who are so good at hating me.

A boy raises his hand. Needs to make peepee. I accompany him. The bathroom is only a little niche separated from the room by a curtain. In its center, a hole in the ground and a porcelain platter. Little piles of excrement all over, and the urinating boy steps in some. I remember the textbooks full of hate and anti-Israel propaganda found by Israeli soldiers twenty years ago, after the war, in the schools and kindergartens. Those books were confiscated, but their content is now transmitted orally. The oral law. It doesn't matter at all who is really guilty of the refugee camps—we, the Israelis, will pay the price. We, and not the Arab countries or the world. It is us they will hate, these children living their whole lives in a colorless world without happiness, who spend long summer and winter hours in a cold and mildewed kindergarten, which has neither a glass window nor electricity. With the all-pervading stink rising from the "bathroom" a grotesque symbol of their situation.

"What games do you play here?"

"Games like everywhere," says the younger teacher. "Tag. Hide-and-seek. There are toys, too."

Two small cardboard boxes hold the kindergarten's toys: old, faded toys. Someone's donation. Not one toy is whole. None of the cars has wheels. Dolls have missing limbs. There is no mercy.

They also have songs, the kindergarten children in Deheisha. The teachers stand them in a line. "What do we sing when the army goes by? One, two, three, four!" And the children break out in song:

"We went out into the street/We waved the flags/We sang for our country the nicest of songs/a song of freedom and unity/a song of victory through struggle/Bloom, my land/By throwing stones and burning tires we will free the motherland . . ."

I recall the Jewish children who sang patriotic songs

when British soldiers passed by. They must also have felt like heroes when they did. It is always the same play, only the players change, and sometimes the roles. It requires a lot of strength to change roles, adapt, learn new lines, inure yourself to the complex significance of the new part.

"And jokes about us," I ask them, as if I am not at all part of the joke, "do you tell jokes about us?"

They think for a minute, astounded that there aren't any. There really aren't. No jokes at all? No slang expression, twenty years old, to describe the border guards, the Shin Bet (the secret security service), the military governor?

We, says the smiling teacher, laugh mostly at ourselves.

Strange that they have no jokes about us. In other places I received the same answer. Really, they asked themselves, how is it that there aren't any jokes? It would be interesting to examine what they do with all that aggression and hatred of us. Who is their Sholem Aleichem? Is it that they unconsciously avoid seeking an outlet in humor? Do they prefer to preserve their hatred and humility unworked, raw, and wild?

"I don't tell the children bad things about Israel," the heavy one says, and adjusts her sweater, "but I tell them stories, stories about animals," she hints.

Like fables.

". . . like, for example, there were small sparrows on a terebinth tree, playing and having a good time, and suddenly came a cruel black raven who coveted their tree and expelled them from it. They were very sad. They almost died of sorrow, until they got up and gathered together, and flew against him as a great and united group, and so were able to expel him from their tree."

"You made it up?"

"Yes. I have a few stories like that. The children already understand."

"And did they succeed in organizing themselves together, the birds?"

"Yes. They are very wise. They're birds, not Palestinians."

Toward evening I travel to Jerusalem. The roads are lined with rusty cars. Metal ruins, tires stuck on barbed-wire fences, old hot-water tanks, discarded doors, walls dirtied with half-erased graffiti, old shoes . . . everything left bare and harsh along the road, everything preserved, awakening pent-up melancholy: all this abandoned, like a rebellion and cry against a destroyed, corrupt, irreparable circumstance.

At six in the evening I arrive at the Ben Yehuda mall in downtown Jerusalem to buy *Dear Brothers*, a book about the Jewish underground by one of its members, Haggai Segel. The evening is gray and misty, and the people are burdened with their civilian matters, isolated so much from the hate and the danger, as I walked among them like the bearer of evil tidings among the unaware. In the thin fog and with the light of the yellow streetlamps it is possible to succumb to illusions and see behind every person a halo, a sort of double peeking out for a split second, the identical twin of this man, his double from Nablus, and that young woman, whose unknown twin I met this morning at Deheisha, that same walk and same smile and same quiet sensuality, and for every child there was a double, and none of them knew, and none of them guessed a thing.

3

What the Arabs Dream

W hat do the Arabs dream about? And what do Jewish children dream about? Is it possible to hope that the dreams of the Jews and the Arabs provide some sort of escape and easing and refinement of the harsh and cruel reality of life—or are dreams only a direct continuation of it?

And why should the mirror mold of dreams not create some sort of closeness, a dialogue unknown to its participants, anti-grammar, unexpectedly creating a new language?

It will not happen.

Dr. Yoram Bilu, a lecturer in psychology at the Hebrew University of Jerusalem, examined with the help of his students, Yussuf Nashef and Tehila Blumenthal, the dreams of eleven-to-thirteen-year-old children in different parts of Israel and the West Bank. Part of his study concerned the children of the Kalandia refugee camp, and the children of Gush Etzion and Kiryat Arba, Jewish settlements in the West Bank.

Every child who took part in the study received a

colored notebook and was asked to record four dreams immediately upon wakening. The age of the subjects was fixed so that they would be old enough to write down their dreams but not old enough to be bothered by sexual dreams.

And one other important comment: the children in the refugee camp did not know that the study was for the Hebrew University. The notebooks were given to them through UNWRA and afterwards were carefully translated. What dreams do they dream?

Seventeen percent of the dreams of the Jewish children dealt with meetings with Arabs. (To the attention of those who wish at any price to prevent such meetings. And by the way: does the law recently passed by the Knesset making it illegal for Israelis to meet with PLO members include dream meetings? Check.) In contrast, 30 percent of the children in the Kalandia refugee camp dreamed during the brief period of the study at least one dream involving some sort of meeting with a Jew. The meaning of this, according to Dr. Bilu, is that the children in the Kalandia camp "are obsessively involved with the conflict."

But whom exactly do Jews and Arabs meet on moonless nights?

Among 328 dreams of meetings (Jews and Arabs) there is not one character identified by name. There is not a single figure defined by a personal, individual appearance. All the descriptions, without exception, are completely stereotyped; the characters defined only by their ethnic identification (Jew, Arab, Zionist, etc.) or by value-laden terms with negative connotations (the terrorists, the oppressors, etc.). The Arabs do not try to refine their stereotyped characters. The Jews make some

sort of effort—in general, the word "Arab" is associated
for them with the word "criminal." "I lived in an Arab
city, full of criminals," wrote an eleven-year-old from
Kiryat Arba. "I entered the grocery store and two men,
an Arab and a gangster, attacked me there," dreamed
another boy from the same town. "We have to educate
the Arabs, so that they will be good, law-abiding citizens," declared another young citizen from among the
Jewish settlers in Hebron. "I taught them to write in
Hebrew, until they became good people, and then they
freed them from the jail, and they didn't make any more
problems."

The Arabs often find escape in apocalyptic dreams, in
which the final, decisive battle is held, and the Arab
armies, dressed in shining white, are ranged against the
Jewish heretics, wrapped in black. The battle is always
won by the good guys.

Jewish children also have trouble facing the constant
struggle, offering no escape, and they find release in
imagination and transference: Kiryat Arba children told,
for example, of a colored flying saucer which landed on
the border between Israel and "the land of the enemy";
of soldiers from Uganda who attacked a Jewish child,
and a twelve-year-old went the farthest when he dreamed
that he was walking, minding his own business, in the
heart of Hebron and was cruelly attacked from the back,
"and I turned around and managed to see that it was a
Chinese boy . . ."

The majority of the interactions in the dreams are
violent and aggressive and end in death. The dreams of
the children of the Kalandia refugee camp indicate a
hard, and threatening reality, a fragile world with no
defense. The typical "plot" of such a dream is played

out in the camp: the boundaries of the dreamer's house
are very permeable, nothing provides him with defense
and security, strange people invade the house and attack
the child. Frequently, they torture him to death. His
parents are unable to protect him. One dream in particular caught my eye: "The Zionist Army surrounds
our house and breaks in. My big brother is taken to
prison and is tortured there. The soldiers continue to
search the house. They throw everything around, but do
not find the person they want [the dreamer himself].
They leave the house, but return, helped by a treacherous
neighbor. This time they find me and my relatives, after
we had all hidden in the closet in fright."

The Holocaust appears in many dreams of the Kiryat
Arba children. An eleven-year-old girl writes: "My friend
and I decided to go to Jericho. Suddenly we heard someone calling us from behind. They were my parents. They
said that I have to take off the yellow star I was wearing.
The star is a large yellow piece of paper, showing that
we support the partisans. The city, Jericho, was against
the partisans. But it turned out that my friend and I had
taken off the star too late, because suddenly someone
came, took us to a grove of trees, and ordered us to
crawl on the ground along with many other people.
Crawling, we reached a tunnel, but only my father was
allowed to enter, and my mother and I had to continue
to the place for the women. Suddenly I saw something
move: it was an old woman starting out of her grave.
Her face was covered with earth."

Guilt feelings appear only among the Jewish children.
So, for instance, in the dream of a twelve-year-old girl
from Kiryat Arba: ". . . suddenly someone grabs me,
and I see that it is happening in my house, but my family

went away, and Arab children are walking through our rooms, and their father holds me, he has a kaffiyeh and his face is cruel, and I am not surprised that it is happening, that these Arabs now live in my house. I accept that as if that is the way it is supposed to be."

It is a long and detailed study, but it seems to me that these few examples are sufficient. The dreams offer neither escape nor relief. There are no moments of pity and no friendly contact. Some of them are nightmares, difficult to read, and more difficult to realize the price being paid by our children and the Arab children for living in this conflict. This conflict, from which there is no escape even in dreams.

The writer J. M. Coetzee, who also lives in a cruel land, complex to the point of being almost insoluble, recently received the Jerusalem Prize; in his speech he recalled the philosopher Nietzsche, who said: "We have art so that we shall not die of reality." "In South Africa," Coetzee said, "there is now too much truth for the art to hold. Truth that overwhelms and swamps every act of the imagination."

Among us, even dreams are crushed under the weight of reality.

One fact is particularly interesting, concerning what does *not* appear in this study: among some thousand dreams of Jewish and Arab children, there is not one which indicates a longing for peace.

4

Don't Pity Them
Too Much

"Let me put it this way," said Jabo at the end of the evening in Ofra. "We conducted a debate here, and we think you lost. But you've got the stronger hand, because you can write it any way you want."

Given the challenge and the heavy responsibility which Jabo placed in my hands, I mean to write cautiously, step by step, and perhaps in doing so I can return the challenge to the people of Ofra, so that they may face up to the implications of what they told me.

For the stranger, the wary, the visitor from afar, Ofra surprises. On Friday afternoon it is soft and green, accessible and unfenced, and its people are welcoming, warm, and unassuming. Quickly, so quickly, the wary stranger is also seduced by the ethereal sense of festivity that permeates the Sabbath here, and in wonder he discovers in himself a tender desire to be absorbed in it in his entirety, to let down his guard, to become worthy of this welcome, of this nostalgic flickering of the candle flame awaiting him at the end of the rough road between the villages of Ain Yabrud and Silwad.

I did not want to make a short visit to Ofra. I wanted an extended one, a weekend, to see the people of this place at all hours of the day, unguarded. With their children. On a typical street I looked for the home of the family which would host me, and found it between, on the one side, the houses of Yehuda Etzion and Yitzhak Novick, and on the other, of Haggai Segel, all members of the terrorist Jewish underground, arrested three years ago. Its members were convicted variously of booby-trapping the cars of the mayors of four West Bank cities, of killing two students and wounding several others in an attack on the Islamic college in Hebron, of planting bombs in Arab buses, and of conspiring to blow up the Dome of the Rock, the Moslem shrine which sits on the site of the ancient Jewish Temple. I stayed, with my family, in the home of Menahem and Na'ama Granit and their four children, warm and pleasant people. The people of Gush Emunim, of the settlements, are used to hosting wary strangers like myself. "We never know when we will get a phone call announcing that tomorrow five or six guests are coming for a meal, for an entire day, for Shabbat," related Ayala Resis-Tal. "Welcome. We're used to it." Gush Emunim, currently somewhat moribund because of the lack of widespread new settlement activity; also as a result of the exposure of the Jewish underground and the sharp internal debates which that event brought on, puts much effort into disseminating its ideas, bringing people closer to its values, and bringing its interests into the public eye. Its publicity machine is well oiled, to the point where you almost don't notice you are being "sold" something, and only afterwards realize that the people here do not listen much, do not display a real interest in you, and that two- and three-hour heart-to-heart conversations revolve, in the end, exclusively around them and their lives. This, perhaps, is the first warning sign of the price they pay.

As for the debate:

To begin with, I did not intend to debate at all, and I don't see that evening—in the book-lined study of Rav Yoel Ben-Nun—as a debate. Furthermore, at the end of twenty years it seems to me that all the arguments, both rational and emotional, have already been made. Only on extremely rare occasions do we hear a crushing new argument, one which requires you to reevaluate your opinions, and in Israel the reality is that it is easier for a man to change his religion, and maybe even his sex, than to change in any decisive way his political opinions. Renounce your opinions—and it is as if you have announced the total replacement of the structure of your soul, and have taken it upon yourself to proclaim that, up to now, you lived a perfect lie. So each bunker peers with its periscope at the bunker across the way, and sees there the reflection of the shining iron of its own immovability. So much for debate.

But debate was, it seems, inevitable. It began in this way: I opened by explaining what I was doing there, in Ofra, on Shabbat. What I came for and what I wanted to hear. I told of my meetings with Arabs in the area, of the pent-up (how appropriate an adjective!) hatred I found among some of them; I told of my visits to the refugee camps. Someone immediately remonstrated—as if by conditioned reflex: Don't pity them too much. Haven't you seen their mansions along the road to Ramallah?

I said that I had seen them, and other things as well, and that I hadn't come to hold forth on that subject.

The Ofrans leaned forward in their chairs. From that moment they lost the peacefulness of the Sabbath eve, and an invisible trip wire joined them all, facing me. I thought that there was no point in contention. They have lived in the middle of the conflict for so many years, trained to resist any attack, justified or unjustified, lacking in their naked vulnerability any sense of irony.

For this reason, and instead of answering, I asked for their goodwill. For their cooperation in one matter that bothers me. A side question, not even part of the debate over who is more in the right, we or the Arabs. The right or the left. Because I am very curious to see if they can imagine themselves in their Arab neighbors' places and tell me what seems to them to be the most hateful manifestation of the occupation.

Someone (it is difficult to remember who, there were about fifty people there) said immediately, "The situation isn't our fault!" And others murmured their agreement.

I said: That is not the question. Let's assume that you are right. Let us assume that your view is correct one hundred percent, and that history will confirm this in time. Now I ask only for a little flexibility of thought, and ask again: What, in your opinions, does an Arab in Silwad or Ain Yabrud, in his everyday life, in his most private meditations, in his relations with his children, in what does he most feel the influence of your (just, you believe) presence here, in a place he sees as his land.

"We haven't taken one meter of land from Arabs," one woman said heatedly.

I saw that I had erred and not made myself clear. So I told them how I describe this to myself, and permit me to record it here with a certain lack of modesty: I related that in my own day-to-day life I attach extremely great importance to time. That sometimes I feel as if time flows in my veins. And I am not willing to tolerate the thought that even one moment of my life might pass empty of meaning, of interest, of enjoyment. I feel great responsibility to the time given us with such meanness, and it seems to me that, were I living under foreign rule, what would torture me would be—besides the tangible things that are taken as given—the fact that I do not control my time. That they can delay me at a roadblock for an hour-long interrogation; that they can impose a curfew of several days on me; that the hours of my life, which are my personal, intimate possession, turn into worn coins in the hands of a wasteful and obtuse malevolence. And this also: that they set me at an unnatural point in the general progress of historical time; that they hold back or accelerate developments and processes in an artificial and arbitrary way, without my being able to make use of all that is inherent in them. And I returned to my now familiar question.

"Fine," said one of the Ofrans. "At the intersection coming into Tel Aviv I also get held up an hour every morning."

Laughter.

"To my mind time is so valuable," said my host, "that I don't waste even a minute on such questions."

More laughter.

But now I was not willing to give up, because it seemed to me that this was an expression of a fundamental and deep difficulty. So, for forty minutes, I continued to ask the same question over and over, and the Ofrans, educated, sharp-minded, and fluent as they are, did not succeed in answering my question, my simple request.

Erlich said that what most burdens the Arabs is actually our, the Jews', indecision with regard to the situation, and that, were we to decide to officially annex the territories, we would make things easier for them. That's an answer to a different question, I said. The atmosphere had already become unpleasant.

Haggai Segel's father stood in the doorway opposite me, erect, wearing a black beret, and his face expressed his hostility toward me. He stated angrily that we did not start the war (absolutely right) and that we won a victory over all our enemies in an almost miraculous way (true), and what do you think, that now we can give up everything we gained. I thought only that this also did not answer that earlier, forgotten question.

Among the myriad arguments thrown at me (sometimes by two or three voices in unison) were some which indicated an attempt to deal with the question. Noga spoke of the Bedouin she saw on television a month earlier, an Israeli Bedouin from near Beersheba, who could not find work and felt himself to be a second-class citizen. Gidele said that he is not comfortable with the way soldiers at roadblocks treat Arabs, and that he even tells them so. These were not real answers, but they showed a willingness to consider the question. Other than these and one or two other responses, the people in the room were not able, even for a little while, to shift their point of view; they did not allow themselves even a split second of empathy and uncommitted participation in the lives of those whose fates are intertwined and interwoven so much with theirs. Like fossils, they did not succeed in freeing themselves from those very bonds which they are unwilling to admit exist.

Then Yehuda said that the answer is simple: that he

does not want to think even for a minute about the situation of the Arabs around him, because he is caught up in a struggle with them, at war, he said, and were he to allow himself to pity, to identify, he would weaken and endanger himself. The people in the room nodded. There was a hum of agreement.

I said that such an answer—even though anticipated—frightens me, because there are things that, when said out loud, become both a judgment and a prophecy. After such things are said out loud, is it possible to say that twenty years of heart-hardening have had no side effects?

"We've heard that kind of talk before," the Ofrans said. I was not sure they had really listened. I expanded on my question a bit more, not only for them, but also to understand it better myself: when we wish to ignore someone, some other person, or thousands of people, we set up a sort of "block" in our souls. A closed-off area, fencing in all the problems we do not wish to touch. Little by little we learn to make detours, to distance ourselves from that same closed area. Our access to it is blocked. Without our noticing, it ceases to be ours. Something is lost and taken away from us, maybe forever. We are social creatures, I told the people of Ofra, and even when we are completely alone we create internal relationships with different parts of ourselves. And when we accustom ourselves to relations like those between master and slave, that division is stamped within us as well. It suddenly becomes a possible mold for our relations with our friends.

The charge most often leveled at you of Gush Emunim is approximately this: Can a person spend years closed off from and insensitive to "certain kinds" of people whom he sees face-to-face every day, without this finding its way into other parts of his life? You probably, by this time, don't hear the charge. You have accustomed yourselves to it, and those who made it have grown tired of it themselves. So it is necessary to pain you even more and ask you: Is the soul a modular mechanism in which specific "parts" may be disconnected, or in which entire sections may be made non-operational for a period of time, in the meanwhile, until the danger passes? Can it be—and this each one of us must answer himself, alone— that in the very making of this dramatic separation you do not turn yourself, in the course of time, into just such an impenetrable mechanism, a mechanism that you sometimes control and that sometimes controls you and is capable of deeds that once were only imagined but today are already—

And I said "the Jewish underground," and they answered me yes, yes, the underground, they always throw the underground at us. And in the same breath, almost, they began to attack my hypocrisy, since I live in Talpiot, which, they claimed, used to be an Arab neighborhood, and I do not make an issue of that, and is that not a sin against absolute justice?

I answered that the person who seeks absolute justice is evading practical decisions, and that I do not seek pure justice, nor the settling of historical accounts, but rather possible life, no more than imperfect and tolerable, causing as little injustice as possible. "And Talpiot?" they pressured me, like victors. "What about Talpiot?" I noted that they were mistaken—Talpiot was never an Arab neighborhood, and that in any case I cannot be responsible for what was done before I was born, and that on the contrary, since today we see the results of earlier wars, we must take care not to bring about further injustice. They speak, I said, as if nothing had happened between 1948 and 1967, no developments, no processes, no Green Line—the border between the State of Israel and the West Bank. They talk as if everything is undetermined and unbounded, everything happening in some sort of vacuum, outside of history, and the debate caught fire, the atmosphere became unfriendly, and we had to decide to meet again, the next day, "to talk about literature and not politics," and in order to make up and get over the resentment.

No one today doubts that the people of Gush Emunim have distanced themselves greatly from the center of the Israeli consensus. At the beginning they meant—under the inspiration of Rav Tzvi Yehuda Kook—"to exalt the soul of the nation" by virtue of their deeds over the Green Line, and to draw after them the entire nation to the land of the forefathers to a new system of values, as in the words of the Song of Songs, "Draw me, and we will run after you," but the condition they set themselves was to be "two steps ahead of the nation"—and no more.

But in their haste they raced forward and were left without troops and without support. Without even the favor of many who at the start thought well of them. It is enough to read any issue of their magazine *Nekudah* to realize this. "The settlers developed a feeling of persecution as a defense mechanism, similar to what was essential in its time to the Jewish nation in exile for its defense and adjustment to an inimical environment," writes clinical psychologist and Gush Emunim member Tzvi Moses. "The existence of such a mechanism in the psyche of the Jewish nation creates a problematic system in which change is difficult, and which may be destructive first and foremost to whoever feels persecuted, even though the aggression is, on the surface, directed against the critical and attacking object . . . Obstinacy and inflexible thinking typify the campaigns of the Gush today . . . There are side effects, such as excessive and nostalgic preoccupation with the early days of the movement, and difficulty making necessary adjustments . . . What today typifies the elders of the Gush—those same people who pushed for quick achievements at the start—is that they have revealed themselves to be functionaries fearful that control will be taken out of their hands, so they retard the organization's normal development processes . . . In fear of the dynamic of change, necessary for growth and development, there is excessive and repeated use of ideological concepts, to the point where they are eroded and emptied of meaning. What has happened to those who have grown tired of the slogans of the left about 'democracy' and 'rule of law' is now happening to those who have tired of the unceasing and overworked expressions 'the people of Israel' and 'the land of Israel.' All difficulties and internal mishaps are blamed on outside forces: the government, the left, the Arabs. There is no self-examination of functioning." (*Nekudah* 108, March 1987)

Because of this self-distancing of Gush Emunim from the central consensus, and mostly because of the underground, the general public has become estranged and hesitant with regard to its members and is reluctant to face up to the problem they present. They are frozen into a tired stereotype, and there are those who fear them in an almost mythic way: "You're going to Ofra? Be careful of them" was the reaction of some people when they heard where I was going; and "They're crazy. They're fanatics. They're blind."

It is obvious, however, that it is not so simple, and that reality never surrenders to a stereotypic view. So I went in order to learn.

Perhaps there are not among them real moderates, but there are those who feel growing discomfort. Like those who in private conversations will finally agree to acknowledge the qualms awakening in them over what they are doing to the Arabs and to the people of Israel. There are people here such as Yoel Ben-Nun, rabbi and thinker, who sees the conflict in a wide historical perspective, and whose ideas are thought-provoking and present a real challenge. I do not want to begin listing the many other names, but I met in Ofra men and women who—when calm—are very different from the public image of them. Sensitive, deep people who stimulate thought and fondness. But again—when calm. Even then it is hard to really get to know them. Theirs is a closed society with a clear internal code of its own, of people with, in general, very similar biographies, interacting with each other over a course of years, people who have been molded since childhood by the same common experiences and struggles. The people I met are diligent, idealistic, and without a doubt courageous and ready to sacrifice themselves. Among themselves they maintain a system of mutual assistance and a high level of ideological and personal obligation. Ofra even became the model of a new type of settlement—neither a cooperative agricultural village nor an impersonal town, like those previously established, but a "community settlement," a small, selective community of independent settlers, most of whom run businesses or work in the city.

Despite this, they are not the elite they like to think they are. In conversations with them, one wonders at the extent to which their way of thinking is sometimes simplistic, provincial, nourished by generations of suspicious self-confinement from the world. Conservatism, an important value in their eyes, disconnects them even more from the world around them and strengthens the "bunker" mentality, and it is hard to know whether they hate this or whether it is essential to their continued survival and faith.

In their conversation and their writing they unhesitatingly make use of empty clichés full of baseless arrogance ("We must move the ship of Zionism forward," Daniella Weiss, Secretary-General of Gush Emunim, said). They speak of themselves as being "a model society," but all their actions already give evidence of, on the one hand, weariness of the model life (and there is already hidden competition over the interior and exterior beautification of the private houses and over the number of electrical appliances they contain), and one may also sense among them, on the other hand, a certain perplexity when they must deal with the little details of everyday life, with long-range actions, since, as Ofra educator Dan Tor said, the nucleus of people which created the "Gush Emunim momentum" was "a group with *'high messianic tension'* " (*Dear Brothers*, p. 219). This tension is diffusing itself. And the tension will want release.

The members of Gush Emunim would like to see themselves as the heirs of the historic Mapai (Labor) movement (and the elders of Mapai never hid their sentimental softheartedness in the face of the adventures of the new pioneers of Zionism), but they do not have an inclusive and deep national vision with "appeal" and wide public support, as Mapai, the predecessor of today's Labor Party, had in its heyday. They have too few great lights, and they rally around them in a rough sort of way, like the inhabitants of a poor Galician town drawing pride and courage from its local celebrated scholar.

They accuse the left of having an exile mentality, but they are not themselves really of the land of Israel. The architecture of their villages is strange to the landscape, proud and overbearing; they know nothing of the language, thinking, or manners of their neighbors; among many of them even the Hebrew language is incorrect, shallow, and trite. Their houses are almost bookless, with the exception of religious texts, and, in general, they have little use for culture. Even the humor of their circles is of the old Diaspora type, of sarcasm and contrariety, and reflexive, nervous contrivances, of mocking one's real and imagined enemies. The whole world is against us, they broadcast to you with every word. Inevitably, they have created their own prison, their spiritual Sparta on the mountaintops, out of which they peek, stiff and prickly, in the face of all other opinions. They turned from people of faith to, if one translates the name Gush Emunim, a Bloc of the Faithful.

Who are these people, I ask myself, who maintain an almost utopian bubble of a society of values, making great demands on individuals, atop a mountain of injustice, impenetrability, and ignorance of their fellow men?

They have established an exemplary settlement here, among the Arab villages. Both good air and a good life. They are fruitful and multiply, and there are many families of four, six, and eight children, *kein ein hara*, and a school for five hundred children, an absorption center for new immigrants, cherry orchards and chicken coops—and of all this I do not write, because there is something else, difficult and threatening and much more important, somewhere under it all, which I want to unearth.

No: they are not hotheaded. It is their complexity that is dangerous, not their simplistic willingness to follow their slogans. They plan their steps with wisdom, in a calculated and pragmatic way. In this sense they are utopian rather than messianic. They are not sleepwalking hallucinators but, rather, very practical people.

When you sit with them, especially with the moderates among them, whom Gush Emunim puts on display, you may sometimes make the mistake of thinking that the differences between you are very small. Yoel Ben-Nun relates a conversation he had with Israeli writer Amos Oz, who supports the idea of a territorial compromise in the West Bank, and his conclusion in the wake of it was: "There is no chasm between us! There is no ideological conflict. The debate is only over the limits of the abilities of the Zionist enterprise today."

But the chasm exists.

It gaped, of course, when the Jewish underground was uncovered. But the underground was only a symptom. It gapes when I see in the house of moderate Yoel Ben-Nun a picture of the photomontage he made with Yehuda Etzion, leader of the underground: the Temple sitting on the Temple Mount (and Yoel Ben-Nun condemned the underground and castigated Etzion—and as a result lost standing in the movement).

And it gapes when Yoel Ben-Nun tells me that, in his eyes, we are not yet in Greater Israel—because the Jordan River is not the border of Greater Israel, but flows down its center. While he does not expect us to achieve that in this generation, he certainly feels obligated by the Bashan and the Gilad, once parts of Biblical Israel and now in Jordan.

Such talk frightens me. Once, the talk and writing about Jews returning to Beit-El and Hebron—such as the writings of Shabbatai Ben-Dov, who called in 1953 to strive for "the full messianic definition of the Israeli kingdom"—seemed daydreams disconnected from reality. Since then we have all learned, the hard way, that in Israel's special climate we must give serious attention to the visions of such people and their supporters. They, after all, see the Bible as an operational order. An operation that, even if its time is yet to come, will come and, if it does not come soon enough, will need to be brought. I fear life among people who have an obligation to an absolute order. Absolute orders require, in the end, absolute deeds, and I, nebbish, am a partial, relative, imperfect man who prefers to make correctible mistakes rather than attain supernatural achievements.

Who are these people who claim that they are acting in my name and in the name of my future (and who actually influence it decisively against my will), who are able to harden their hearts so much against others and against themselves, over the course of an entire generation or two, and become the kindling of the historical process they desire? What do I have to do with them? If they succeed in getting what they want, and if the opportunity presents itself (and in the inconstant Middle East it will eventually do so), and if they could proceed immediately to the next stage of realizing their grand plan, they will then be even stronger and more determined, wonderfully trained in hardening their hearts.

Who are these people who hurl themselves forward with spiritual devotion like a stone thrown from here into the clouds of the future and the promise, and all during their flight they are stone and solidity, splitting the air with power and determination, and when they finally hit ground, on a mountain or hill, they turn suddenly into a house of soft candlelight and the "warm Jewish heart"?

Who are these people who are able to pilot their lives with logic and clearheadedness into the very heart of a doubtful reality and then, upon arriving at a barrier which seems to all others impassable, metamorphose themselves into some other realm of existence, execute a sort of instant takeoff with the help of an Uzi, crossing the Messiah with a vertically launched aircraft, enter into an apocalyptic trance, dance like kids on the hill-tops, shout ecstatic and ridiculous prophecies, and so, with determined blindness, with elimination of the self in order to allow the "together" to fill the soul, they are carried skyward, to the next target, and to the one after it, and wake up in the end with dawn on another hilltop, or in the heart of Hebron, red-eyed and battered by their drunken senses, fluttering toward us like spoiled children, and afterwards in provocation, and in the end in impudence and insolence?

I am too small to understand it.

Two weeks later, in the settlement Alfei Menashe, I heard Rav Levinger, the leader of the Jewish settlers in Hebron, say: "Fifty years ago our opponents argued about Jaffa; today they argue with us about Alfei Menashe; in another fifty years they will argue with us about Amman. That's the way it is."

I do not comprehend people who set history in motion. The impresarios of history are beyond my understanding. They amuse themselves, I feel, with overly large toys, and the game may come down on all our heads. For instance, the game called "Blow Up the Dome of the Rock and Wait One Turn for the Arab World's Reaction." Historical games often end in historical mistakes.

There will be a second underground. A second and a third and a fourth. Just writing the words sickens me, but it has to be said expressly: it will happen. They will happen. Not from among the generation who gave birth to the first Jewish underground—it was dealt a mortal blow and is greatly broken, not necessarily because of the deeds, but because a cruel mirror was placed in front of its face. The first underground was not an accident of history. It was the inevitable result of reality. So the second one will be. I have noted elsewhere that the major educational problem in Ofra is the lack of discipline among the children, and that one of the women there suggested that this is linked to the lawbreaking of Gush Emunim.

In all that touches on the underground, the children of Gush Emunim receive double messages from their parents. It is enough to spend one evening with a family in Ofra to realize this. Even the most prosaic of them can evoke sudden wonder with their verbal acrobatics. The bottom line of all this twisting and turning is this: there is no regret. "We oppose the murder of the two students at the Islamic college," the Granit parents say, "but no one regrets the attack on the Arab mayors."

And the children—five and ten years old—listen, and are meant, it seems, to patch together some sort of philosophy and system of moral values in which one attempted murder is acceptable and another is not.

Would it be too much to believe that the leader of the Jewish underground of the 1990s is now studying in one of the yeshivas? The climate of the national religious public creates a sort of internal hierarchy, headed by those who are more committed than others to the absolute order. The mental steamroller which created characters like underground members Novick, Segel, and company has not stopped working. From the do-nothing clubbiness of what they lovingly and in awe call "our circles" will emerge now and in the future the hard and dim seed of absolute commitment. The mixed reaction they heard to the deeds of the underground from within Gush Emunim, as well as the indulgent attitude of some national leaders, was well understood by the potential terrorists now rocking over their books.

It is difficult for me to connect the pleasant people I met in Ofra with the obliquity of those who chant the words of the prophet Isaiah, "Take counsel together and it shall come to naught," but they are the same people. It is hard for me to understand Avital, who spoke with pain of the sufferings of Israeli Arabs, on whom we have forced Israeli citizenship, saying, "And I can justify every one of them who joins the PLO," but cannot feel the same emotion with regard to the Arabs of next-door Ain Yabrud, to whom she herself is a thorn in the side; it is difficult for me to grasp the declarations that "we hire no Arab laborers," but when I ask who built their houses, Shalmai, a sensitive and wise man, answers, "I don't know, little dwarves came one night and built them."

And these are the same people. I saw them in their calm days. Almost in their slack days. Not in the season of their messianic heat. Not at a time of "high messianic tension," but it lies in wait for them always, like a disease. These are historical people, and historical people become—at certain moments—hollow and allow history to stuff them, and then they are dangerous and deadly.

Until this is fully understood, we will all continue, gone foolish from abundance and apathy and feeling inferior in the face of "activism" and "realization of ideals," to sit in the hall and watch the *gushnikim* playing before us scenes of horror—at every opportunity that presents itself—yet stimulating some pleasant impulse in some hearts, as well as dramas of authentic pioneer idealism, and snatches of scenes of madness and instigation, except that sometimes, while we watch the events in that circular field and pay the small price of not doing anything, someone will awaken in the back corner of the great auditorium and will discover, when he sees the ground moving slowly under his feet, that this wonderful circus is a traveling one, traveling with determination, and that its goal and direction are known to him without any doubt.

5
Life Sciences

I told a friend of mine that I wanted to visit some classes at one of the West Bank universities. He said: "Classes? They go to classes there?" and laughed in amazement. "It never occurred to me that they go to classes. All we hear about them is that they throw stones and burn tires."

The doors on the classrooms at Bethlehem University have small glass windows. A stranger can peek through them and see the lesson in progress: the teacher, the pupils, and mostly the attentiveness. That is the first impression: the forward tilt—unconscious—of their bodies. The students hang on the teacher's every word. I have a green notebook in which I write as I listen to people, as I stand and as I walk. A long day of studies awaits me today.

In the hallway, near the stairwell, stand a lecturer and his students, conferring together. They speak about Freud. Humor as a way of expressing aggression, she says. I did my master's thesis on humor, he says. I also once took an entire course on humor, I remember, at the Hebrew University. We studied Freud and I wrote a long paper; I laugh quietly, to myself, like someone making a toast to another.

Hanging on the wall of the hallway is a very large bronze plaque depicting a lion cruelly overpowering a doe. Sitting under this familiar Palestinian symbol, on two chairs pulled together, are a boy and a girl. They whisper between them, her hair almost falling into his face. Ask people here about the role of politics in academic life, I note down to myself, and ask about permissiveness.

On the basement floor, the physics-department faculty lounge. Three professors take counsel with each other. Professor Zurub Abd-Al-Rahman explains their problem to me: the summer session generally runs six weeks, but because of the frequent closing of the university by the army, they have to make do with only four weeks of studies.

They refer to the calendar again and again, shaking their heads at each other with concern. We may need to give up on Electromagnetism B, one says.

The students won't be able to grasp the material, another says, making question marks next to the courses in danger of being canceled.

The third, an American professor working here on a Fulbright grant, tells me: "We can offer only the basic courses, the ones most necessary for their degree. Nothing else that can really enrich them, or expand their horizons."

Bethlehem University is fourteen years old. It was established by decree of the Vatican and has its backing.

About 1,500 students study at the university; the faculty numbers about 130. The West Bank has five accredited degree-granting universities. They enroll about ten thousand students. The largest of them is Bir Zeit, at this writing shut down for four months by order of the military administration, in the wake of violent demonstrations there. A few thousand more Arabs study at teachers' colleges, religious seminaries, technical schools, and commercial colleges. Bethlehem University is considered no less extreme in its politics than more-well-known Bir Zeit, and is known to be a stronghold of the Democratic Front for the Liberation of Palestine, a Marxist Palestinian faction. But because of the Vatican's support for the institution, the administration treats it with a bit more delicacy than it does the other West Bank universities.

Professor Hana Halaq suggests that I come with him to see the laboratories.

"When were you last closed?"

"We opened just yesterday, after three days of closure imposed in honor of your Independence Day. Here, this is our laboratory. Modest, I know. We make most of the equipment with our own hands. In the carpentry and metal shops."

Poor and primitive equipment. Microscopes and measuring instruments and Bunsen burners, all ancient-looking. A demonstration for students was in progress, and I had a quick lesson in the refraction of light. To the extent I could judge, the explanation was on the level of an Israeli high school. But more impressive was how the students related to the material—with respect and interest. Their expressions were totally concentrated.

Could I sit in on a class session?

Caught off guard, Hana Halaq removes his glasses and polishes them.

Not at all?

He avoids my gaze.

"Are there things you prefer to hide?"

"It is not a simple matter to let an Israeli into a class session. It would cause some tension."

"You mean that the students would be suspicious of a teacher who brought an Israeli to class? Even to a mathematics lesson?"

"Let's continue our tour. I will show you our greenhouse."

"Do you have courses in politics and current events here?"

"Take a look at the catalogue."

The catalogue is attractive and written in English. On the cover is a photograph of the university's stone quarters—the carved steeple with the statue of the Madonna above, and a large clock with its hands pointing to five minutes after twelve.

Course 201—Political Science 1. This course deals with the following subjects: social environment, the society's metamorphosis into a political entity, types of sovereignty . . .

Course 304—The Palestinian Problem. Detailed study of the problem, focusing on decisive events. Historical documents, people and organizations involved in the situation. Object of the course: to clarify the problem, in an effort to understand it in perspective.

But there is also Course 311—Drama. Critical study of the development of the drama as a literary genre.

There will be an emphasis on the influence of the classical and European theater on dramatic works in the English language . . .

Course 431—The Exceptional Child. Through comparison with the normal child, the course will survey the gifted, the creative, the retarded, the blind, and the socially inhibited child . . . There will be an emphasis on personal and social problems and on modern methods of treating them.

And this, too: Course 438—Israeli Society. This course is aimed at acquainting the student with Israeli society, and how its melting pot brought together groups so different and heterogeneous in their customs, traditions, and cultures, and made them into one homogeneous society composed of subgroups.

Hana Halaq leads me to the almost-empty greenhouse. A few shrunken cactuses and geranium plants. Biology students learn plant anatomy from these plants. From the greenhouse in which I stand I gaze outward, toward the wonderfully beautiful campus lawn—flower boxes, stone buildings, stately pine trees, gravel paths. Hundreds of students and they make hardly any noise. Most of them are sitting, during their break, in the sunlight, studying alone or in groups. It reminds one, slightly, of the pictures of Plato's school in Athens.

I absorb their seriousness, penetrating even the glass walls of the greenhouse. Hard work is in the air of this small campus, an atmosphere of study. Whoever says that the universities are hothouses of terror does not understand the complexity of the issue. There is something deeper and more fundamental here. I wrote the following in my notebook: "There is no idleness. Not like the campus quadrangles I know. Here they seem, somehow, determined. Even during their breaks."

Back to the bustling corridor. It is very crowded. A new, elegant wing of the university has just been completed, but the military administration approved it on condition that it not contain a single classroom—only a restaurant and administrative offices. It will not solve the overcrowding. Here, over the large stones of the floor, someone guides a wheelchair: the body and face of a small boy. Maybe a young genius. His chin droops on his chest. Thick glasses over his eyes. Everyone races between the classrooms. The space is full of youth and chatter. Boys and girls exchange glances. By the way, there are as many women studying here as men, and the teachers say the women are the best students: first, because the most talented men find their way to other countries, and a girl, as talented as she might be, will not go far from her father's house; second, because they are less involved in politics. I note that almost all the students are well dressed. None is sloppy. You can feel that people come here with respect, almost in celebration. I try to guess at the backgrounds of those passing by me. Who is the son of the rich man, whose father and grandfather are educated and learned and sent the young man to continue the family tradition, and who is the son of the poor fellah, peasant, who only reluctantly gave up his son's labor because the boy insisted on continuing his education and pleaded that the father allow him to change his life, because the neighbors said that the boy has the head of a government minister, because even if the family eats less bread during these years, the father himself feels that in making his son a student he is rebelling against the fate which is strangling him.

From among the milling crowd I make out a crown of red hair. The face of a young boy. Striding in the middle of a knot of students. This redhead from Bethlehem jokes non-stop, eager to entertain. I join them in their walk to class, look for the girl he is trying to impress, and think I have found her. I don't think he'll succeed.

Two short conversations:

Professor James Connolly, chairman of the English department: "I am here because it is an important service to the population. The students here are eager to learn. They are never satiated by their studies. In many ways I prefer them to those in England. Their motivation to gain knowledge is immense. Of course, the general level here is lower than in a Western university. We try to admit as many students as possible. There are difficult entrance examinations, but we accept mediocre students as well. We have to meet a great demand."

"What do you teach here?"

"I teach English poetry. They are so sensitive to lyric rhythm! Maybe because the rhythm of the Koran flows in their blood."

"What will you be teaching in your next class?"

"The poetry of John Donne."

"How do they relate to his wild sensuality?"

"At first they are very confused. Then they are conquered."

"And does what is called 'the situation' make its way into the class?"

"I try to prevent it. My status here as a foreign lecturer is very sensitive. Other teachers have been expelled from the West Bank after being accused of incitement. Sometimes, in English-language classes, I ask them to write a composition on what concerns them. Then I get not a few compositions on their suffering under the occupation."

"And what do you do in such cases?"

He throws me a blue-eyed, British, sly smile: "Why, I correct the mistakes in the English, of course."

Muhammad Haj Yihia teaches social work. He is a native of Teibe, an Israeli Arab village, and a graduate of the Hebrew University of Jerusalem.

"The first year here is hard for every student. Don't forget that they generally come from a traditional society, that they are the products of an unadvanced public-school curriculum, and that they have for the most part studied only with others of their own sex. All this affects the students' spirit and intellectual ability. They are not an open people. They are used to learning by rote, memorization, to having to guess at the desire of the authoritative teacher. At first they are incapable of working on their own and thinking as individuals. They lack even the tools needed to develop self-awareness.

"I, as a teacher, endeavor to pass on to my students the approach I learned at the Hebrew University: independence, critical thinking, and curiosity. I tell them not to base themselves on a single source of information, that they not accept anything I say as dogma, that they should always question. At first, they actually get angry at me: they do not succeed in overcoming the obstacles within them. Afterwards, they do overcome them and break loose. This is the most important education I can give them. I could have found work at the Hebrew University, but there I would have been only a lecturer in social work. Here I am also an educator. That is a big difference."

A loudspeaker suddenly barks outside. From the window I see a student in a black leather jacket gathering people around him. Students from every corner of the courtyard come to listen to him. He voices a furious protest against the university cafeteria serving food today, at the height of Ramadan, the Moslem holy month of fasting. "Oh, it's only a demonstration of fanatical Moslems," says a Christian student working in the room, but those around me exchange quick glances.

As the demonstration continues, I talk with a student with an official position in the student government, who refuses to give me his name and who dictates a stream of tired and insincere declarations. He finds it necessary to raise his voice in order to be heard over the noise of the demonstration outside. The shouts coming from the demonstration now turn into the regular chants of a chorus. I get up to look and see that the pastoral courtyard already contains hundreds of students, gathered in tight circles around the speaker. He shouts a phrase, and they answer him with a roar, waving their fists in the air. To my surprise, they are now crying hostile anti-Israel and anti-occupation slogans. The object of their anger has switched so quickly. In the crowd are many white-kerchiefed women. They are the most extreme of the female Moslems who study here. Someone pulls me gently away from the window. Better that they not know I am here. Bring that man out to us, like Lot in Sodom. But even a stolen glance allows me to make out that redhead among the sea of darker ones. Now he is completely foreign, waving his fist with the others and thundering with all his might. Oddly, that is the main thing that remains in my memory from this moment—being totally disappointed with a person whom I did not even know.

One of those present in the room walks away from the window, looks at me, and says in a swallowed voice: "We have a little problem outside." I examine the energetically moving lips of the official student, flower of the politicians, dictating to me his tired text, in which the sentences could easily be switched around without any damage to its actual intention, and as he speaks I write the following in my green notebook: Now, the truth. Are you afraid? Yes. And if something happens to you here, if they hurt you, do you think it will cause you to revise your opinions? To begin to surrender to hate? And if they were to hurt your child?

I set down the answer for the record and as personal testimony, and it is all written there, in the green notebook.

The campus calms down within half an hour, and I emerge into the courtyard. I present myself to a group of students and ask to talk with them. They giggle awkwardly and suddenly look very young. One of them takes up the challenge and rises. I am willing to talk, but not here. Her name is Raula, from Ramallah, and she is studying social work. "I wanted a profession that would allow me to give something to people. Something that would give me an opportunity to work with my heart and not just with my head or hands." She leads me through the bustling courtyard, through the piercing glances, to a room that looks like the office of some sort of cultural committee: metal cabinets overflowing with posters, tables piled with pamphlets, stacks of newspapers. A red-tinted map of Palestine is stuck on a wooden board, with the caption "Palestine Is Ours." On one wall is a picture of Che Guevera, and on another a drawing of a long-haired girl, with strong brown eyes. "Her name is Taghrid Batma," Raula tells me, as her voice takes on a special color, as if she is telling a folktale. "Israeli intelligence agents killed her in '82. Why? Because she was a good Palestinian. She organized many demonstrations and was an activist. That's why."

For some reason I do not feel like speaking to her about the side the Palestinians present to us, the Israelis, and I ask about the couple I saw whispering to each other in the corridor, about the glances exchanged between boys and girls in the courtyard, about that hardly hidden fluttering of eyes that makes the atmosphere of this campus more charged and potent than at Israeli universities. Raula laughs for a minute. "Relations between men and women here are very free. Why are you surprised? We are educated, progressive adults, and we know what to do with the culture we have acquired."

"Did your parents agree that you live this way, so close together with men?"

"My mother knew exactly what happens here, and she sent me here anyway. Besides, we all know that the university is the greatest matchmaker for educated young people, so maybe Mother was thinking of that, too."

"And does the situation allow you to study as well, or are your minds distracted by other things?"

"The occupation weighs down on us here. We never know if there will be classes tomorrow, or if they will allow us past the roadblocks on the way to the university. In class we are afraid to express our opinions freely, because we are afraid of spies. You know, two years ago they caught some collaborators here. They beat them and expelled them from here. Afterwards, some of them were found dead, and they never discovered who killed them. There is always tension in class, because everything is connected in one way or another to the situation. We really live under pressure, but that is what creates the motivation to keep at our studies and to continue with our daily lives. It is a pioneer challenge, because with all the disturbances and closures and pressures we still exist and study like in any other university in the world, and we do our best to get through all the material. That's an iron rule with us, with the teachers and the students, a rule we accepted of our own volition: we make up all the required material, no matter what happens, even if it means classes in the evening, during vacations, at people's houses. Here every class lasts at least an hour and a quarter, not forty-five minutes as at your university. We aren't lazy. We have a goal, you know." Her small mouth forms a determined circle. "We must educate ourselves, in opposition to what the occupation wants us to be. The occupation can numb, and we must fight that numbness. That is our mission. There are those among us who fight with weapons, and there are those who fight with speeches. We will fight with the help of education and thought."

6

The Yellow Wind

And there are also refugees for whom a miracle happened and who were returned to their land.

Such an instance, of incomprehensible mercy, is that of those who reside in the village in Wadi Alfuqin: in 1948 they were uprooted from their village, and for twenty-four years they lived in a refugee camp, or with family members who took pity on them, or in rented houses, the houses of strangers, in Jericho and Deheisha and Husan and Amman, and suddenly, in 1972, some remote emperor lifted his little finger and gave the order: "Return them!" and they returned to the village from which they were exiled, and they, perhaps, are the only ones to have returned from refugee life to that of human beings, and they can testify to the differences, and can say something about the chances for reconciliation and forgiveness. I went there.

Wadi Alfuqin is a fertile, watered valley. Springs flow, the ground is productive and benevolent, and everyone has a storage pool for springwater, and kitchen gardens full of produce, and olive groves bordered by grapevines planted shoulder to shoulder. And at the top of the mountain which stands over the valley are the foundations of the ancient city of Beitar, and the new settlement Beitar Elit.

After the War of Independence, the valley was the focus of attacks on Israeli Army patrols passing nearby, along the border, and after the army took several retaliatory actions, the village was abandoned and its natives dispersed. Nearly all the houses in the village were demolished, and the ruins on the mountain slope are still bleached by the sun, and the remaining houses have become a training site for the army. On some of the ruins one can still make out the marks of the bullets fired by soldiers in the fifties.

Imtiyaz (the name means "excellence") had not yet been born when her parents fled from the village. They moved from place to place in the West Bank over the course of several years. When she was a baby, they came to the Deheisha refugee camp. She lived her entire childhood and youth in the camp, and a year ago she returned to Wadi Alfuqin: she married a man there. Her parents, who could not afford to build a house in the village, remained in Deheisha. She remembers the day, fifteen years ago, when the people of Alfuqin left the refugee camp and returned to their village. "Of course we were mad at them," she says. "We were angry that they were returning here to real life, and we remained there, in prison. They cried with happiness, and we cried out of jealousy and pain. There are still some there today who are angry with those who were able to return."

"They are mad at the ones who returned? What are they guilty of?"

"Whom should they be angry at?"

Whom, indeed? "The Jews threw us out of here, and the Jews brought us back." A wide-eyed old woman sighs as she listens to us from the roof of the house next door, between clumps of just-sheared sheep's wool hung out for air: the Jew taketh away and the Jew giveth.

It is a cool day in early spring. We are sheltered in a shady, broad yard, and the little valley lies at our feet, and the storage pools sparkle in the sun, and despite the Ramadan fast, my hosts bring me a glass of tea, and little by little people from every corner of the village gather around us, listening, nodding their heads, and telling their stories—but not freely. These are things people do not like to recall.

"Life in the camp is bad," one woman of about fifty says shyly. "You are always with your head down, waiting for the next blow. After a few years there you have nothing left but fear and poverty. You become like a dead person: you do not want anything and you do not hope. You wait for death. Even the children there are old. They are born with fear. Here, children are like children: they almost do not know what the army is. Only the *mustawtanin*, the settlers, are frightening."

Everyone glances upward, to the bauble of a settlement stuck into the mountain.

"When the families left Deheisha on their way back to the village and we stayed there," Imtiyaz relates, "I cried for nearly a week. They can return and we can't, because we didn't have the money to build a new house. I was small, and I didn't understand that. After all, we all lived like one big family, we shared everything, we suffered together for years, so why them and not us? After a while, when they began to come visit us in the camp, we would pelt them with questions. We wanted to know everything about the village: how the land was and the spring and the vegetables . . ."

"They would bring us vegetables in bags," remembers Hanan, a rounded young woman who knows a few words of Hebrew. "And we would kiss those vegetables. We would kiss each tomato a hundred times before we ate it there."

"But I actually like Deheisha and miss it," a woman says hotly. She has strong features and had come to sit across from me on a stool, her legs held apart, and had immediately begun vilifying our hosts for serving me a drink during Ramadan. "Even if your brother comes," she says to the taken-aback woman of the house, "do not give him anything to drink! Ah, when the Jordanians were here, they would shoot anyone who desecrated the fast. Since you came here, everything has changed. There is no respect for religion anymore."

You miss Deheisha?

Even the retarded woman, kneeling by the wall and hollowing out green squashes to be stuffed with rice and meat, stops to make a circular motion with her hand and looks at her in amazement.

"Yes. I miss it. I get goose bumps when I think of it," she says, and bares an arm to illustrate her meaning. "But there it's bad! Frightening!" Imtiyaz counters her, and she responds: "The fear is their doing"—indicating me with a movement of her head. "And I miss the people who were there. I miss my house. What, aren't they people, the ones there? Weren't we close to them? That's what I miss."

Apparently she is right, I think. A person can miss even a hard, bad place, if there were beautiful moments there, and if he has a memory of a single instance of grace, and maybe loved someone there or was loved. I thought of the army bases in the Sinai where I once served, jumbles of iron and cement thrown at random on a mountain, and how we made our lives there full, and how those neutral, dead places became dear to us.

Another woman joins the group, greeting us and sitting by us, and another young man, who brings us mandrake fruit to smell. Here it is called the "madman's apple," and it has a faint and wonderful aroma.

The name of the woman who just arrived is Wadha Isma'il, and she listens for a while to the stories of the others. Afterwards, she begins to speak, in a moderate tone, without any reproach in her voice, and tells me this: "After they expelled us from the village, we would come back to work our land. The Israeli Army pretended not to see us. They would have maneuvers up on the mountain, and we would work the land in the valley. We would come every day by donkey from Hebron in order to work our land. One day I came here with my father. I was young then, almost a girl. We worked a few hours, and we started on our way back home. Suddenly the Israeli soldiers surrounded us and separated me from my father. I saw that they blindfolded him with a rag and pushed him into some bushes. I remember that he still had a chance to turn to me once and call to me through the rag. Immediately afterwards I heard shots. Many shots. I began to cry. The soldiers who had stayed with me asked me: Who is that man to you? I said: He is my father. They said: Go to the garden down there, and you'll see that he is harvesting lettuce and eggplant. When I was some distance from them, I glanced back and I saw one of the soldiers aiming his rifle at me. I was frightened and bent over. His bullet hit my neck and came out on the other side."

I don't know what to say to her, and she interprets my silence, apparently, as disbelief. "Look," she says, and her work-hardened fingers undo her kerchief, and she smiles a sort of apology about having to bother me with her wound. I see an ugly scar in back, and another ugly scar in front. Young Hanan cries. It seems that Wadha is her mother. "Every time I hear that story, it is as if it were the first time," Hanan says.

Wadha lay among the bushes and played dead. The soldiers distanced themselves from her and then left the area. She rose, oozing blood, and bound her wounds with a handkerchief. Afterwards, she found her father on the ground, his hands tied behind his back, a large rock on his neck. There were thirty bullets in his body, the village elder, Abu Harb, told us later. Wadha, who is for a moment a girl once more, describes with movements of her body how she walked and tripped through the valley, at night, scared that the Israelis would shoot her from behind, or the Jordanians from in front. She concluded her story as she began it, quietly, with no tone of accusation, and her daughter Hanan stood and cried for all of us.

I pondered then about how much one must be suspicious of people who testify about themselves morning and night that they are merciful. They always taught us that we do not know how to be cruel or to hate our enemies, really hate. We are cleanhanded types. And despite that, every so often another ugly incident takes place, carried out by the merciful hands of people like us, people who never hate, and maybe the fact that we do not allow ourselves to hate actually testifies to the disparagement we feel toward the Arabs, since you do not hate a person whom you see as lower than you. It is hard for us, for instance, to hate children, because we sense that they are not our equals. In this context I recalled a story told me by a reserve soldier I met during the course of these seven weeks. It has no connection with Wadi Alfuqin, but it is very much connected to the entire matter.

"Once, when I was on reserve duty, there was a terrorist attack in the Old City in Jerusalem, near the Rockefeller Museum, and we set up a detainment area for Arab suspects in the courtyard of police headquarters. We picked up all the Arabs we caught. We brought entire truckloads. How I beat them that night! There was another reservist, a young guy, with me, and I saw that every Arab he catches, he bites hard on the ear. Actually takes off a piece. I ask him why he did it, and he answered me: 'So that I'll know them next time we meet.' "

At the top of the village, in a small, dark house, next to the house of his extended family, the village elder lives. He is called Abu Harb, and he is eighty-five years old. He is, according to the residents, the village historian.

He sits on a colored reed mat, his shaking hand playing with a large, antiquated transistor radio. His eyes are much swollen, and his nose is oddly reddish. He remembers the Turks and the English and the Egyptians, who were here briefly, and the Jordanians he remembers, and now us. "In October 1948 we were exiled from here," he says (the only one in the village, he says, who knows the precise date), and for twenty-four years we were not here. We wandered from place to place for twenty-four years, and everywhere we went we would bury our dead, and afterwards we would wander onward, and for twenty-four years I did not sleep at night, I would lie awake and think, and the first night I returned to my village and slept in it was the happiest night of my life, because I slept on my own land."

In 1972 the people of the village received a notice from the military government that they could return to their village. They do not know who made the decision. They received a notice, and that same day the news spread to all the village's exiles, who had been dispersed to the four winds. When Abu Harb describes how they gathered and came here, I recall the book of Ezekiel, the vision of the dry bones which join together, cover themselves with flesh and sinew, and return to life.

"The military government gave us one month to return to the village," Abu Harb relates. "They told us that whoever did not build a house within that month would not be allowed to return. We came that same night, from every place, and we set up booths and tents in the place that was once the village. Afterwards, we collected money and paved an asphalt road to bring construction materials in trucks. It was a harsh summer and we worked day and night, and we would sleep under the floor of the house we were building. Each one of us built a single room with a roof, and that was our claim."

He tells his story, and his wife, Ratiba, enters the room. She looks younger than he and her face is still smooth. Her face is dark, "but that is not my color from birth, it is only because of the damned sun of the camp, in Jericho," she explains. They have been married for sixty years, "and he never took another wife, other than me!" she boasts.

I asked them if they know why the Israeli authorities so suddenly allowed them to return to their village.

"We heard that the Israelis needed our place in Deheisha. They intended to bring to the camp a large group of Gazans whom they wanted to remove from the Gaza Strip. So they evacuated us."

"And did Gazans actually take your place there?"

"They came. But afterwards they stopped transferring people there from Gaza."

I do not know if that is the correct interpretation of this singular act of mercy. The fact is that it was all done in secrecy, under wraps. Maybe so as not to arouse demands from other exiles in the territories, or from Israeli Arabs who had been expelled from their villages. I tend to think that the explanation given by the people of Wadi Alfuqin, concerning their exchange for Gazans, is correct. In the twisted climate of the occupation, when one act of mercy is performed, it must almost of necessity be crooked and bent, and be nothing but another of the many faces of arbitrariness.

I ask my conversants how the return to their land affected them.

"Everything changed," Abu Harb says. "We now live here among real people. The people who stayed behind in Deheisha and in Jericho are miserable. They are going mad from sadness and longing for their land. They come and plead with us to give them a little garden plot. Just so they can regain a little self-respect. Something to live for. After all, it is not just land, it is everything. They are cut off from everything there. They have ceased to be people. We have been planted anew. Not only in the land. The land is the beginning: we are planted in life as a whole. In normal relations with other people. In tradition. In all the right things. We are no longer strangers in the world. We have the milk of our cows, the flour of our wheat. We are now complete people."

I have one more question. Maybe the most important question: The Israelis brought you back to your village. Do you hate them less now?

They exchange glances. The very old man, his wife, his daughter-in-law, his many grandchildren and great-grandchildren, all of whom have gathered in the room. The daughter-in-law speaks. She relates that her husband has been arrested on suspicion of taking part in terrorist acts. Immediately after his arrest, Israeli soldiers came and destroyed their house. It was a new house, just completed. The family was not given enough time to remove all its belongings. When it was destroyed, it collapsed on ten sacks of sugar and ten sacks of flour that had been bought at great cost and had been stored in the house for the housewarming celebration. The husband was released right afterwards without any charges having been brought against him. As she tells the story, her lips go white with fury and look like a whip scar on her face. Two other sons of Abu Harb are now under arrest in Israel. One is in prison and the other is awaiting trial. Abu Harb says: Both of them are innocent. And if they did something, they apparently had no choice. The injustice and bad effects of the situation are what turns normal people into criminals.

The mother, Ratiba, says: "The settlers come down

from the mountain at night with dogs. They frighten us. They stole our spring, and call it sharing."

"The bus that takes their children to school," ten-year-old grandson Hazem says, "blocks the way for our bus every day, and we have to walk about a kilometer to school."

"They will expel us from here again," says another young man, about eighteen, and everyone nods in agreement.

"And then we will really go mad," says Grandmother Ratiba.

The old man, Abu Harb, sighs a long sigh, passes his hand over his face, and presses it against his eyes. The small children watch him. Returning home did not turn the heart of any one of them into one which loves us, the Israelis. Maybe it was foolish even to hope for that. Abu Harb rises to his feet with difficulty, and sees me to the door. We stand and look together over the beautiful and peaceful valley, and the smoke from the straw fires curls up into the air, and the thistles and wildflowers bloom as far as one can see. Now is the time of the yellow flowers. I tell Abu Harb that I called my book *The Yellow Time* in Hebrew, and he asks me if I have heard about the yellow wind. I say that I haven't, so he begins telling me about it, and about the yellow wind that will soon come, maybe even in his lifetime: the wind will come from the gate of Hell (from the gates of Paradise comes only a pleasant, cool wind)—*rih asfar*, it is called by the local Arabs, a hot and terrible east wind which comes once in a few generations, sets the world afire, and people seek shelter from its heat in the caves and caverns, but even there it finds those it seeks, those who have performed cruel and unjust deeds, and there, in the cracks in the boulders, it exterminates them, one by one. After that day, Abu Harb says, the land will be covered with bodies. The rocks will be white from the heat, and the mountains will crumble into a powder which will cover the land like yellow cotton.

7
Catch-44

The military court in Nablus. An ugly, dirty, dark building. As soon as I was inside I felt a need to contract, make myself small, to keep from touching other objects; the windows are broken and filthy. Through the spiderwebs one can make out the silhouette of barren Mt. Ibal, the mountain of the curses. Outside, storms frequently cut off the electricity, and in the dark it is sometimes hard to see the justice being done here. I enter the courtroom in the middle of a trial. The accused—a skinny boy with a scarred face—is charged with membership in an enemy organization. The defense attorney summarizes his arguments. He recalls that the boy merely expressed interest in joining the Fatah, and did not actually become a member, and furthermore, he is sick, his knees jut forward, from birth, your honor, stand up for a minute so they can see, here, and his father is over there, your honor, he would like to say something, he promises to be responsible for the behavior of the boy in the future, there's no time, your honor? So if the father can only stand up, so you can see what kind of person he is.

From among the public benches the father rises. A man of about fifty, short, with a wrinkle-lined face. He crumples his hat in his hands. Takes a hesitant step forward, and slowly, slowly, raises his eyes to the judge, as if laying out before him a complex and delicate exhibit for the trial, and actually, his face is all he has to exhibit in his defense: his son's guilt is absolutely clear. A stupid and simple boy, the father's face says, perhaps your honor also has young children and he knows how it is with them, the face murmurs, and I can see that even the judge has been caught up in the fear of that expression.

He may be seated.

He sits down beside his overgrown wife, thick of limb, whose lips mutter unceasingly. The rest of the family look frozen at the judge, hanging on his words. The father's face calms little by little.

The military judge, Major Yair Rabinowitz (himself once a military prosecutor), sentences the accused to four months in prison, with a one-year suspended sentence in force for three years. The defendant goes to prison, throws a smile of relief at his brothers, not at his parents. He is surprised at the leniency of the punishment. The mother looks at the father in agitation and bites her lips: four months!

Next case.

When lawyer Leah Tsemel arrives at the parking lot opposite the military court in Nablus, her clients pounce on her car, besiege her in fear and supplication, thirsty for the news she brings. In her office in East Jerusalem, in a broken house with a shattered roof, Arabs whose actions have brought them, or members of their families, up against the Israeli judicial system wait for her from the early morning, confused and ignorant of their rights and obligations and what is going to happen to them. The office teems with people, mostly villagers, who sit there for hours, and who greet Tsemel with awe. She is a small woman, always smiling, resolute in her speech, most extreme in her opinions, sympathetic and honest. She conducts several conversations at once with all those massed around her, speaking with them in excellent Arabic with an unmistakable Jewish Ashkenazi accent, chainsmoking, arguing over the telephone with police investigators who are preventing her from seeing a client of hers in jail, curses, forgives, puts on glasses missing one sidepiece, sets out on her way, to Nablus or Ramallah. The high energy she exudes threatens any calmer beings close by with adrenaline poisoning. Something else ought to be noted: in her relations with Arabs there is something you don't come across very often—straightforwardness and equality, without a trace of sanctimony; she places herself neither above nor below her clients, and there is no soft and self-effacing paternalism. Very rare.

And now—the trial of Jafer Haj Hassan, accused of having made contact with an enemy organization.

He is different from the prisoners shut up in the small, filthy confinement room. He stands tall and has delicate features. His movements are moderate and quiet. The prosecutor explains the charge: a few years ago Hassan asked his father for a sum of money in order to study in Germany. His father applied to a friend of his, a Fatah member in Jordan, and asked for assistance. Jafer Haj Hassan did not receive money but did receive a scholarship to study German in Germany. After half a year's work, he decided that he did not want to study German and changed his field. His patron in the Fatah told his father that the organization would support him only if he pursued a subject of some benefit to the organization. He refused—and his scholarship was immediately revoked. Hassan remained in Germany several years, with no links to terrorist organizations, married a German woman, and then came home. A week later he was arrested. He has been in the Nablus prison for forty-four days. A security detainee.

Forty-four days. They did not beat him there, he tells me afterwards; the treatment was reasonable. Even so, he says, do you know what forty-four days in jail is? Previously, he had not been involved in politics at all. Did not even know what it meant to be a Palestinian. One may assume that in prison he learned something. Forty-four days. A trimester course in national consciousness.

The judge listens to the prosecutor's arguments. He wears a knitted *kipah* and has a pleasant face. He also has a businessman's black swivel chair, which may be moved in any direction, and which may be bent backward, rising and falling with ease. The prosecutor, a young officer in the standing army, enumerates the charges. The room is dim. Uniformity is congealed on the faces of the reserve soldiers guarding the courtroom, on the face of the prosecutor, the translator, the woman soldier-stenographer. Only the judge rocks back and forth on the raised platform. For a second, his head disappears entirely behind his desk. The court holds its breath. Then he sweeps up slowly, raising with him an interesting argument: from the charge, it would seem that the suspect never had real, active contact or connection of any sort with a terrorist organization. There was never any direct connection between them. He maintained—so to speak—contact with his father. What is wrong with that, the judge asks. After all, it was his father—who is now in Jordan—who had made the contact, etc.

The prosecutor, lacking a little experience, here makes a mistake and does not accept the hinted advice of the judge. He sticks to his arguments: the accused should have distinguished between those conversations with his father regarding family matters and those regarding terrorist organizations. The translator—a heavyset Druse soldier with no expression resident on his face—had some time ago ceased to translate the proceedings for the accused. He picks his ears with his finger, whispers something to the stenographer, and again sinks into a deep vegetative stupor, accompanied by additional unconscious bodily movements. The relatives of the accused gaze at him in supplication: he is their sole connection with what is being said, but he has become habituated to them and pays no attention. Only an angry admonition from the judge brings him back to life: he resumes translating for several minutes, and then, little by little, is reabsorbed into that addicting oblivion.

Defense attorney Tsemel rises from her seat and protests the use of the term "terrorist organization." The judge asks to hear the reason for her objection. Tsemel reminds him that British law calls it a "proscribed association."

The judge: But the term "terrorist organization" has been used here for years!

Tsemel: That's because of Mehahem Kornwitz, the

prosecutor who was from Gush Emunim. He changed the term at his own initiative, and suddenly all the charge sheets were filled with "terrorist organizations." So, inevitably, every accused person is a "terrorist," and that, of course, influences the judges in making their decisions.

The prosecutor (slightly mocking): And Madam, of course, has not come to terms with that distortion.

Tsemel: Correct. I have refused on principle to accept charge sheets in which the term "terrorist" is used. Judges have always conceded me the point, but I did not want only consideration.

The judge: So what did Madam do?

Tsemel: I applied to the chief counsel in the territories and asked that he instruct prosecutors not to use the term "terrorists" when drafting charges.

The judge (amused): And what, Madam, was the counsel's answer?

Tsemel: He said that I am right, but did nothing. For a year and a half I have been sending him requests. Just this week the corrective instruction arrived, and I demand that from now on it be adhered to with care.

The judge: As far as I'm concerned, it can be called a "charitable organization." The prosecutor will now continue to relate the accused's connections with the Salvation Army.

The accused understands neither the amused trialogue nor the reading of the charge sheet. No one explains to him what is being said. He is caught in an incomprehensible nightmare and does not know how it will end. His situation is, however, better than that of an ordinary defendant here, because most of them who arrive in the courtroom have already confessed their guilt at an early stage, while being interrogated by the security service. In 95 percent of the cases, the defense attorney is forced to satisfy himself with bargaining over the severity of the sentence, rather than over whether punishment should be imposed on his client in the first place.

Here, however, the charge sheet may be disproven easily. The judge is also aware of this, and he wavers out loud: Is maintaining contact with his father sufficient to convict the defendant?

The prosecution and defense finish their presentations. The judge withdraws to his chambers. The prosecutor, the defense attorney, and the translator wait for him in one of the secretarial offices of the court. The place is humming with young men and women soldiers, who while away their military service here. Several of them are currently sprawled on a pile of mattresses, chatting. The walls are decorated with cutouts from an Israeli teen magazine and with the same pseudo-clever posters which hang in every army office: "The Lazy Man's Ten Commandments," "Today Is the First Day of the Rest of Your Life." To think that they serve three years of life experience and routine here, organize going-away parties ("And from all of us success in civilian life, and don't forget us"), to think that here they fall in love.

"He has to free him," Leah Tsemel erupts. "It shouldn't be open to question. The matter is completely clear!" The prosecutor, young, blond, and bearded, smiles with a sort of strange wisdom, older than his years.

Both he and she know that the decisive majority of trials in the military courts in the area end in conviction. They both know that the defendant—if convicted—will not be able to appeal the judgment, because in the "territories" only a single level of courts functions, hearing

every kind of case, without any appeals court above it.
There is always tension between the civil jurists and the
military people dealing with the law: the army, of course,
prefers to see the court as part of the executive arm of
the military. The regulations regarding the legal handling
of prisoners reflect this: in the "territories," a suspect
may be held prisoner without a court order for eighteen
days (in Israel, no more than forty-eight hours); in Israel,
the police must allow the defendant to meet his lawyer
as soon as possible, within, at the most, forty-eight hours.
Under the military government, the court responsible
for the prison may delay the meeting between the prisoner and his lawyer for as long as it cares to.

The judge still wavers.

I recall the George Orwell essay "Shooting an Elephant." Orwell, while serving in the British Army in
Burma, is drafted by a Burmese mob to kill a giant
elephant in heat. As he strides toward the elephant—
pressed by the expectations of the crowd—he first understands that he may not be as free to decide his own
actions as he thought beforehand.

In his chambers, the judge delves into the case of Jafer
Haj Hassan. Hundreds of thousands of inhabitants of
the West Bank and Gaza have, as defendants or as relatives of defendants, passed through the military courts
of Israel. They have waited in the mildewed corridors,
have raised frightened and confused glances at the judge
determining their fate and the fate of their families; have
listened without comprehending to the defense and pros-
ecuting attorneys bargaining in the hall over the severity
of the punishment to be inflicted. There is not, it seems,
any way to impose security and order in these areas

without military courts, but there must be a way to make this massive friction between Israelis and Palestinians more honorable and tolerable, and minimize the hate as much as possible.

The judge still wavers.

Orwell says: "And suddenly I realized that I should have to shoot the elephant after all. The people expected it of me and I had got to do it; I could feel their two thousand wills pressing me forward, irresistibly. And it was at this moment, as I stood there with the rifle in my hands, that I first grasped the hollowness, the futility of the white man's dominion in the East. Here was I, the white man with his gun, standing in front of the unarmed native crowd—seemingly the leading actor of the piece; but in reality I was only an absurd puppet pushed to and fro by the will of those yellow faces behind."

The judge's chambers are still closed.

Because there is a catch.

Catch-44.

Since the defendant, Jafer Haj Hassan, had already spent forty-four days in prison, the judge faced a serious problem. Can a military court of an occupying power admit that the military government of the occupation made a mistake? And how will that influence its authority, esteem, and power in the eyes of the inhabitants?

Everything depends on the answer to this question.

Perhaps it is because of this question that the judge has been wrapped up in himself for two whole hours.

Here. He returns.

All rise!

The judgment: I sentence the defendant to forty-four days in prison. The crime: bringing money into the area in violation of section 2a-1.

The defense attorney does not believe her ears. Even the prosecutor smiles uncomfortably.

This requires a brief explanation. After two hours of uncertainty, the judge has decided to convict the defendant of a new charge not included in the original charge sheet! The law establishes that such a conviction ("a conviction without informing the defense counsel that the defendant is liable to be convicted on this charge, and without giving the defense counsel notice of intent to convict on this section") is directly contrary to section 23 of the order on security regulations. In a case in which the court revises the list of charges, it must (according to the same order) "allow the defense counsel to postpone the hearing or reexamine the witnesses, before the court may continue with its judgment."

None of these things was done here.

And note well: the accused did not bring money into the area. He received a scholarship. That is, a benefit. In Germany. And Germany is not in this area.

All rise!

Catch-44 is a combination of two Catch-22s.

One of them says something like this: If his honor the judge acquits the defendant on all charges, the inhabitants of the "territories" may interpret this as weakness. His acquittal is liable to call into question the sensitive system of relations between the inhabitants and the government authority, and riots, demonstrations, and so on may break out. General and personal security will be put in danger, and the defendant himself is liable to find himself in prison in the wake of a general escalation of tension, which may sweep him along with it. So that if he is acquitted, he is liable to be arrested.

The other catch is this: If his honor the judge imposes

a punishment of forty-four-day imprisonment on the accused, the inhabitants will understand immediately that the occupying power cannot allow itself to appear in error even in an unimportant case like this one, and this implies a great and dangerous weakness, which may, God forbid, endanger the sensitive system of relations ... riots ... arrests ... and the accused will find himself again behind bars.

In this light, the retroactive sentence of Jafer Haj Hassan to forty-four days in prison should be seen as a preemptive acquittal.

The defendant is freed immediately. The judge disappeared even before that. The black, authoritative chair still rocks up and down in a suspicious way, and I instinctively examine the ceiling.

All rise!

"I perceived in this moment," Orwell, the colonial officer, says in his essay, "that when the white man turns tyrant it is his own freedom that he destroys. He becomes a sort of hollow, posing dummy, the conventionalized figure of a sahib. For it is the condition of his rule that he shall spend his life in trying to impress the 'natives' and so in every crisis he has got to do what the 'natives' expect of him. He wears a mask, and his face grows to fit it. I had got to shoot the elephant. I had committed myself to doing it when I sent for the rifle. A sahib has got to act like a sahib; he has got to appear resolute, to know his own mind and do definite things. To come all that way, rifle in hand, with two thousand people marching at my heels, and then to trail feebly away, having done nothing—no, that was impossible. The crowd would laugh at me. And my whole life, every white man's life in the East, was one long struggle not to be laughed at."

An Unfortunate Mishap

During the period in which this book was in preparation, there was a hunger strike involving three thousand convicts in a West Bank prison. The strike ended of its own accord, without the use of force by the prison authority. Lawyers for the strikers were not allowed to meet with them. The prisoners' families were in deadly fear: the methods used for ending hunger strikes in the prisons have acquired a bad reputation.

For example, in 1980 there was a large hunger strike in the Nafha prison. Until that year the prison authority had the practice of giving the prisoners a "subsistence diet"—milk enriched with vitamins, meant to keep them alive. The prisoners themselves agreed to accept this diet, and did not see it as a violation of their strike. In the case of the strike at the Nafha prison, the prison authority decided to physically break the strike: they transferred twenty-one of the strike leaders to the prison in Ramallah, did not give them the subsistence diet, and insisted on pumping the milk directly into the stomachs of the prisoners. The prisoners refused. The medic on duty, an employee of the prison authority named Ruhami (he was later laid off for a morals violation), forced the pipe on some of them, but due to a lack of expertise the pipe entered the lungs of three of the prisoners. The enriched milk filled their lungs and they began to choke.

The lawyer of one of them happened by, and at her insistence her client was taken to the hospital and saved. He died three years later of a heart attack. The other two prisoners suffered all night. Only in the morning were they brought to the local clinic. From there they were sent to the hospital. One died on the way, and the other in the hospital.

A commission set up to investigate "hunger strike practices in the prisons" (the Eitan Commission) examined the circumstances of the deaths of the two prisoners. In their report they "recommended considering their deaths as an unfortunate mishap."

The Yellow Wind

8

Jews Don't

Have Tails

In the heavy fog I almost did not find the village. It was a white and thick night, and low clouds rose in front of the car. I searched for the house, but the fog led me astray into the wrong alleys and sent me over dirt paths. Then I stopped struggling and allowed myself to travel at a crawl through the village, and then, for the first time, I could feel something soft and free before me, maybe because of the fog lying over the village, maybe because of the quiet and the late hour; in any case, the air was completely rid of that thing bitterly called "the conflict," from the poison of the facts and interpretations and the enmity and the lingering memories. The Arabs were alone, and I was simply an undetected voyeur, and they were without us. From between the scraps of fog I saw a woman come out toward the doorway of her house, wiping up the drops of rain with a mop; a broom seller walked bent over, returning home after the day's work; in a corner of the street the headlights of a car lit up the warm secrets of a small grocery store, where two men sat playing backgammon. It was already

10 p.m. when I found myself outside the Tahers' large house. Taher is not his real name. He asked that I call him that, because the people here are still not willing to listen to his ideas. "Here they want to understand what you think right away: to know whether you are against the occupation or a collaborator and traitor. Black or white. They don't understand that there are several grades in between."

Taher is middle-aged. Somewhat heavy, with glasses, and quick of movement. His speech is swift, a little musical, as if each of his sentences were a question, and movements of his hands illuminate his words with improvised drawings.

He asked me what I had heard from the people I had met in the area.

I told him that only two days ago, in Beit Jala, one public figure told me that if we, the Israelis, were to leave the area, there would be a "second Beirut." The Moslems would slaughter the Christians, and then each other.

Taher answered immediately: "There will be a great slaughter. They will butcher each other on the bridge, anyone who is armed. Afterwards—the others: first they will kill whoever had any connection with Israel, and those who did business with Israel. And those suspected of collaboration with the *mukhabarat*, the intelligence service, and after they kill half of the population here, they will begin killing each other in a struggle for power. But I think"—he smiled—"that if you leave our land, there will be a second Beirut among you as well, because your debate over us, about the territories, is what keeps you from the real disagreements you have among you, which you haven't pursued for twenty years."

And if we stay here, I ask.

"Even if you stay here, it will be the end of you. We are dismembering you from the inside. You are small and want to be a great empire. And as you grow, you will approach your end. Like a child's balloon. And we are gaining strength in the meantime. We have more money, from working for you; we have identity, and that didn't exist before; and we learn many things from you. And today there are many people among us who can send their children to college to study literature and history, as I did—who ever heard of sending a child who can work and bring in money to study, of all things, humanities?"

And if we arrive at some arrangement under which we leave here and you have a government of your own? How do you see the country which will then be born?

He smiles broadly. "That won't be in my time or in yours. It's a dream. If the Jordanians didn't give me a government, do you think that Shamir will? Or Sharon? Peres won't, either. Why waste strength on dreams? Even without that, life is hard for us. Here we live in constant fear that the time is approaching when you will expel all of us from our land. That, after all, is the only difference between your parties, the good ones and the bad ones: when to expel the Arabs. I need all the strength I have in order to live with that fear, and in order to live without freedom, and you ask me about dreams? We need to think only about the possible."

The conversation, by the way, was conducted in Hebrew: twenty days after the Six-Day War began, Taher went to Jerusalem and registered for the intensive Hebrew course at the Beit Ha'am community center. "I knew that the Jews would be here in the West Bank for a long time." How did you know? We ourselves weren't sure that we would. "That's because you still didn't know how much it suits a person to be a conqueror. You thought then that you didn't know how to be like that. But don't forget that I had lived for twenty years under another occupation, the Jordanian, and that I am a much greater expert on conquerors than you are."

And what did your neighbors in the village say when you began to learn Hebrew?

"At first they said *jasus* [spy]. Afterwards, they quieted down and saw the truth."

And what is the truth?

"What I said. That we need to learn from you, and take from you what you can give us.

"If you leave here now and leave us alone—it will be very hard for us." He explained: "You accustomed us to many things, and we aren't what we once were. It would be as if you were to take us to the middle of a stormy sea and say to us: Get along on your own now. We aren't ready for that yet. Maybe in another ten years, twenty years we will be. Not now. And we know that in our hearts—it's just that no one dares say it out loud."

And in the meantime?

"In the meantime, stay with us for a little bit longer. But change your attitude. Change your views. And start thinking about us in a totally different way."

How differently?

"Start thinking about us not as your Arabs, asses that anyone can ride, people without honor. Start thinking about us as your future neighbors. In the end we will be the people with whom you will have to live here and come to an agreement with and create ties with, and do business with, and everything, right? It's not the Japanese you will have to come to an agreement of peace and trust with, right? Even if there are five more wars here, the children of my grandchildren and the children of your grandchildren will finally get wise and make some sort of agreement with each other, right? So I say: Change your attitude a little, make some effort in our direction. Even try—and I know that it is probably hard for you, right?—try, God forbid, to respect us.

Taher speaks a fluent and special Hebrew. He studied for three years at the Hebrew University. Then he went into business. He has extensive links with Israel and his economic situation is good. Because of his Israeli connections, and because of the things he says, I at first suspected that he was telling me what he thought I wanted to hear. I wondered whether he was not deprecating himself; but I did him an injustice. I wanted to be sure that I was not mistaken: in the two months I traveled in the land of Ishmael, I heard once or twice the sickening sound of the groveler. I was acquainted with the whisper of one who makes himself a partner in my crime and tells me: Stay here forever. Only you can save us. You brought us wealth. Liberty and freedom won't buy us bread. And this, too: We, the Arabs, need to be treated with a strong hand. We respect only the person who hits us. I listened, and tried to find out if the speaker could say something more than that, about what awaits the two peoples if the current situation continues, and about the reality coming into being here. But I heard no more than the same whispers over and over again. There is no point in going into details: it does not matter who said these things—they are said by an enslaved man who has lost his divine image, and maybe doesn't realize it himself. More than likely he believes what he says with all his heart, but I want nothing to do with such people. You can never trust them. Not when they are under our control and not when we are allied with them.

Taher, however, speaks his own free, original thought, without a trace of groveling or desire to be liked. "Twenty years have passed," he tells me, "twenty years during which we have been together. You already know that Arabs know what theater is, and we know that Jews don't have tails. True, not everyone understands it fully. Sometimes I hear a mother here in the village shout at her child: If you don't eat, I'll tell a Jew to come and kill you! I tell her that she should be ashamed to speak that way, because if you teach your child to fear Jews, you ensure that he will do so all his life, and, after all, he needs to live together with them here, right?"

He speaks with emotion, with urgency. Sweat gathers on his forehead, and his thick eyeglasses fog over, despite the coldness of the large, unheated house. For a moment he looks like a frightened attorney caught between two hotheaded disputants, trying to appeal to what remains of their reason, knowing that if they pounce on each other he will be the first to be crushed.

"You also have much to learn: not to get into our souls, for example. Why do your soldiers need to stop me five times when I go to buy a sack of flour in the main street of Hebron? Why do they need to humiliate me at a roadblock in front of my children, who can see how the soldiers laugh at their father and force him to get out of the car? Of course, you have to behave like conquerors. I don't deny that. That's the way history is:

you won the war and we lost. I say, all right. Be conquerors. Push us, but with delicacy. Because sometimes
you push so hard that we see how scared you are."

Scared? Explain that.

"Yes, yes. You should know that you're in a bad
position. When I return from Amman, from visiting my
brother, and one of your soldiers tells me to undress,
and pokes his fingers down there, and checks my underwear, my hair, I look him in the eyes and think, My
God, look how the entire Israeli government and the
entire Israeli Army are scared of you, Taher. And then
you seem to me like a great king who sits in his palace
and places many guards around him, but doesn't sleep
at night, because he knows that at any minute someone
might come and take his crown away."

But you know that our fears are well-founded. We
have enemies, we are in danger, and we have to defend
ourselves.

"Yes, yes, that's right. But even if you are certainly
justified in your searches and your roadblocks and all
that—you yourselves feel in your hearts that this is not
the right position for you. You want to be great conquerors like the Moslems of Mohammed were, like the
Turks and like Napoleon, but on the other hand you
want to be merciful and democratic like the English and
like America, so what do you do? You make mistakes.
Look, every year you have a new political party; anyone
with any sense sets up another party, and why? Because
no one understands what your country was originally
meant to be, and no one remembers what they wanted
to do, and believe me, when I sit down with a Jew (and
I work with Jews all the time) I feel as if we are both
of us in a prison under Israeli occupation."

Then the door opens, and a sleepy child in pajamas comes in, turns to Taher, and jumps into his lap. A small boy, curly-haired, who walks barefoot across the painted floor tiles. Taher speaks to him with movements of his hands, mouthing words for emphasis, and the boy answers with more movements. Taher excuses himself and goes to put the boy to bed. When he returns, he tells me that he has two deaf-and-dumb children. They even studied for a time at the school for the deaf in Jerusalem, but they don't teach Arabic there. He speaks of his children naturally and lovingly, without a hint of reproach in his voice, and I understand without any explanation from him why he so urgently seeks to bring the extremes to reason together, to open their eyes to moderation and caution, and why he cannot surrender to any sort of dream.

9

The Essence of Being a Sabra

On the way to Kfar Adumim, a settlement just off the Jerusalem–Jericho road, Moni Ben-Ari points to a budding green olive grove to the left of the road and says: "That—that I planted. The people from the JNF laughed and said that nothing would grow, that this is the most barren desert in the world, but I planted anyway. And I'm not a farmer and my father was not a kibbutznik, I was born in Rehavia, in Jerusalem, but I said, They have no choice, these olives, they will grow here."

And afterwards, in his back yard, he leads me among the avocado, pomelo, plum, tangerine, lemon, fig, pomegranate, and orange (one of every variety) trees, and lingers by a young mango tree: "He has to grow . . . no . . . he has no choice . . . you think he has a choice? He has to."

I had wanted very much to meet Moni (Menashe) Ben-Ari. Everyone had told me about him. They told me that he is a real mensch. That's what almost everyone said, as if they had coordinated it in advance: a real mensch.

He is almost forty-five years old, father of four, teacher and settler. His father was Arieh Altman, a member of the Knesset, a Revisionist and one of the leaders of the Herut Party. (Revisionism was a Zionist faction founded by Ze'ev Jabotinsky which called for the establishment of a Jewish state on the entire territory of the British Palestine Mandate; that is, including what is now the Kingdom of Jordan. The Herut Party, founded by Jabotinsky's disciple Menahem Begin, is the Israeli successor to the Revisionist movement.) Moni was at the head of those who founded nearby Ma'aleh Adumim, now the largest Jewish West Bank settlement, and after living there four years under difficult conditions, left to settle in Kfar Adumim. He went out to "this point" (the people of Gush Emunim still speak of "points of settlement," as did the first Zionist settlers of Israel), and here, in Kfar Adumim, established a community settlement of religious and secular Jews together.

Moni, secular, is today a member of the secretariat of Amana, the settlement movement of Gush Emunim; up until seven years ago, he was a member of the executive committee of the secretariat of Gush Emunim, but resigned: "I checked all the time to see if their dreams were in tune with reality. How they come into being. Today I'm no longer part of that [Gush Emunim and its secretariat] for two reasons. The first one is that it is an anti-democratic body. No one elected its leaders, nor did anyone ordain them from above, as a rabbi is ordained. They are not accountable to anyone. It's auto-election. The second thing that sets me apart from them is that, in my opinion, they are a small religious cult, which therefore has no interest in the wider public, and I am a simple Jew from the land of Israel. They're a cult.

They're a *schteibel*. That's not to say that a cult can't be a nice thing. You can meet at night, conduct cere- monies, and read interesting things, have music, but that's not enough to do something on a national level. Some- thing that I would call 'all-Israeli.' That's my personal obsession."

Moni speaks the way Israelis used to speak. Slow, heavy speech with a nostalgia-awakening mixture of slang and Talmud, with those special and characteristic cutoff sentences. Not rude, but tough: "I'd also be happy to see their, the Gush's, bylaws. Some sort of document, anything. Maybe there once was one. I don't know. It'd be interesting to see it sometime. In Amana, though, there's popular rule. General meetings, elections. Or- ganized. And there I work. We settle all over the land of Israel. Here, I'm now advising a new settlement in the Galilee. There are about four groups in the Galilee. Little by little. An acre here, a goat there."

There are eighty families in Kfar Adumim. Four hundred people. There is no friction between the religious and the secular inhabitants. This year they received the Speaker of the Knesset's award for quality of life and tolerance. In the school, everyone wears *kipot* while studying re- ligious texts, but non-religious students are allowed to be excused from studying Talmud and Jewish law, in place of which they learn another subject. People drive on Shabbat within the settlement. It's not co-existence, Moni says; it's existence.

A third of the residents work in the town, in agricul- ture, workshops, and greenhouses. There is also a horse ranch. The settlers built the houses themselves. They refused to take money from the Jewish Agency. The Agency officials said: We should pay you for going to this mountain, but Moni said that a house is too important a matter for state finance.

"I don't have any dreams about what the future will be. My dreams have been realized already. I even thought that in order to grow artichokes I would have to work down in Jericho. But look, I have them here. What more do I need? Only to progress with Israel as a whole. To create something new here. To absorb immigration. Secular and religious. Ashkenazim and Sephardim. White collar and blue collar. Those are things that you can try to do something with only in a small community. I don't have any other dreams. Only that we grow. That we plant. Listen: they're going to bring Jerusalem sewage here. That will bring water. Don't laugh! Things will be great here, thanks to the sewage.

You, I said, you speak of Israel as a whole. Unity. But Gush Emunim and the settlements over the Green Line have created, for the most part, division and polarization within the nation.

"Here—again I want to talk just about my corner, only about what I'm responsible for. Let's take this place. So, in the first place, it is state land. This whole area is a tract that was never inhabited. And now let's examine what the big boys say about our location. We won't talk about the Likud, just Labor. Labor has talked for years about Jerusalem, afterwards they added 'the Jerusalem area' (and none of the Mapainiks, the old Labor regulars, noticed the change) and the Jordan. Now, if you like, this place is on the Jordan, or if you like, it's Jerusalem. And I, I put the national consensus to the test. National consensus is wonderful. It's democracy, and I like that, democracy, and if we sit down and look at the platforms of most of the parties we can see that according to eight out of ten Jews we are sitting within the national consensus. That's what I understand in life. That is, this nation, on paper, wants this place—and here I am! What, it's not Jerusalem? I can see Mt. Scopus, where I was born, from here, and the Mount of Olives, where my father is buried, he's also a sort of settler there, and the Augusta–Victoria Hospital on the Mount of Olives, which I liberated in the Six-Day War. This isn't Jerusalem? You have to understand, it was Labor that built the army bases at Beit-El and Bamat Givon, and Labor didn't set up bases in places that it didn't think we would serve, right? We need to wait until the people love their entire land—and as for me, I have no problem with the east bank of the Jordan, but the reality is that for now that is something else. And in reality I know exactly where my power ends. I live within my own bounds.

"And if another two or three million of ours were to come here, my appetite would be bigger. But dreams—oho, I'm free of problems in my dreams. The Bashan and the Gilad and the Horan and all those other Biblical places across the Jordan. Do I want them for my people? Of course I want them, what a question! Understand: I didn't say we should conquer them tomorrow! You think that all the great Zionists didn't want the Horan? They wanted it."

I want to understand why Menashe Ben-Ari, a secular Jew, a Sabra like me who was born in Jerusalem, dreams about the Horan.

"Because I have a right to it. What, rights aren't a serious thing? You don't stand on your rights if someone tries to put even something small over on you? We have to demand our rights. Our rights to the Horan were acceptable to the League of Nations two generations ago, not two thousand years ago! In my terms, in my childhood, it's my land, the Horan, yes, I grew up when the British ruled here, and after that there were still books to learn about the land, pictures of the Arnon River and all that, they are my pictures, that is, Jews like me took them, it's Jericho, the Dead Sea, this area here, what are you talking about?!"

And the Arabs who live here?

"Look, it depends how big our country here is, and where we put the borders, but the Arabs who are in this country will be citizens of the country. There's no room for argument—they are citizens here. And as far as I'm concerned, the military government—its time to go has come. Enough. What we need to make now is interim agreements. After all, everything in life is interim. Here, twenty years have passed, so we need to make an agreement. The basis of that agreement will be, first, a wide national consensus, and that the country preserve a large Jewish majority, almost like today, with the addition of relatively uninhabited areas, and a small addition of Arabs in essential areas, and they'll have full rights. Autonomy. And if none of them wants to make a deal with us, we will establish autonomy unilaterally in the heavily populated areas. Not a state. If they make themselves a state, they'll see that someone will take it apart, one-two, with an iron hand. There's no room for another new country between the Jordan and the sea. In my opinion, the most we can give them now is autonomy. Autonomy is not lack of rights. It just doesn't include RPG bazookas, that's all. Now there's the trial of the Nazi Demjanjuk, right? So, in my opinion, what we have to learn from that is that we can't give them RPGs. That's all. If the world wants them to have RPGs, then I'm against the world, what can I do? No wise stuff. And you asked about Hebron. Good, Hebron is a special case from 1929, when the Arabs massacred the local Jewish community. You can't reward slaughter. I think justice is a serious business. There are things you let go and things you don't let go. In the case of Hebron, there are accounts to settle. We have business with them. No one should win a prize for even one successful massacre. Here there is a great account between peoples. History has accounts. And when you return to the old Jewish quarter in Hebron and rebuild the Avraham Avinu synagogue, which the Arabs used as a latrine—that's an answer. When you build and live, that's an answer. Now, I have a lot of criticism about how it was done, I wouldn't suggest going and settling in the middle of Nablus, like they did in Hebron. We don't need anything like that in Nablus. We can settle on the mountain over the city. Above them. Then I'm calm. I feel good. But in Hebron, within Hebron—that's something."

And are historical accounts so important to you today? Are you willing to endanger the present because of them?

"It bothers me. What do you think? I have accounts going back three thousand years. Of my people. I carry them with me. No one asked me before they put them on me. I'm carrying a burden! The only thing I need to think about is what I do with that burden and how I make another generation possible. That's what directs me. If I go to Spain, let's say (I've never left Palestine, you understand), but what do you think, among the Spaniards I wouldn't suffer? Five hundred years of accounts! So there is at least an interesting part to historical accounting, and that's what expelling and destroying us does to those who hate us: it takes them down several levels. Look at Germany without all its Einsteins! They only have Krupp and those types."

So maybe the solution is to leave the territories, hm? And in that way to take revenge on those who hate us?

Moni laughs his heavy, heart-winning laugh. Outside, strong winds are blowing from the wadi, from the Syrio–African Rift. They cry like *shakalim*, jackals, I say, and meditate that not for nothing did I use the word *shakalim*, like they used to say. Because in a strange way Moni, among the major initiators of settlements in the territories, is precisely the man who symbolizes what we lovingly call "good little Israel." Because he is kibbutz. And manual labor. And sensuous love of the land without God as an intermediary. Honesty, self-sacrifice, and simplicity, and also clumsy speech, but of a type backed up by actions. That, after all, is sabraness, actually, the essence of concise definition of sabraness, so stereotypical, to the point that when you meet it, it seems refreshing and invigorating. Like a greeting from a world that no longer exists. And that world already isn't, partly because of the actions that Moni Ben-Ari himself took part in. Because of the circumstances he and his friends brought about, tangling himself into a helpless state. Very confusing.

"Here, I'll tell you what I tell, say, the guys from the Peace Now movement who ask me about the settlement here: I tell them—guys, it's all right, let's see where we have something in common. How many of you will go to settle the Negev? How many to the Galilee? How many of you will decide to be teachers? Simple ones, second-grade ones, right? How many of your guys will you require to sign on for the standing army after finishing compulsory service? Right, right, you'll make them sign up? How many officers? How many construction workers? Now, if you won't set up any settlements in your way—your way, mind you, not mine—if you don't do anything, then we have nothing to talk about. Nothing. And all your words and all your books and articles—it's nothing but paper. *Kalam fadi*, like they say in Arabic—words without value.

"And understand: the debate should be the way it was forty or fifty years ago. It has to be that both sides do things. In the dispute between the great sages Hillel and Shammai, we accept Hillel's rulings. Of course. But we say of Shammai—also the words of the living God. You can't not settle. But Peace Now, when I see, say, the Labor Party set up fifty settlements a year in the Negev and the Galilee with the best of the youth—hoopa! That's already serious. Then you have someone you can trust. But that's far off, really far off. Labor doesn't offer anything. And does Peres? He doesn't make settlements. Doesn't do it. And we do. And it's hard work building a settlement. And we do one and another one and every year there is something. And there are people. They come. You know, it's really startling: I go to Neveh Ya'akov in Jerusalem, to any apartment, blue-collar workers sit there: What do you want? We want to set up a settlement. Hard to believe but that's the way it is. And they're not from a youth movement and not from Ben-Gurion and not from flags and not from songs. There, somehow it comes to them and that's what they want. And the left—they're in trouble. The whole matter of unaccountable individualism, of everyone for himself—they're in trouble. We're all in trouble because of that. Every man for himself is opposed to the instinct for survival. To the simple instinct for life. And among them—when you get out of the army, they give you money to travel around the world. And they don't have money! And they send the kid for as long as he wants! And then he begins finding himself. And that's all during the ten best years of his life! Between twenty and thirty! Those are the years that you have children and study and develop. What do our sages say? 'At twenty for pursuing a livelihood.' And they—it's a waste of those years, they don't come again. They're not for living out your fantasies in the jungle. They search for pointlessness and become pointless themselves. Finding myself, what am I, those are *kalam fadi.* Horrible nonsense."

Moni talks and outside it grows dark. Actually, it grows purple. Outside the window is a desert void, and past that, brown hills softly joined one to another, contentedly, like the cords of a braided challa, and at twilight they exude a pale amethyst glow. People turn on the lights in their small houses. A point on the mountain. And facing us, through a thin gauze, Sartaba and the eastern approaches of Jericho, and Mt. Ba'al Hatzor and Kiprous, which is the palace Herod built for his mother, and Jerusalem, where Moni was born.

"It really was my dream to see Jerusalem liberated and Jericho and Bethlehem and this place here. I can't deny that. Really a dream. I really wanted that all those years. In my heart. In my head. I had dreams."

I apologize for the next question, silly to my mind, but anyway, it seems to me that I have to ask if—that is—maybe you also laid out, in the secrecy of your room, plans for conquering the city?

"Why is that a stupid question? Listen well: One day, one Jerusalem night, it was two years before the '67 war, what terrible shouts suddenly emerged at eleven at night from Ramban Street in Rehavia, next to my parents' house: 'Moni!!!' I go out, it was Yossi Langotzki, my company commander from my army unit, the son of the first pioneer of the Dead Sea. A Mapainik, from the Labor movement! A Mapainik to beat all Mapainiks, no both-sides-of-the-Jordan Revisionist like me! 'Get down here fast!' Of course I get down there. When Yossi says get down, you get down. I go down in my underwear. He says to me: Listen! I was at Schneller today, at the regiment headquarters, and I said show me the plans for conquering Jerusalem. And they all laughed. Plans? What plans? Where are you coming from? He was in shock. So I was, too. Because I always took it on faith that someone had taken care of that. That is, that someone was looking out for my interests. That's what I believed. Then I didn't know that here you have to do everything yourself. I was naïve. Anyway—I told him, Yossi, that's amazing, what you say. That's not right. I was shaken. He said to me, *Yalla*, come on, let's begin. Do you understand? No one appointed us. It wasn't auto-election, like the people from the Gush. We didn't mean to tell anything to anyone. Just two Jews, civilians from Jerusalem, with maps, notes, whatever; we sat in his apartment, his wife made coffee, and we began to think. Yes. After all, we would be there when they started to shoot. Not anyone else. So there's your answer."

And could it be that today you spend time sitting with someone poring over the plans for the Bashan, for example?

Moni again laughs a slow and warm laugh. "I'm already old. Enough. I only deal with settlement. Now people will come and say that the situation in the ter-

ritories causes corruption. So I state sadly that the corruption existed before, too. It's true, a military government corrupts. We have to get rid of that. Decide one
way or the other. Now, I'll tell you something about
justice. I hate being unjust. It eats away at me if I'm
unjust. But still no one has proven to me that I'm unjust.
The Arab nation is a great nation. Huge. I don't accept
that every two Arabs is a country. The Arab nation is
not a nation without a motherland. Forget that. It has
a tremendous motherland, of which it sees us as just a
part. This people that lives here, the one that calls itself
Palestinian, has not up to the present day realized itself.
And it had many opportunities: it could have realized
itself under the Turks, under the English, under Hussein.
His brothers, no? And I, from the outpost at Notre
Dame, saw what Hussein did to them before the Six-
Day War. How he cut them down with gunfire. What
did we say then? The Arab nation has many motherlands
and countries, and in truth it doesn't bother me that
much. As individuals—of course, a person has a house,
a field, he has rights to that. And if he is a citizen of the
country—he can vote. That's why I don't want two million of them. We'll make an arrangement so that there
will be less than that among us. And whoever belongs
to us is equal. Like me and like you. So I don't say we
should annex tomorrow morning. Because if we do, they
will get the right to vote, but if not—let the noble Arab
nation take care of them. Noble! And by the way, as
long as the gap between the Arab nation's image of itself
and reality is preserved, it is to our benefit."

Moni Ben-Ari does not preach. He explains slowly,
like someone who is figuring out for himself, as he talks,
the facts he presents. Something in the structure of his

face—the crook in the nose, in direct line with his chin—
hints at a personality that always bangs its head against
the wall, and the things he says in such a friendly way
hide in them the hard kernel of the entire conflict: two
nations which still don't recognize each other's legiti-
macy. The Israelis see the Arabs as another branch of
the Arab countries, and the Arabs see us as an artificial
stooge of world imperialism. Dr. Meron Benvenisti argues in this context that any possible solution, of those
now in the air, would be an artificial, political solution
which would not take into consideration the power of
the primal fears, the traumas, the memories, and the
historical accounts, which did not allow either side to
risk even recognizing the other. "And this land," Moni
says, "is very small. How do they say it: Can two kings
sit on one throne? And we are, after all, two beggars.
There isn't even a proverb appropriate to our circumstance. That's right. So we are a beggar who needs to
get along here. Because where can we go? I don't have
another piece of land. Somehow I never learned English,
I learned only about what is here. And as for me, if they
put me somewhere else, I will wither immediately. Only
what is here is mine. Only here."

And what if the government decides that we have to
evacuate Kfar Adumim?

"I will get up and go. Immediately. With horrible
sadness. Understand: I didn't come here for my own
private reasons. I came because I think that my people
need to be here. And I try to persuade others through
what I do here. I told you. An acre here, a goat there.
But if my people decide that they don't want me here—
I will get up and go."

It is already dark. We go out into the garden, and

Moni shows me in the dimness the goldfish pond and the fruit trees, and the young mango tree that has no choice. Moni has four sons; his wife died eight months ago. She is buried in the settlement. That was the completion of the settlement, Moni said: a settlement isn't complete without a graveyard.

The Mountain That Went

I had the privilege of enjoying much help from Nisim Krispil, and I want to thank him. Krispil, an Israeli, once of the Society for the Protection of Nature and the author of many books on nature and outdoorsmanship, spends much time wandering through the West Bank, and in his direct, heart-winning way, establishes immediate rapport with every person. He walks the streets of the West Bank, in the refugee camps and the villages, speaks Arabic like a native, and knows all the smallest customs and manners. During the last few years he has been studying the material culture of the Arabs in Israel and the West Bank in all its aspects—the structure of the villages, the houses, agriculture, traditions and customs, superstitions, and the arts. He calls the Palestinians "the masters of the place," and in his words, they remind him entirely of his forefathers. "We missed a chance to create good relations for the future with the villages here," he says. "We could have built something with them in partnership. In mutual assistance and friendliness. Today, the only people who come to them are people with demands. Teams of surveyors looking for state lands, security police, building examiners, and so on. No one has taken an interest in what can be improved, to distribute clothes to the needy, to bring toys to kindergartens." Krispil himself brings clothes to families he meets, helps out his friends when they have problems with the administration, and performs other small deeds, so simple at first sight, but tremendously valued by the Arabs. He goes everywhere unarmed, even to the most inimical villages. He says that no one has ever tried to hurt him. "Carrying a gun angers the Arabs and humiliates them," he says.

"The occupation," he relates, "has penetrated even the more traditional folklore: for example, there are certain places which have changed their names. The Mt. Gilo range, where the village Beit Jala is located, was once called Ras-Beit-Jala, and today, Jabal-Ma-Rakh (the mountain that went). And there are no few other places which became Ma-Rakh for the Arabs."

Circumstances have also influenced traditional poetry. Nisim gives as an example a traditional gasidah (a long poem, structured according to a classical rhyme scheme and divided into verses), telling of a hunter who hunted a doe and treated it cruelly. Over the last few years, the poem changed, and the hunter became a Jew:

"Pray for our prophet Mohammed/so that he may help you and us./The doe went to graze in the meadows;/the Jew caught her./He chained her;/she began crying for her children./He said to her: Why are you crying, doe?"

The song continues to describe over the course of several additional verses the sufferings of the doe at the hands of the cruel Jew, and in the end an Arab comes to save her. Not only does he save her—he makes the

Jew a surprising proposal: "Lock me in chains instead of her/and free her to her fawns."
And how does it end?
"The cruel Jew saw this./His heart was taken with the nobility of the Arab—and he freed them both."

10

The Other Barta'a

The "situation," like a stage magician, draws another card, links another inseparable ring to the chain. This time it is Barta'a, and actually, the entire problem of the relations of the Arabs of Israel to the Arabs of the West Bank.

The village of Barta'a is situated about three kilometers east of the Wadi Ara valley, between the Israeli cities of Afula and Hadera, in the area called the Little Triangle. The village is built on the two slopes of a ravine called Wadi Elmia, and the huge Kabha clan, with a family tree reaching back to the eighteenth century and inscribed on deerskin, lives here.

The village received its name from Hawali (holy man) Sheikh Muhammad, buried on the mountain peak over the village. Sheikh Muhammad had been a scout in Saladin's army and had participated in the wars against the Crusaders. When he returned from a victorious battle, he would jump with happiness, and they would say of him *bart'a ash-Sheikh*, which means "the Sheikh hopped with joy."

The village was one until 1949. In that year the representatives of Israel and Jordan, meeting in Rhodes, decided that the border between them would run through the ravine that divides the village. It would seem that the drafters of the Green Line saw the ravine their maps indicated as a natural border. It may be that they didn't realize what they were doing.

One morning, the village was divided. Members of the same family and friends and relatives were torn from each other. The village spring remained on the Israeli side, and the mosque in Jordan. Everything was split in two by the sure and powerful hands of maliciously indifferent giants.

During the first years there was no fence between the two countries or between the two villages, but Jordanian and Israeli soldiers prevented free passage of civilians. When the two armies began clashing in this contact area between them, a "proper" border was built. At the insistence of the villagers, a canal was dug to bring water from the spring in Israeli Barta'a to the center of Jordanian Barta'a. The Israelis drank by day and the Jordanians by night. The children in Israeli Barta'a would urinate in the water to taunt their friends on the other side of the border. The women would launch paper boats containing letters to their friends.

The villagers, suffering from longing and frustration, felt their existence split and their lives disconnected. The meanings of so many primal things seemed suddenly to be on the other side of the fence. The two parts of the village did all they could to maintain some sort of illusory fabric of cooperation. Smugglers would bring news from across the border. When Jordanian Barta'a celebrated a wedding, the residents of Israeli Barta'a would

stand on the other side of the border and watch the celebration from afar, with binoculars. When a couple married on the Israeli side, the famous singer Abu Leil would
arrive from Kufr Qar'a to entertain the guests, and his
voice would fill the emptiness of the valley; the Jordanian
soldiers on the other side would shoot into the air out of
joy. When a child was born in one of the Barta'as, the
proud father would station himself on the hill and shout
the news across the border with all his might.

Only once, in 1964, did a Jordanian officer allow the
villagers from both sides to meet their relatives. The
entire divided clan descended into the ravine for three
hours and mixed with each other, touched each other,
talked without stopping, and cried. It was then that they
saw for the first time babies which had been born and
couples who had married. One young man from Israel,
who had loved a Jordanian girl during the years of separation and had been able to gaze at her only from far
off, asked her hand from her father. The *hutba*, the
marriage contract, was drafted immediately, and the girl
"infiltrated" and came to live in Israel.

Then came the war, the war of 1967, and the border
was lifted. The two halves, the two lovers, could finally
make their unification a reality. They descended into the
ravine, looked at one another—and were strangers.

"We suddenly saw how different they are from us,"
Riad Kabha, the young mukhtar of the Israeli village, said
to me during my visit there. "We had been with the Israelis for nineteen years. We were more modern than they
were, more open and free. It was hard for us to get used
to them. Their internal rhythm was different. The whole
way they thought about things was different. For example, our attitude toward women is liberal and advanced,

and with them there was—and is today—complete separation of boys and girls from school age onward, and equality between the sexes is not even a subject for discussion. Along with that, we felt that they somehow looked down on us. As if they had remained more faithful to tradition and to Islam. They would lecture us haughtily, feeling that they were better Arabs than we were.

"Contact with them was awkward and unpleasant. They had been all that time under oppressive Jordanian rule, and their links with the outside world had been extremely limited. Jordanian soldiers lived among them and intimidated them; they were trained to say 'yes, sir' and 'no, sir' and it affected their entire behavior. Our Barta'a, the Israeli one, was richer and more active. Our houses were more luxurious, and every family lived on its own. With them, a married son would continue to live with his father. People pay less attention to their fathers' advice among us, and every person sets out on his own. Individualists. Even in daily life there are differences: they go to Tulkarm and Nablus for shopping and enjoyment, and those cities are their focal point in every way. Our focus is the Jewish city of Hadera. There is a gap and there is distance between us."

In 1971, a young man from Jordanian Barta'a described the young people on the Israeli side as follows: "They are shallow politically. They do not have a serious foundation for understanding current events and lack a proper outlook for the future. They are influenced outwardly by the Jewish people; they took the shell of modern society and threw away the content. They do not have strong family connections. They change their opinions as the situation changes, and they have no principles."

Riad Kabha's comments on this criticism were in a way defensive and apologetic. "We have not taken only the shell of the modern world," he said. "We have taken more than that. We have many positive characteristics—higher social awareness; we are more active than they are, better able to organize ourselves in order to help ourselves, and in the framework of the political problems, we do everything possible in order to . . ."

Kahba continued to speak, and it was possible to guess in advance what he would say and how he would say it. He is a nice person, wise and moderate, and he is caught, to his sorrow, in the trap that captures every uprooted person. He has abandoned one way of life without having absorbed another. People like him speak very carefully: they are well acquainted with the tenuousness of uncompromising statements untested by threats and temptations. I supposed that in the other Barta'a I would hear more uncompromising, determined, strong language, but Riad Kabha and the people of Israeli Barta'a had personally felt how life can erode the totality of the ideal, and of natural, primal aspirations.

The other Barta'a (the people of each call their sister village "the other Barta'a") winds up the face of the ravine, and is poorer and more crowded. Lines of cactus break through the fences of each house, and herds of sheep kick up dust in its alleys. 'Amar Kabha notices me talking with some teenagers in the street, and suggests I come with him to his house. He is twenty-six years old, but looks much older. He works in the poultry slaughterhouse in Hadera, and does nicely. His new house is large and sunlit, built like the houses in Israeli Barta'a.

His small children play on the floor mats, and there is a wide, open view from the window.

"I was a boy when the village was reunited. I remember not knowing my grandmother until the reunification. Other children had grandmothers and I was jealous. I would run over the hill facing the other Barta'a, and I would call out *"Siti Siti,* Grandmother" to every old woman I saw there, but I didn't find her. When my grandfather died, we learned about it from hearing the shouts and wails from the Israeli side. My father could not go to his funeral, of course.

"Every so often, the Israeli authorities would bring a movie to the other Barta'a, and the people there, with us in mind, would project it on the side of a house that faced us. I remember how we would bring benches and chairs and sit out at night to see those movies. They were very popular among us, at least as much as Egyptian President Nasser's speeches on television."

"As-salam and aleikum."

Judat and As'ad, friends of 'Amar's, enter the room. They are also, of course, of the Kabha clan. Judat, tall, curly-haired, delicate-featured, studied economics at Irbid University in Jordan. He cannot find work in his profession here: "I worked for a while in a pub in Tel Aviv, and I spoke to Israeli students there. They studied exactly the same material I studied. Afterwards, I worked as a dishwasher in a restaurant. Until I couldn't stand it anymore—they paid me so little, and treated me like a servant—so I came back to the village. You're surprised? We have an Oxford-educated engineer here who works picking oranges and repairing cars. We have some street cleaners with college educations. I know a dish-washer who has a master's degree in economics. Can you imagine how someone like that feels? We made a mistake when we went to college. We had great aspirations, and we forgot where we come from. Our parents spent their life's savings on us, sold their herds in order to pay for our studies, and we come back to the village, no longer really belonging here. But they won't accept us anywhere else. I sit and read newspapers all day, hang out with my friends, and grow older."

I ask him if he knows what the people in Israeli Barta'a think of them. He laughs and says, "You talked with them, didn't you? You tell me." I say that on my way here I recorded an unflattering description of them from an Israeli Arab, a native of nearby Um el Fahm. I qualify it in advance by saying that it is very derogatory, on the most general level, but authentic nevertheless. "Immediately after the war," the young Arab told me, "without even waiting for the cease-fire, we all ran to Barta'a. All those years we had heard the adults talking about how Barta'a had been cut in two, and about the wonderful people there, and we wanted to see for ourselves. So what did we see? A filthy village. People dressed shabbily, in clothes from twenty years ago. We had bell-bottom pants, they had straight-legs. When we started wearing straight-legs again, they started wearing huge bell-bottoms. We, when we got older, didn't grow mustaches. They all have mustaches two meters long! We had a game when we were kids of counting the mustaches of *dafawin*, that's what we call them, *dafawin*, you know, people who live in the *dafa*, the West Bank, and every Arab will put down the Arabs of the West Bank Barta'a by saying, 'What a *dafawi*!' "

"It's not a serious study of us," Judat says, "but simple things like that really do reflect a lot. When we met Israeli Arabs, and from the other Barta'a in particular, they thought we were simply backward. Like the Negroes in Africa, for instance. They still like to think they are better than us, but there are statistics, and they say that there are more high-school graduates among us, and more college graduates. Maybe the conditions of the occupation are what keep us from making the most of our abilities; after all, the whole world knows that the Palestinians have great potential, knowledge, and experience of life. Israeli Arabs have already lost that gift, that 'spark.' They have become spoiled and rotten. Their thinking is already lazy. So they have color televisions and I have only a black-and-white, and he eats meat every day and I have meat only once a week. He thinks that's culture, but he is wrong. Israel improved their standard of living a great deal, but their minds have gone to sleep. Maybe it's because they try very hard not to think of their complex predicament, so they busy themselves with unimportant things: they spend their lives competing with their neighbor over standard of living and external wealth. The most important thing for them is who can build their son a house first. It's the opposite with me. I have a sixteen-year-old brother. He could get married tomorrow, but I won't let him: he needs to finish his studies first. To build his life. And another thing—we are better than them when it comes to human relations. Israel was a bad influence on them in that area as well. Friends and relatives aren't as close. They've become like the European Jews among you"—he laughs—"and we've stayed like the Middle Eastern ones."

'Amar: "When we go there for a wedding, they laugh

at us. 'They've come to get some food!' And afterwards they laugh and say, 'The *dafawin* came and ate everything!' They say they're just joking, but we know they mean it."

As'ad (twenty years old, baby-faced, works in the village, getting married next month): "They have Israeli identity cards, so they can go to Tel Aviv and hang out all night and no one does anything to them. I have to return to the village at night, or hide if I want to sleep there. My car has the blue license plate of a *dafawi*, and they have yellow Israeli plates. They feel like kings because of that, because the police will stop me at a roadblock and let them pass, like Israelis. Once I was driving along the road and the car behind me honked the whole time so that I would get off the road and let him pass. I looked in the mirror and saw an Israeli Arab. It didn't help me any—he almost threw me off the road, and as he passed he even shouted, 'Move aside, move aside, you dirty *dafawi*, go back to Nablus where you came from!' "

The other two nod their heads.

As'ad: "If you ask out a girl from there, she says, 'I don't go out with *dafawin*.' "

'Amar: "Still, there have been some marriages with them during the last few years. At first they didn't want to, but now they're getting used to it."

As'ad: "It's like an Ashkenazi Jew not wanting to marry a Yemenite Jew."

'Amar: "And there's something interesting. Whenever they have a fight with someone over something, they run to us and ask us to fight for them."

The three of them laugh. "As if we were their bodyguards."

Riad Kabha from Israeli Barta'a confirms this with an awkward smile. "In 1972 the Israeli border guard wanted to fence off part of our land for training. We didn't know what to do. We sat and talked about it. People from the other Barta'a, the Jordanian one, suddenly appeared, and asked us, What are you planning to do about it? We said, We'll shout, we won't let it pass quietly, we'll have a press conference! They laughed at us and said, Come out to the land itself and we'll fight. We fought together with them. They came and lay down in front of the bulldozers. They had a lot more nerve than we did."

Judat: "They always brag about how much like the Israelis they are, yet they don't sense what the Israelis think of them. Israeli Arab towns like Faradis and Kufr Qar'a don't get the same kind of government support Jewish settlements get. Here a week ago the government decided that the Druse and Circassian communities would be granted equal rights with the Israelis. They're not giving equality to Israeli Arabs. I don't envy them—they don't have any pride. They only take things from the country, but they don't do anything for it. While you do reserve duty forty-five days a year, they go to the beach. If I were in their position, I wouldn't take anything from the country at all—not social security, not social benefits, nothing."

I read them what the young man from Um el Fahm told me: "They'll tell you how miserable we are and how much Arab pride they have. Sure! We were in Israel twenty years, and we collaborated with you a little, but not excessively, and never of our own volition. They did. True, there were some among us who sold you land, but you took most of our land by force. And here they came, the *dafawin*, and within a year or two they had sold land, received weapons from you, collaborate with you even more than you need them to, maybe! They look down on us? They haven't suffered a tenth of what we have! They took all our lands. We suffered horrible oppression under the military government before 1966. And them? What do they know? They can travel freely wherever they want. At the most they get stopped at a roadblock here and there. And I'll give you one small example why I hate the *dafawin*: once an Israeli took his cigarettes out of his pocket and offered them to me and to a *dafawi*. I said no thanks and nothing more. The *dafawi* kissed the Israeli's fingers and said he didn't smoke. Kissed his fingers! That's the difference between us."

'Amar, Judat, and As'ad listen and laugh derisively. Judat says: "They suffered more than us? How many years did they live under a military government and how many years have we lived under one? And with us there's no end to it in sight! They talk about oppression? What do they know about oppression? They say we sold land? Sure, there are some who sell land, and there are others who sell their souls . . ."

The three of them talk together excitedly, interrupting each other in an odd, almost Jewish, competition over how much they had suffered at the hands of the Jews. Judat adds: "They cry about being second-class citizens. But the truth is that they are fifth-class citizens!" The three West Bank Barta'ans give me their ranking of all those who live under Israeli sovereignty: first come the Jews, who are first-class citizens. Then come the Jewish immigrants from Ethiopia, who are second-class. Then come the Bedouin, and then, they say, we come, because we lack rights but we have pride, and at the very end come the Israeli Arabs.

"Understand," says Judat, "that in living here, in the West Bank, I constitute an international problem. The whole world talks and argues about me. No one talks about him. I am free in my soul, I know that I can say what I feel toward you and the occupation with a full heart. He can't. He is too tied up with you. He can't even think about it. He prefers not to think about it."

As'ad: "That's why they feel uncomfortable when they meet us. They suddenly have to decide who they really are."

'Amar: "They call themselves Israeli Arabs, but they don't call us Palestinians, because that is problematic for them. They call us West Bank Arabs or just *dafawin*. Their children even talk that way—instead of saying, 'I'm going to the other Barta'a,' they say, 'I'm going to the *difa*,' to the West Bank."

Riad Kabha, the mukhtar of Israeli Barta'a, said of that: "They really see themselves as part of the Palestinian people. We see ourselves as part of the Palestinian people, but also as an integral part of Israel. The sad part about it is that the Israelis reject us because we are Arabs, and the Arab countries reject us because we are Israelis. The Arabs in the other Barta'a continue to see us as part of Israel. But despite that, if you write about us, you should write the whole truth: in recent years the differences between us are starting to blur. After all, twenty years have passed. There are more marriages between them and us. There is more contact. They are beginning to be a bit influenced by our way of life. We've also gained something: our national consciousness has grown stronger as a result of contact with them. As if we had remembered our roots again. Our economic superiority could not stand up to their political superiority."

"If, in the future, they ever decide to set up a Palestinian state," said the young Arab from Um el Fahm, thirty years old, university graduate, now living and working in Jerusalem, "and if Um el Fahm were to be included in that Palestinian state, I would not want to live there under any circumstances. You have to understand that I was educated here. My way of thinking is from here. I'm already used to this life, even to our special status among you, on this quarter-democracy you have given us. Do you think I could go now and live with them in Nablus?"

Just before I left West Bank Barta'a I met a young, embittered man who works as a laborer in Israel. After asking that I not print his name, he told me: "If we act like fools, the gap between us and Israeli Barta'a will always remain. If we are smart, we will learn it all from them. There are lots of things worth taking from them. The future lies in their direction, not in ours. Look how they enjoy life, and what dogs' lives we have. With us, the father decides everything, and he doesn't always understand how life has changed. Their women study, ours don't. Among us, a father has many children, so they all remain poor generation after generation. With them, every family has three children and stops. A guy my age and with my intelligence who lives there will succeed more than me, and will be happier. But if we are smart, if we learn from them exactly what they learned from you, when you come here twenty years from now, you won't see any difference between Barta'a and the other Barta'a."

11

Swiss Mountain

View—A Story

Gidi raced lightheartedly up to the edge of the village, where he slowed the pace of his gasping Peugeot truck, and turned calmly and considerately onto the main road. It was early afternoon and only a handful of villagers were out in the street, and they nodded at him in a slightly summary way. Gidi was a little disappointed, because he expected that they would be happier to see him: he had not been there for six weeks. He supposed, however, that they were waiting to find out what his extended absence and sudden return meant for them.

He stopped by Al-Sa'idi's small grocery store, checked routinely to see if his pistol and case of maps were on him, pushed his sunglasses up above his forehead, locked the car, jiggled the key in the lock—and just performing those actions filled him with a feeling of power and joy.

"Abu Dani! *Ahlan*, Abu Dani!" The storekeeper, small and quick to serve, called out to him, went out to greet him, dragged him inside, and seated him on a stool. "Sit, sit. We haven't seen you for so long!" At the crook of a finger a small, barefoot boy hurried behind a filthy curtain to make coffee.

Gidi looked over the shelves and smiled at Al-Sa'idi: "How's business?"

Al-hamdu-lla. And where have you been, Abu Dani? It's been maybe a month that we haven't seen Abu Dani.

Work.

The storekeeper bared yellow teeth and laughed, as if party to some dark secret:

Your work—I won't ask any questions!

The coffee arrived. They drank.

He didn't want to spend too much time here, with Al-Sa'idi, in the unlit store. He was too happy right now to waste his time here, and wanted to be in the light, at the top of the hill, taking in the view. He wanted to shout what he had to say to the whole world. But he didn't mean to start in Al-Sa'idi's grocery. Not that it mattered to him that Al-Sa'idi know in the end, too—after all, everyone would know—but his heart stilled for a split second when he imagined himself telling Al-Sa'idi first. Even though Gidi liked him and was grateful to him, because this crafty little storekeeper had been the first one to dare offer Gidi a cup of coffee, when he came to the village after the war, to work.

Gidi had been young and inexperienced then, just through a crash course put together to provide for the immediate needs of the war, and was sent out to fend for himself. When he came to the village, six years ago, at the end of '67, his muscles had been a frozen lump of fear and tension. He had caught his reflection in the window of the Peugeot and had seen his shoulders bunched up almost to the level of his ears. The villagers followed his movements with concern, not with enmity. From the way he walked, they could identify immediately who he was. They had endured not a few years of occupation under the Jordanians and had already been under the thumb of people like him; he slipped easily into the territories they had evacuated in their souls to make room for deference and inaction.

He told them that his name was Abu Dani, "the father of Dani," Arab custom being to call a man by the name of his eldest son. They would often send regards to his Dani, and he answered them with a smile and invited Allah to bestow his blessings on their children. Over the course of the years, he came to know them all: the children, the grandchildren, and the great-grandchildren. As he passed through the streets of his village, he would feel a slight bureaucratic throb of satisfaction, of a type he had never known, like a shopkeeper examining the merchandise in his store.

The basic work had been hard, and there had not been anyone to help or instruct him: all the senior members of the unit, all the instructors from the course, were busy those days gathering and absorbing the endless intelligence that victory brought with it: documents and people, suspects and collaborators, cities and villages to be utterly penetrated, to crack the code of relations and alliances and allegiances of the people, the leaders, the clans, a great quiltwork, intense study, no holds barred— knowledge is power.

Everything had to be brought to light quickly, before the people had a chance to think twice, before anyone had an opportunity to apply counterpressure: family ties, acquaintances, intimate friends, letters, secrets, diseases, hidden defects, all types of perversions—Gidi worked tirelessly in those days, in a fever, grabbing the village from the underside, exposing it to the sunlight, knowing that he had to hurry and preserve what he found out, before the sun had a chance to parch the delicate, bashful frescoes he uncovered.

Six years. Three thousand people. He knows almost all the men by their full names. He can recite in his sleep the number of children Hashem Al-Masri has, and the names of all of Fa'ad Abu Saliman's creditors; nowadays he barely needs to exert himself here, today he is already responsible for three additional villages, but he keeps a warm place in his heart for his first one. Proof: he came here immediately when his vacation ended. Here he wants to break his news for the first time. A sort of slightly foolish gesture of thanks, but it is that naïve, unprofessional foolishness that makes him tremble slightly.

A quiet village, Gidi thought, walking again in the sunlight, greeting the vegetable man, shaking hands here and there, regaining the authoritative gestures of his job. An easy, dignified walk, so different from the way he walked in Israel, and belying the wild joy he felt inside, which he felt he must bellow, roar.

Nimr, ten years old, rolling an iron hoop with a stick, almost ran into him, and was aghast. A nice boy, Nimr, and Gidi felt like his godfather: when Nimr was small and suffered from kidney disease, Gidi saw to it that he was operated on at the Hadassah Hospital in Jerusalem. It was in that way, using such simple and humanitarian means, that he succeeded in winning over an entire clan. Gidi smiled at Nimr and winked, and the little boy made off on his way, rolling his hoop and trumpeting. Gidi made a mental note to talk to Nimr's father about his cousin, Aref, who had traveled to Amman three times

in the past year. And another detail he had meant to
find out about before leaving suddenly on his long vacation: Is Bassam Abaida still meeting his beauty in Hebron? Unimportant details, which will be of use some-
day.

My Arabs are quiet, Gidi reflected, I can leave them
for a month and a half, and they stay quiet. In other
places there are always disturbances, but in my village
it is always quiet, and that is because I know how to
handle them.

He walked past two women drying watermelon seeds
on a blanket, joked with a few construction workers
who were setting up a scaffold, exchanged macho jibes
with them, and shook their brown, hard hands. They
asked him where he had disappeared to, and he was
almost tempted to tell them, but stopped himself, because he felt that the first time he wanted to tell it differently; he didn't know exactly in what way it would
be different. Maybe—with more festivity. In any case,
he had a feel for how he did not want to say it. And he
did not want to now. That is—not to them.

It was a hot, good day, full of shining light. Gidi strode
through the street, his hands behind his back, lost in his
thoughts, greeting with a nod of his head the figures
appearing before his eyes. The long separation from the
village—the longest since he began working here—gave
him a more disinterested and slightly celebratory way
of looking at his work, and everything that had happened recently in his life made him—so it seemed to
him—wiser and more mature; he reflected on how easy
it was for him to control this large population, he had
almost never needed violence to do it, and with the

exception of one or two cases of discontent and shouting, the villagers had helped him perform his job in a dignified way.

They would come to his office in the next district over and report to him all he requested, almost without opposition and without enmity, as if humoring the unpleasant eccentricity of an insistent relative. During tense times he would tighten his hold on them a little, and when the tension passed, he would let up. He was always on guard, but was amazingly good at hiding it. They did not sense it, and he also trained himself to live with his guard up, though invisible, so that it wouldn't interfere with his private life. He never forgot, though, that he was in enemy territory, and the news which flowed out of the teleprinter did not allow him to forget. Terrorist cells were active everywhere, performing cruel, animal-like deeds, and he and his colleagues were the main buffer against them. Without their work, there would not be a minute of peace either for the Israelis or for his tranquil Arabs. Gidi began his job as a professional, and stayed with it as an idealist.

Over the course of those four years, Gidi spread his net wisely over the village. He preferred to see it as a commercial venture in which the villagers provided information and in exchange gained security, as well as the licenses and permits they needed. Gidi tried not to force anyone to provide information. But every villager needed, along the way, various documents, building permits, or permission to cross the Jordan bridges, so that they had to go through Gidi's modest office and talk with him over a cup of coffee.

I've studied them, he told Billie when he met her four years ago, I study them the way you study Hebrew, a new language. With all the fine points and nuances. When you know a language well, you can suddenly make out when something isn't right. In what way? Billie asked. So that I can feel even the smallest change in my village. Any tension. Or if a stranger appears. Billie, who was smart, asked: The question is whether you understand it for real, from inside, or whether you only know how to press a button and get your output, like, say, from a machine, right? And Gidi, who was an honest young man and did not ever allow an illusion to lead him astray, and who was cruel in his demands on himself, was thrown off by her comment, and turned it over and over without finding an answer to it.

There were also villagers who showed up at his office without having been invited. Sometimes in order to report something about their neighbors, or about their enemy in the village, and sometimes they just came in order to sit with him for fifteen minutes, drink coffee, and make up a story. The grocery-store owner was one of those. At first Gidi thought they were coming to look him over, to feel out his intentions, but after a while he realized foggily that there were people who had some strange compulsion to be around him. To expose themselves to a vague temptation which he embodied for them.

But most of the villagers came to him only at his behest. He scheduled appointments, and arranged it so that every year he would meet all the adult males living in the village. It entertained him to think that they themselves knew nothing of his clever planning and could not guess what role each of them played in the picture as a whole. They would sit with him for a short time, try to satisfy him, embarrassing him a little by treating him like a father. Like someone older than they, experienced and very powerful. It was necessary for him to adjust himself to a small change in his internal image of himself when he crossed the Green Line which separates Israel from the West Bank, and again became Gidi. They would tell him with quiet, choked voices all he wanted to know. They in any case felt that he knew everything about them, about their public and private lives, and they had already stopped wondering which of their friends had given him that particular piece of intimate information about them. They could no longer trust anyone, not even members of their families, and that made them even more submissive and apathetic than they had been six years before. He himself noticed that for a long time they had not been able to tell him anything he did not already know, and he somehow felt that they had given him all the information they had and their whole selves as well.

But he did not want—he really did not want—to think of those kinds of things on this wonderful summer morning, as he strode among them, bursting with happiness, looking for the one person worthy of being told of the birth of his first son, slightly disappointed to discover that all of these old acquaintances of his had become somehow transparent and hollow, as if they were all very old or very childish, and that none of them was his age: that is, not really his age, but, how to put it, close to him. That is—a sort of uneasiness came over him. And impatience.

Gidi never believed that they hated him for what he did to them as part of his work. He was sure that they knew how to appreciate his delicacy, the respect he showed for them. Not like certain colleagues of his who accomplished their work through the use of overt and covert power and violence. Gidi did not need that, and was happy for it. Only once, about two years ago, he had had to make small use of the "starling" procedure on one of the village teachers, who had suddenly turned into a young and disgruntled "crow," darkly shrieking. Gidi warned him a few times, surprised him with an exact quote of things he had said to his pupils during a Koran lesson, and explained to him reasonably what those things would lead to. The man refused to take the hint. He had a bitter soul and was full of hate, and blasted Gidi with strident words, so strange to the spirit of the tacit and unwritten agreement Gidi had with the village. Gidi really had no choice but to use the "starling" procedure. It was almost fun to see in actual use a simple and subtle exercise from the course. Officers, friends of Gidi's who had borrowed senior officers' insignia, would arrive in luxurious military cars, not the usual trucks, and would invite themselves to lunch at the house of the "crow." At the end of the meal they would ask him to show them out, and outside the house, in front of everyone, they would slap him on the back and shower him with smiles and winks. The village was soon muttering and giggling. It had been necessary to direct the matter wisely and with great sensitivity. Not to awaken a real uproar against the teacher, but only to ostracize him. Within two weeks the pupils in the crow's class were boycotting his lessons, and a month later he took his wife and four children and moved to another village. Eviatar, Gidi's colleague there, reported that the man was quiet. He became a canary.

Someone ran and called out after him. Gidi turned around. The village elder, the mukhtar Harbi, ran after him, calling him with a smile, his feet getting tangled in his robe. Gidi thought—Here, this is the man I will tell, with him it feels right. He waited without moving until the mukhtar approached him, obeying an unwritten law that the villager must approach the officer and not the opposite, and then he shook his hand, gripping it with determination, in order to keep the slightly excited man from falling on his face.

The mukhtar pelted him with questions, his words running into each other in emotion: where had Abu Dani been, why had he suddenly disappeared, had he come back for good, the village had been very worried, they sent some other officer, not as nice as Abu Dani, we were getting scared he would stay here, and he didn't want to tell us where Abu Dani had gone, we thought Abu Dani didn't love us anymore—the man chuckled, pulling Gidi toward his house—after all, he can't go without having coffee with Harbi, who almost didn't sleep at night worrying about him, because Abu Dani is like a brother to him; what do I mean brother, son.

With a certain reluctance Gidi allowed the heavyset, heavily clothed mukhtar to lead him toward his house. He would really rather have remained in the sun, in the clean light, filling up with the clear air, but he knew that he could not refuse Harbi, and not only that, he had already returned to work, and would have to sit with Harbi anyway and hear what was new in the village.

The house was large and handsome. They sat in the light-filled living room, sinking into the greenish velvet armchairs, smoking the Israeli Time cigarettes that the mukhtar saved specially for Gidi. He would always open him a fresh pack and Gidi was somehow flattered by that: a sort of personal gesture.

So, where was Abu Dani all this time?

He gazed at the brown, large face gazing at him from close range, baring before him its lines in a too open way, intimate and embarrassing. Over the last six years Gidi had seen those lines rearrange themselves into varied and different expressions—he had seen deep, heart-rending fear, desperation without hope; he had seen them cry, and seen them greatly calmed. Sometimes he thought he saw sincere, instinctive affection as well, affection which transcended the limitations of circumstances. The first few times, he saw the mukhtar Gidi was very impressed with the man's nobility. He was like a legendary Arab hero. Afterwards he began liking him as a person, not as a legend: the mukhtar was an emotional and stormy man, and knew how to win Gidi's heart. Gidi was thankful to him, because he had given him, actually, the key to the riddle of many of the villagers.

Your health is all right? the mukhtar asked, worried by Gidi's silence. Is the family okay? The children? How is your Dani?

Sometimes, and especially during the past month, when he had spent much time at home with Billie, Gidi had reflected on his previous life, after he left the army, and before he began his new work. He told Billie that he thought he had once been much more naive. Really, I was so naive, he told her, his hands running over the long brown hair spread out around her head, and she said: "You? Naive?" and laughed the short, nervous laugh that she had made her own during the last months of her pregnancy, and said that she was sorry she had not known him then. You were probably nicer, she said, and she pouted, slightly resentful.

Gidi did not want to start another argument with her, so he only smiled and was silent, but he thought to himself that people once seemed much better to him than they really are. Much more proud and interesting and natural. I really did live in an incubator at the kibbutz, he thought, embarrassed at remembering his immaturity then, and the things he used to write to his previous girlfriend, stupid ideas about how in every man there is a riddle that makes him special and different, some deep-forged secret . . . I was like a kid, he thought, a kid who looks in from outside at the adult world.

I had things to do for work, Gidi blurted out in the end at the earnest face of the mukhtar.

Ah! About work I don't ask any questions! Work!

And the mukhtar leaned back, wearing a discreet expression, almost a caricature.

And will Abu Dani stay here with us? We're the only ones for him, right?

The only ones. And from now on, everything will be like it used to be.

Ah, good. That's very good. Very good.

The coffee arrived, and the mukhtar told Gidi about the grape honey he plans to concoct this year, and about his intestinal troubles, and about Fufu, the village eunuch and idiot, who had suffered an epileptic fit and had been taken to the hospital and had almost died there. Yes, Gidi thought, suddenly having a hard time keeping himself within the shower of the man's chatter, today I know people for what they are. Work taught me a lot, no question about it. They have no secret and no riddle. If anyone can be sure of that, I can. Because they tell me their most hidden thoughts. And I see them in their most intimate circumstances. They have no mystery. They are so predictable and banal. And what moves them, always, is just a few simple, miserable urges: the same fears, the same appetites, and they are really nothing but machines, really, machines without independence and without souls, so easy to operate and direct according to one's needs.

The mukhtar told him the latest news. Gidi listened and filed it away in his memory. Suddenly he asked about Abu Khatem, and saw how the mukhtar's face went yellow with repugnance. Leave Abu Khatem alone, the mukhtar said. They sipped their coffee in silence. Abu Khatem was the richest man in the village. He had little to do with the rest of the villagers, nor did he allow his wife and two children to talk too much with the neighbors. There was a sort of mystery about him, but no security risk. Gidi visited his house once or twice and felt uncomfortable there. The mukhtar sighed, and said that nothing was new with Abu Khatem, no one visits him, and he doesn't leave his house, and why did Abu Dani have to bother himself about him.

Gidi rose abruptly, almost rudely, bade the mukhtar goodbye, and went out. The air was transparent and clear, but still lacked something to expand the lungs. Gidi walked along the path that went up the side of the mountain, kicking stones and picking bunches of yellow and white daisies, only to throw them away. He had surprised himself by his hurried exit from the mukhtar's house, but he had suddenly felt himself suffocating there. He thought about the child born to him two days ago, his first child, and he was not filled with happiness. A boy leading a few black, scrawny goats passed him and greeted him with deference, and Gidi glanced at him angrily and did not answer. He reflected on the fact that things which once seemed to him to be the most basic principles of a moral life—honesty and courage and self-respect—now seemed pathetic hypocrisy. Courage was only fear that had not been put to the test. Honesty was only deceitfulness that had not had to face temptation. All noble virtues were now in his eyes only signals which pointed the observer to their opposites, their ruin.

Almost without meaning to, he knocked on Abu Khatem's door, not understanding why he had come there. He had, after all, always tried to refrain from going to this house and to this rich, reclusive man. Abu Khatem possessed something that demanded a different attitude from Gidi, quieter and more subtle, and Gidi had always felt that he did not want or could not respond to that demand. The mistress of the house opened the door, and her expression cooled at the sight of him. She led him into the dimly lit living room, curtained on all sides. He sat in an armchair and admired the carved amber columns and heavy chandeliers. A huge Swiss mountain view, complete with a peaceful stream, a snow-covered alp, and greenery, covered the entire wall opposite him.

The master of the house entered, tall, thin, and dark, like a magician's hat. Two small children defiantly peeked out at Gidi from the hallway. The woman served tea. Gidi waited for the man to say something and break the silence, but Abu Khatem did not open his mouth. Gidi was forced to speak, and found himself mumbling trivialities. Abu Khatem answered curtly. Gidi knew that the man had not left his house for six years, and had barely seen the sun. The villagers did not know how to explain the change that had come over him: even before the war, they said, he had not been a sociable man, but he would leave the village and return, talk with people, and people even remembered that he knew how to joke. Now it was as if he had placed an interdict on the village and denied himself to the villagers. Maybe he holds them in contempt, Gidi thought in a flash. How did I not see that before, maybe he holds them in contempt because they are so miserable and docile, he thought, and suddenly he felt a strange surge of compassion for this stern-faced, ascetic man sitting silently opposite him, a sort of pleasant burning sensation in the depths of his lungs, as if something of the Swiss mountain air from the great wall picture had made its way into them, and he asked the man about his elderly father in Jordan, and expressed his surprise that Abu Khatem did not submit a request to visit Amman, or to allow his father to visit here. After all, it is pretty easy to arrange something like that, and everyone does it, and Abu Khatem said he was not interested, nor was his father, and Gidi, who now felt very close to this silent, proud man, decided that he would not leave this house without persuading Abu Khatem to submit a request for a visit. Get out a little and get some air, he said with an odd enthusiasm, see how the world has changed, see that we've given you some good things, too, and anyway, your father is not a young man, it's worth seeing him because, who knows, and you are his only son, right, you see, I remember everything, and to be an only son is a special thing, I can say that with certainty, because when you have a son—and Gidi almost felt for a split second the precise joining of the desire and the necessity to tell his news, finally, to someone here, to one of the thousands under his management, those into whose lives he had been prying for six years and with whom he had drunk thousands of cups of coffee and tea. And here, with Abu Khatem, he really felt that he wanted, had to tell, tell and hear how it sounds out loud and in Arabic, even though were he to say it he would reveal finally that there was no previous son named Dani, and his relations with the village would go through a sort of clarification and purification, but something nevertheless stopped him, maybe the expression of warning, disapprobation, and enmity on the man's face, or the knowledge that Abu Khatem would not even get up to shake his hand, and the news would remain hanging in the air, deflated, and Gidi quickly sat up straight, bid the master of the house goodbye, and left even before they rose to accompany him, and feeling as if he had been expelled. He descended swiftly from the hill, resentful and angry, acknowledging in spite of himself the unquestionable nobility of Abu Khatem, the natural and annoying authenticity he possessed, something which reminded Gidi of his father, of all people, and he hurried to his truck, passing along the way villagers who greeted him with weary gestures, now seeming to him without any life or sincerity, and he returned them an angry wave, feeling like an art collector who has filled his warehouses with cheap forgeries and has just seen the originals.

He tore out of the village, pressing the gas pedal of the Peugeot to the floor, as if fleeing from an infected place, but not really knowing the object of his travel, because he suddenly did not want to return to the empty house, or to the hospital, to radiant Billie and the parade of friends who came devotedly to visit her every day of her confinement, and of course, after the birth, the professors from her department and those bleeding-heart doctoral students, who could shed with suspicious ease their vocal consciences and declare to him privately—a

chummy hand on his shoulder—that they also think
people with tendencies to violence have to be dealt with
sternly, concluding with a sort of co-conspiratorial smile
of distaste, saying that they can imagine how hard it is
to work there, in the dark, with those animals who
would sell their mothers for a penny and who will stab
anyone who turns his back to them, and he would smile
at them, for Billie, and while doing so look into them.
It was actually during the last few weeks that he began
seeing them for what they were, and wondering which
one of them would be the first to break down in a third-
degree interrogation, and who would sneak of his own
accord into his office to inform on his best friend, and
which of them would turn in his parents in order to gain
a favor. No, he decided that he did not want to go back
there just now, home, or to Israel at all: he deserved a
rest, too. He had gone through several difficult weeks,
yes—and he turned the truck off the road and stopped
and smoked a cigarette. Afterwards, he walked into the
field, stepping between the thistles and smelling them,
drawing stalks of grass through his fingers, sucking his
cheeks in. He meditated on the locals (as he called them)
he had seen that morning, and on Billie's friends—he
himself had no friends other than her—and pictured
them one after another on the background of the disk
of the fierce sun, saw how they became completely transparent, so that you could see the simple gears of their
insincerity and their fears and mostly—and this was most
surprising of all—their insignificance.

Gidi sat, leaning against the trunk of an olive tree,
thinking in a monotone: I have a son, I have a son. He
felt that he had to shout it, in Arabic, and he slowly
turned his head toward the tree and pressed his face into

a wide and pleasant hollow in its trunk. It was dim and full of a far-off fragrance that he loved. Gidi wondered who was guilty, he or other people, in that he could no longer believe in anybody, or in anything visible, or in the simple emotions which had become in his trained hands handles to be pulled and pushed.

Then he thought that he did not want to be there, in the twilight area created when two peoples turn their dark, corrupt sides toward each other, and the thought startled him, because he loved his work and believed in it, and felt that it gave him the necessary rules with which to navigate through his life. But he also knew clearly that when two apples touch one another at a single point of decay, the mold spreads over both of them.

He hunched his shoulders, curled up tightly, and lay that way for a few minutes. Then he rose and returned to the truck, guiding himself heavily and knowing that he felt very bitter, and something in his eyes clouded everything, even in the fierce light.

12

Sumud

"A year has passed since I stopped writing . . . I have overcome my despair, as other people have overcome their despair, and I emerged from it wiser, perhaps, but certainly more adamant in my decision to maintain my *sumud*, just as the Israeli government seems more determined than ever to empty the West Bank of us, the *samadin*. I now feel, more than my immediate personal fears, an objective fear of the tragedy awaiting all of us. I am now once more able to see what vanished last year—the individual faces on the wheel of death, Palestinian and Israeli faces, all struggling to halt its progress."

So wrote Raj'a Shehade, lawyer and author, in the epilogue to his book *The Third Way*.

Sumud means to endure. To stick to one's guns. To remain firmly planted on one's land. The term was coined at the Baghdad summit of Arab states in 1978 (*samadin*—the endurers) as a name for the million and a half Palestinian refugees who live under the Israeli occupation. The summit established the Steadfastness Aid Fund, meant to direct $150 million a year to these Palestinians—including those who have lived under Israeli rule since 1948—but this has become but a trickle in recent years, because Arab countries have not met their commitments to the fund.

Five years have passed since Shehade wrote those words. When you are not a free man, time passes more slowly: your soul is delayed and defeated along the way. You unconsciously moderate your actions and responses in order to be prepared for any evil. Any unexpected capriciousness of the occupier. Or of the situation itself. The time which passes for the inhabitants of the West Bank and Gaza under Israeli rule cannot even be measured in prison terms. Its end is unknown, and this makes it even harder to deal with. I asked Shehade if he had not tired at the end of these five years, at the end of twenty years, of being *sumud*.

"No," he said, "I go on believing in it. Of the two ways open to me as a Palestinian—to surrender to the occupation and collaborate with it, or to take up arms against it, two possibilities which mean, to my mind, losing one's humanity—I choose the third way. To remain here. To see how my home becomes my prison, which I do not want to leave, because the jailer will then not allow me to return."

Sumud expresses tenacity and stamina, and a sort of passive combativeness, gritting one's teeth to keep from giving in, and to keep from losing one's mind. *Sumud* means to bow one's head and live, somehow, until the storm passes. Shehade is consciously *sumud*—and was even before the Baghdad summit labeled him as such.

Other Palestinians are almost unconscious *samadin*, practically turning their expert passivity into an art.

I tell Shehade that there are such *samadin* among the Israelis as well: many people who do not accept the situation but who do not know what to do about it. They cling to the desire to remain ignorant and unaware. Faithful to their half-closed consciousness, they immerse themselves in a despairing, miserable moral slumber: "Wake me when it's over."

And what does the occupation do to us, the Israelis, in your opinion?

"I think about that a lot," Shehade answers (our conversation was conducted in English). "First, you must remember that it is not just an occupation. From a legal point of view it is an occupation, but it is actually much worse than an occupation: after all, you do not work among us just to prevent violent attacks upon yourselves. You have taken other, exceptional steps, such as establishing settlements. Nor do the civil administration and the military government work for the benefit of the local population, as they like to say they do. The military government itself is confused. The people there will tell you how much they have improved our lives. They won't tell you about the twelve hundred amendments and new laws they promulgated in the West Bank. Those are laws meant to make the current situation permanent, gradually but irrevocably. The occupation is selfish. It only acts in matters which affect it directly. Security matters are seen to with great care, but the police station in Ramallah has no sign that says "Police" in Arabic. Only in Hebrew and English. The Israeli policemen don't even pretend that they are there to protect the locals. West

Bank crime is growing and becoming more serious, but Israel is doing nothing to prevent it. It doesn't affect the occupation.

"What happened to you is what Professor Yeshayahu Leibowitz predicted immediately after the '67 war. He said then that it is impossible to be occupiers and remain moral. Even people with moral intentions are led slowly into an immoral situation. The situation turns into a sort of monster with a life of its own, which can no longer be controlled. An unjust and immoral monster. You have two kinds of people in Israel. One is the kind you called 'the *samadin* of ignorance.' They simply disconnect themselves from what is going on. The second kind uses every means to achieve its goal. The first kind of people say: An honest, sensitive man of conscience like Efraim Sneh [until recently head of the civil administration] should not do the work of the establishment. They want to cut the Arabs off from all the positive forces in Israel. Afterwards, you can't understand why the Arabs are so wild and violent. You see, you can't treat people in a certain way for years and not expect that they will react to it, right?"

Israelis sometimes ask the mirror image of that question: Why is it so easy to control you? How can you explain the fact that we rule more than a million and a half Arabs, almost without feeling it? After all, were the situation reversed, wouldn't we make your lives miserable?

Shehade smiles sadly. He is a small man, of delicate appearance, and projects a strong presence. And exactly because he is so fragile, it is clear from the start that it is hard to frighten him with any sort of physical threat: he has already come to terms with that, as it were, and the discussion passes on to other, deeper subjects, where he is very sure of himself. In his book he writes: "How easy it certainly is for the Israelis. It takes no effort to rule a society accustomed to paternalism to the point that people do not even ask who is giving the orders. We make use of and accept authority so naturally that we do not even see the humiliation and shame it engenders. The Israelis need only glide down the path prepared for them and rake in all the profits."

He tells me of the Jordanian occupation. Those are his words: the occupation. Of the intentional Jordanian effort to rewrite Palestinian history and obliterate Palestinian identity. Of the breaking of the Palestinians and the destruction of their society. "Imagine it—when King Hussein would come to Ramallah, we were all required to go out and stand along the roads, waiting for him for hours—he never came on time—and applaud when he arrived. Yes, there was oppression then, and today, too. You see, I am becoming an expert on oppression. You ask why it is easy to rule us? Check out how many people have been exiled. Many thousands of people have been exiled [more than two thousand have been expelled from the area since 1967, according to data collected by Dr. Meron Benvenisti—DG]. Whenever someone has expressed an opinion about anything, he has found himself on the other side of the bridge. Today there are far fewer expulsions, because there is no one left to exile. You have not allowed any leadership of any kind to remain here. You have ripped our society apart."

In any case, what do you do with your emotions about the occupation? How do you take out such constant frustration?

"I write. I work against injustices inflicted on Palestinians by the administration. I established the Law in the Service of Man organization. I do things so as not to fall silent. Whom do I hate? I am filled with repulsion when I meet some of the fools who manage our affairs. It is not hate but pity. There was a case in the military court—I generally prefer not to represent clients there, it is too emotional a matter for me—when I told myself: Take it easy, don't get excited. But I could not help it. I boiled over. The Israelis there were so rude and unfeeling! That is, they were rude, noisy, vulgar, and uncultured, just as they are everywhere. I asked the secretary there, a nice girl, not all there, and not herself responsible for anything (that's what I thought then, but today I think that there is no such thing as not being responsible; everyone is responsible), I asked her why I had to leave all my human qualities behind me at the door when I entered your building. And she said blandly, What are you talking about? It didn't matter to her! I stood there and vented my anger, in an unfeeling world that neither paid attention to it nor understood it! What kind of life do your people have, your people who manage our lives? That girl, still so young, and she has to work in something that has no connection with what is real, only with the oppression and humiliation and the violation of the natural rights of every man! And there are thousands like her! After all, all your young people pass through these territories!

"Or another instance: The authorities were going to destroy a house in the neighborhood where I grew up. A house full of memories and emotions for me. I stood there and I saw how the soldiers measured the thickness of the walls in order to decide where to lay the explosives. They did it with such matter-of-factness! We stood there, I and the owner of the house, and we saw how they measured, and it was horrible. It was like seeing someone measure a live person for a coffin. I looked at the soldiers. So young! It is a challenge for me: to understand how they can do it. One of the answers is that they are racists. They simply don't see the family that lives in that house as their brothers, human beings."

Have you ever tried to put yourself in their place? How would you act if you were in a similar situation?

"I certainly understand the dilemma Israelis find themselves in. I don't mean to imply that Arabs are angels. Not at all. I understand the importance of military service for Israelis. But if you serve in the army you support something that is out of your control. On the other hand, as an Israeli you cannot decide to serve and yet not to serve. I think that, were I Israeli, I would devote the same energy I devote to military service to attempts to make peace. That would, perhaps, be one way to deal with the contradiction."

I asked him what he feels with regard to the settlers. Here, for the first time, Shehade lost his keen sense of humor and abandoned the low voice he had used until now.

"In my eyes they are criminals. Criminals and lunatics. Sometimes I have to meet them. They are racists. Look, racism is hard to diagnose precisely. There are many things that seem to be racism but are not. Real racism is when you don't see another person as human. They ask—with deep inner conviction—why the Arabs don't accept what they want to do here? They don't understand that, as human beings, the Arabs desire everything that any human being desires. They simply are not willing to understand that!"

And after so many years of contact and mutual acquaintance, don't you see something positive in Israel's effect on the Arabs?

"At the beginning I believed that the Israelis really were a sort of new race. And there really are some good things about you: friendship, frankness, the strong feeling of mutual responsibility. That impressed me. You definitely have created something new in liberating yourself from the past and attempting to create a new life for yourselves. The problem is that when it clashes with my freedom, in the West Bank, it is a little difficult for me to be enthusiastic about it. Israel is, in a way, a positive challenge for the Arabs. It has momentum. It is the resuscitation of something that was almost dead. It is hard to come to any clear conclusion about this, because, in comparison with the Jews in Israel, the Jews in the world at large have progressed much more intellectually, culturally, and even economically. Your legal system is impressive. Of course, it is regressing as a result of the occupation. That corrupts everything. The occupation continually presents strange, twisted challenges that it is hard for a system of justice to provide answers to. The truth is that you suffer greatly from the occupation. Britain conquered half the world, but it was then a mature nation, prepared for it. Israel was not prepared. You were too young."

Have you met Arabs who have adopted or who imitate—as a method of assimilation—Israeli modes of behavior?

"There are people like that here and there. Mostly those who work with the authorities. I once met, in the context of my work as an attorney, an Arab whose job was to interrogate security detainees. He sported a pistol

on his belt. His work is hard, you know—there are
prisoners who are very hard to break. Sometimes he has
to beat them. Sometimes even his Israeli commander has
to chew him out for that—really. His life is much easier
under the occupation. They also taught him to shoot.
But there aren't many like him. And I have more proof
that, for you, the occupation is not successful, and that
we have not surrendered completely. You would think
that, if the Hebrew language is part of a higher culture,
it would be a strong influence on Arabic, right? But the
only Hebrew words which have been absorbed into Palestinian Arabic are 'roadblock,' 'traffic light,' and, oh,
right—'walkie-talkie.' And what has happened to Hebrew during the same period?"

I tried to remember. A large number of Arabic words
had been naturalized by Hebrew even before '67, probably as a result of our acquaintance with another group
of Arabs, those who live in and are citizens of Israel.
But today you hear many more Arabic words in daily
conversation, in all different contexts. Raj'a Shehade,
Christian, thirty-five years old, single. Son to one of the
families of the Arab aristocracy. His father, also a lawyer, was murdered, apparently by Palestinian extremists,
and the murderers have yet to be found. Raj'a Shehade
himself has many connections in the United States and
in Europe, and he has many Israeli friends. In the twilight
region between the conqueror and the conquered, Shehade stands out as a man sensitive to nuances; he seems
to me to be one for whom the blind, anonymous occupation threatens his personal sense of individualism,
rather than his Arab or national identity. For this reason,
perhaps, he keeps his head above water, exposing himself (sometimes dangerously) to critical Israeli eyes, chal-

lenging Arab society as well, confirming again and again
his uniqueness, his existence.

I asked him how he feels when he leaves Israel for
another country.

"That experience, of foreign travel, is very important
to me, for the very reason that Israel continually claims
that it is a part of Western culture. You should understand: the Israelis are not satisfied with having conquered us. They want to turn us into a colony of theirs,
in every sense of the word, culturally as well. That means
that they don't want only to confiscate land, but also to
impose themselves on the soul and thoughts of the conquered. It is very important for Israelis—in a sometimes
touching way—to impress us. To convince us how much
Israel is superior to us. And by the way, there is a huge
difference between the propaganda that Israel directs
toward the West Bank, where it wants to appear omnipotent, and the propaganda it directs toward the West,
in whose eyes it wants to appear as a victim, surrounded
by powerful enemies.

"Overseas travel was important for me, because I had
become accustomed to your occupation. I had become
accustomed to Israeli rudeness, cynicism, idiocy, and
arrogance, and it was very important for me to see whether
that was the only true reality. A person begins to forget
things after a few years. Is that the price that people
must pay for the progress they have achieved? Must they
become rude technocrats, suppressing values they have
buried deep inside them, lacking sensitivity to human
emotions and suffering? So every time I leave the country
I look for alternatives. I look for standards by which I
can correctly evaluate our situation here, and reconfirm

to myself that it is not inevitable, that what I see here is a counterfeit of the truth. It gives me more strength to face reality. And when Israel tried to impose its patterns of thinking and behavior, and tell me that it is the best, I can respond to that challenge and prove that other nations have done it differently. That it's possible to have a national consciousness, as the English and the French and the Americans do, and remain yourselves, and not lose the most positive human elements that you have. There are peoples with strong feelings of national pride who, despite that, are completely different. That encourages me and shows me that in the future the Palestinians can have an independent and proud nationalism, and behave completely differently from the way you present yourselves. For that reason, whenever I left the country and was asked about my destination at the airport, I answered: 'Civilization.' Here there is no civilization. You try to impress us—and yourselves. You say: We have highways and fighter planes and tanks that we made ourselves, we are liberated people, and you Arabs are primitive; and I had to leave here to discover that it's not true."

You certainly know that there are many Israelis who argue that "time is with us." In your opinion, is the fact that the political situation with regard to the territories has been frozen for so long to Israel's benefit?

"It seems to me that the long term is more dangerous for Israel than for us. The Arab world is now in a miserable state, there is no denying that. It is a world that is bad to live in. A world of oppression. But Israel is founded on so many contradictions, and on so many opposing forces, that its existence is always in great danger. For example, there is a huge gap between the self-image of Israelis and reality. You think you are omnipotent, because of your success in controlling such a large Arab population. But the truth is that foreign support is the decisive factor. You remind me of the spoiled son of a rich man, who thinks he can do anything, until he has to face life on his own and discovers a few hard truths.

"Another thing: you are still misled by your belief that millions of Jews will still come here. That, after all, is one of the important arguments you have for settling the West Bank! But the Jews of the Diaspora have no intention of coming here. They have a good life where they are!

"And you have another mistaken assumption: you think that Israel will be strong forever, and will get out of the present situation in one piece. You prefer to forget that the Arabs are developing. Part of that is to your credit, of course. We are now more exposed to the world. There are many foreign visitors. We are not standing still. You, however, are stuck. You are prisoners of your conceptions and refuse to recognize reality. It seems to me that to live in an area full of hostility and think that you can do so forever, without making any effort to come to terms with your neighbors, is simply not rational. You display no creative thinking about how to solve the conflict. You . . ."

Excuse me for interrupting, but do you hear creative thinking of that sort from Arabs?

"For now, we are not in a position to propose attractive or inspired things. We can only respond to proposals that reconfirm our humanity and our personal and national pride. That, unfortunately, is the state we are in. We can only respond to proposals, and they don't arrive. The Likud voices its opinions. They are not, in my opinion, correct, but they express them clearly and influence the public. The Labor Party plays a cynical game. It could have certain political effects, of course, but it contains nothing new or earthshaking that could bring about any real change or solution to the problem. Look at the blindness of Ber Borochov [the early Zionist who inspired the fathers of today's Labor Zionists], who wrote in 1900, in Russian: 'They [the Palestinians] have no reason to greet us with unfriendliness. On the contrary: they believe that the land is justly that of the Jews.' That blindness continues today in the supposedly enlightened Labor Party, which still believes it deep inside. And now, if all these mistaken assumptions determine your policy, consciously or unconsciously, how can your policy be successful?"

I still cannot understand how Shehade does not tire of and despair from his *sumud*.

"I do not despair. I only fear for the future. The occupation is steadily destroying us. It destroys the entire fabric of civil and traditional life. We are caught in a totally false reality, and are beginning to think that it is the truth. That is a great danger. But I do not despair: there are so many things to fight for. There are so many things to improve! From looking after mental-health institutions to the effort to set up a law school. There is not a single law school in the entire West Bank. There are a million things that a person can devote himself to. You can't give up. Independence, for me, is not only a piece of paper or a declaration. You have to work hard to achieve it, and it is possible to do so much even now."

Later, Raj'a Shehade said: "One of the things which, for me, gives meaning to my life is that the situation is a challenge: to remain human even under the conditions that prevail. To answer honestly the questions that the situation presents. Questions that a normal person can live his entire life without needing to deal with. Not to surrender to despair. Not to allow myself to give in and become a hater. People who speak a language of violence speak a very tempting language. And when I say violence I don't mean only physical, concrete action. There is also quieter, camouflaged violence. Sometimes I feel that I would very much want to take on that language for myself. I have to fight against that constantly. I am always on guard."

The Censor

In a chance conversation with two Arab intellectuals— the poet and critic Muhammed Albatrawi, and the author 'Ali Alkhalili—both made reference to the military censorship of their writings.

Albatrawi: "Every word of mine goes through the censorship office. In my poems, I am forbidden to write Yafa, *the Arabic name for the city Jaffa, and must use the Hebrew form* Yafo. *I can't write* 'Askalan *and must write* Ashkelon. *Instead of* Falastin, Palestine, *I write 'my land.' Sometimes I write a simple love song and the great Israeli censor decides it is a nationalist Palestinian poem. For this reason I try to write with great clarity, so that they won't mistakenly ascribe to me other intentions and red-pencil whole lines and verses. It goes without saying that this affects the work's literary value. I have to guess and take into account what the Israeli censor will think, and refrain from getting him angry at me. You have to remember that there are more than two thousand books banned in the West Bank. Some of them are works of Israeli Arab writers, which we are forbidden to read in the West Bank, poets like Samih Alqassem and Tawfiq Zayyad. I can never know in advance how the censor will react: sometimes I write something risky and he approves it without a comment, and sometimes I write something totally innocent and it is banned completely. It can drive you crazy, because there is no logic to it.*

"I've often wondered who the man is, how he can shred my thoughts with a wave of his scissors. I sometimes try to guess who he is by the way he crosses things out: sometimes I think he must be a recent graduate of the Arabic department at the university who feels some holy and juvenile calling to wipe out every threat, even the imaginary ones. There are censors who, I sense, are pedantic bureaucrats, because they consistently cross out only certain words, no matter what the context is. I think the censor must be a very frightened man, bored with his work, maybe even ashamed of it: after all, it is so much easier to cross out a verse than to delve into it and try to grapple with what it means."

Alkhalili: "If you don't want all the copies of your book to be confiscated immediately upon publication, you must send the manuscript to the censor. I think it is horrible, because a writer needs to act with complete freedom. What happens to me now, after twenty years of battles and censorship of my work, is that I find myself, to my horror, developing a little Israeli censor inside me, who keeps an eye on me. It has suddenly become clear to me that in a way I am no longer a free man.

"I spend a lot of time thinking about my Israeli censor: he must be some low-level clerk who wants to do his work without getting into trouble with his superiors. That is why, when he has any doubts, he prefers to delete. Sometimes I can feel how angry he is at me by how deep his pen has gouged the manuscript. I don't think he really likes his job. Somewhere inside, he certainly must feel that he is like an executioner. Words, after all, are things full of life, of humanity, and his job is to cut their heads off.

"Once I carried on an indirect dialogue with the censor. I wrote, for a newspaper, a story about Juha, the great fool of Arab folktales, and the censor banned it. Then I wrote another story about 'the man who does not laugh.' I portrayed him as a bitter man, ugly inside and out, who sits in a dark corner and hates everyone, himself included. The censor approved the story without any deletions, and added a note in his own handwriting: 'But I like stories about Juha.'"

13

A Doll at
the Allenby Bridge

"My cousin from Amman came to visit me for my birthday," Raj'a Shehade tells in his book *The Third Way*. "He cursed me for two days after his arrival, and accused me of being responsible for everything that happened to him at the Allenby Bridge when he came from Jordan. The cries of the children when he was stripped for a body search; the sight of a corpse, in transfer for burial in the West Bank, taken out of its coffin for a security search; the stink of the feet of travelers after hours of waiting for their shoes, which had been sent for X-ray examination; the heartrending wails of a mother whose fourteen-year-old son had been taken for inter-rogation and had not yet been returned. All this, and the long hours that each person waits for his name to be called."

I must go see for myself. Is it as he says it is?

A hot wind blows north from Arabia. Far off, Jericho shimmers behind a veil of dust circling lazily over the bottom of the world and of memory: Jericho. Along the way there, the absurd refugee camps, ruins of ruins, with a bicycle path alongside the road, as in Europe, and young people walk along it reciting their lessons, not because they like studying outside that much, but because it is too crowded at home. An energetic boy sails on his bike, carrying behind him a box containing a few chicks, some of them already dying in the heat.

Closer up, it is a different Jericho, a shady, slightly unruly resort city set out around its squares and the whispers of its springs and trees and the red splashes of the bougainvillea and the scandalous summerhouses of the West Bank wealthy. Capricious Jericho.

I stop briefly to talk with the Governor of Jericho ("A governor must be a father to the inhabitants," he says with much self-importance) and continue on by way of the plain, choking under the layers of dusty air, past the banana and date groves and the abandoned monasteries, and arrive at the Allenby Bridge.

There is nothing like the open bridges between the West Bank and Jordan for illustrating Israeli policy with regard to the territories. When then Minister of Defense Moshe Dayan decided after the war in 1967 to allow people and merchandise to pass over the bridges, he wanted to break down psychological barriers, create the possibility for Jews and Arabs to become acquainted with each other, and create tight economic dependence and a sort of de facto coexistence. The open-bridges policy was also meant to demonstrate that Israel allows freedom of access to holy sites in Jerusalem and freedom of worship to all religions. Another goal which guided Dayan, also very important, was to turn the open bridges into a safety valve for releasing the excess tension that he expected would build up among the West Bankers as a result of the occupation. The knowledge that it is possible "to go out and get some air," to enter, for a time, the Arab world, to study there, to do business there, to visit relatives, has a huge influence on the people of the West Bank and Gaza Strip.

The bottom line of Israeli policy in the conquered territories, says Shlomo Gazit, Israel's first Coordinator of Activities in the territories, in his book *The Carrot and the Stick*, has been to create a situation in which "they have something to lose." And in fact, Israel's ability to close and open the bridges has become a powerful tool in its hands, and the most important of its deterrents. There have been cases in which the travelers crossing the bridge have jeered the inhabitants of Nablus or Ramallah who arrived at the bridge only to find their crossing prohibited because of some crime which took place in one of those cities, while the bridge remained open for all others.

On the other hand, Gazit notes, the open-bridges policy has, paradoxically, been an obstacle to progress toward a comprehensive political solution. This great pressure valve has made it easier for Israel to control the territories, and in doing so has dulled the urgent need to find a long-range political solution. Dr. Meron Benvenisti told me that the open-bridges policy is an efficient weapon for Jordan as well, in its efforts to impose its will on the West Bankers: when the director of the East Jerusalem Chamber of Commerce, Fa'ik Barakat (the man responsible for granting passage certificates for the bridges), once made an anti-Jordanian comment on the radio, he discovered upon arriving at the bridge that Amman had forwarded instructions not to grant him an entrance permit. Jordan and Israel apply such pressure on entire villages, if one of the two countries discerns irregular activity in them. This quiet "war" can take on even more critical forms: Israel, in its desire to encourage the emigration of young Arabs, decreed that West Bank residents between the ages of twenty and thirty cannot return home within nine months of their exit from the West Bank. Jordan responded to this with a measure of its own, forbidding (between 1980 and 1982) that such young people reside in its territory for more than a month. In these power struggles it is the Palestinians who suffer, of course—"asses that anyone can ride," in the words of Taher, the man from the village near Hebron.

At the entrance to the waiting area by the bridge sprawl a group of Israeli soldiers, reservists. I had already noticed that the reservists who police the West Bank have a special expression and build: something which projects an unconscious detachment of the man from himself. Reservists are always good at suppressing their individuality, but in the West Bank they become exceptionally talented at it.

A surprising silence reigns in the waiting area. The dozens of Arabs waiting their turn to be examined by the soldiers sit motionless on the plastic benches, and bide their time until their name is trumpeted over the loudspeaker. When your name is called, you must get up, approach the soldier holding your belongings, and answer questions while he examines them. The soldier empties the suitcases on the counter, fingers everything, confiscates anything with writing on it (including plastic bags with store logos and T-shirts), forbids the entry of all electrical appliances, wooden items, and cosmetics— in short, anything which might conceivably be a security threat or which might contain explosives. Toys must be

confiscated, because they have in the past served as con-
tainers for detonators. That is the reason why you often
hear the bitter crying of children here. Afterwards, your
shoes are sent to be X-rayed, and you yourself enter a
small cell for a body check. A woman soldier performs
the examination on women and children. Even the baby's disposable diaper must be removed, because not
long ago a young woman was caught trying to smuggle
explosives in one of those all-absorbent Pampers.

I have come on an easy day. Relatively few visitors.
Everyone breathes freely today, and the examinations
go quickly. It takes only three hours from the moment
you arrive from Jordan until your exit from the waiting
room. But it is not always like this: an average of 400,000
people cross the bridges every year. During the summer
visiting months, the place is intolerable: flies fill the air,
the heat is oppressive, children scream, and people are
stuck here for many long hours. Sometimes as long as
ten hours of such waiting.

The reservist serving as a bag searcher at the bridge
relates: "On a busy day you cannot be judicious and
polite. I've seen soldiers who throw out clothes and belongings of Arabs out of spite and in order to hurt them.
More than once I've seen a young, angry soldier use his
position to humiliate an elderly and venerable man, making him run all over the place in his socks, jeer and
degrade him in front of people from his village. You can
only guess what that man feels about Israel after such
treatment."

The shoes of the travelers return in a single crate,
which the travelers then storm. You can often see an
Arab, by his dress penniless and poverty-stricken, worm
his way out of the mob, shiny patent-leather shoes in

his hands, while a wealthy-looking lawyer is left disappointedly holding a pair of battered sandals from the bottom of the crate.

Porters and janitors, Arabs from Jericho who undergo a security examination at the hands of the soldiers when they arrive every morning, also work in the waiting area. The reservist with whom I spoke said, "An odd system of masters and slaves is developing with these Arabs. They work with us—but they are always suspect. It is an unclear and unpleasant situation."

One can see the authorities' efforts to make it easier for the incoming travelers at the bridge. The reserve units sent to serve there are made up of top-flight soldiers, there is air conditioning (but in the summer you would not know it), and recently five young stewardesses from Jericho have been added to the staff, their job being to mediate between the perplexed civilian and the authorities in charge of the passage point, and to explain to him what the process is and what he is expected to do.

There can be no doubt that, under present conditions, the discomfort suffered by the travelers over the bridge is unavoidable. That is, as long as Israel oversees the passage of Palestinians from Jordan to the West Bank. The damage done to Israel here is, however, very great. Even on an easy day such as the day I visited, I could feel immediately how this place becomes a hothouse for the growth of enmity toward Israel; how, as a result of the unpleasant friction between civilians and soldiers, the hate always lying in wait under a thin cover of surrender and silence is quickly bared. Today the travelers over the bridge accept this right as self-evident. They are not aware of all the political considerations behind it. They know only that an Israeli soldier fingers their personal belongings, the hair on their heads and in their groins; that he makes their old mothers wait five hours in the heat to be examined; that he steals their children's teddy bears. Any one of us who has had a similar experience—even if immeasurably milder—in any European airport, and anyone who has had any personal belonging of his confiscated for ten minutes—certainly knows the feeling of rage and insult that came over him, and how easy it is to judge, bitterly and without distinction, the entire country at the gates of which it happened.

"Once," the reservist went on to tell me, "one traveler under examination thanked me, in English, for having refolded his clothes, which had been disturbed during the examination. He was very surprised by that—he had never encountered such treatment. Another time a woman came to me with a three-year-old girl. The girl held a plastic doll, and according to orders toys are to be confiscated. Since it was a quiet, unpressured day, I decided to take the doll apart, in order to make sure that it was 'clean,' and to allow the girl to take it with her. I carefully took apart the mechanism that says 'Mama,' the hands and the feet, the stomach and the head. The soldiers around me made fun of me. They called me a 'peacenik.' There was nothing in the doll. I put the doll back together and I was about to give it back to the girl. Then the bridge commander came and told me to confiscate it. I explained that the doll was no danger. He insisted. The girl cried horribly, and her mother pleaded tearfully. The commander said: 'We cannot make exceptions.' The doll was confiscated."

The Arabs themselves display no emotion. From the minute they disembark from the buses which bring them from their visit in Jordan, they place an impenetrable mask on their faces. I saw them as they came. Their expressions reminded me of what I used to feel when I came back to basic training after a short furlough. Even during the examination, they do not change their expression. The children learn to put on that expression from a very young age when faced with a soldier. Sometimes, at the end of the procedure, you can see a quick glance of hate or pain, or a calming hug—so tight as to hurt—that a father gives to the crying son on his shoulder. Something is recorded somewhere in their memory.

Later, on my way to the bridge, I passed the great red bridge trucks. Merchandise can be transferred from Israel to Jordan only in these trucks. They are special trucks, most of their parts visible to the examining eye. Every part of the truck has a special seal, the absence of which immediately alerts the examiner that a change has been made in the vehicle. On every such truck, there are hundreds of such seals. A transparent window has been added to the gas tanks, in order to allow examination of the contents of the tank. They have thought of everything here, but even so, terrorists manage to smuggle weapons into the area from time to time. The war continues.

And at the end—the bridge itself, over the Jordan flowing lazy and brown, running around the clumps of reeds. An Israeli position opposite a Jordanian position. Two machine guns yawning at each other. Jordanian soldiers in blue uniforms and blue berets stare at me from behind torn sandbags. Once each day, the commanders of the bridge from both sides meet exactly halfway across, in order to make necessary technical arrangements. Each day, they trade newspapers. I stride to the middle of the bridge and halt. The border and the river awaken strange and unexpected urges in me. Then I return.

I went to the bridges mostly because of the harsh section from Shehade's book. And because of another story told me by the reservist, who has known Shehade well for several years:

"One of the things that was like a nightmare for me was the fear that I would meet Raj'a Shehade at the bridge. And then, one day, in the early afternoon, I raised my head and I saw Raj'a. He came with a small parcel. I asked the soldier examining him to let me take care of him. Raj'a was returning from the United States by way of Amman. The major part of the material he had with him was posters from the New York exhibition of paintings from the Hermitage Museum in Leningrad. He had some clothes as well. It was an indescribably awkward meeting. We both said something like 'What a place to meet . . .' I could, actually, have avoided examining him, but I remembered the passages he wrote in his book about going over the bridge, and I wanted to save him one time from that experience. At least once."

14

The Wastonaires

An unofficial public institution functioning alongside the Israeli military government and civil administration, the "wastonaires" are a product of the occupation. In the local slang, *wasta* means "mediation." So the wastonaire is an intermediary—or, in other contexts, a pimp. In the special context of the West Bank this is not, however, just the name of a profession.

The wastonaires are usually from the middle or lower classes, some of them former criminals who have come up in the world and won wealth and power by grace of a sharp and no-nonsense instinct for spotting the opportunities presented by the existing complex and murky situation. Most of them began as collaborators with the security forces, and then, when their relations with the military government had become well established, they began to present themselves to the populace as possessing contacts and influence within the administration. There were men of similarly sharp and quick instincts in the military government who immediately understood that it was worthwhile fostering such contacts and helping the collaborators refurbish their image.

So, when a local Arab presents a request to the administration—for a building permit, for example—and his request is rejected, justly or unjustly, he now has the recourse of turning to the man with the connections, the wastonaire, who has the run of the corridors of the military government headquarters. These intermediaries have become the representatives of the populace, which has no choice but to make use of them, galling as it is. The wastonaire approaches "his man" in the military government and presents his clients' petitions. The military government official, interested in furthering the reputation of the wastonaire in the eyes of the locals, frequently approves the requests. In exchange for this, the wastonaire is expected both to provide the military government with information and gossip and to influence and direct those with whom he comes in contact. It is not hard to imagine how this process is managed, what it has achieved, and what things are understood but never spoken.

Since, for all intents and purposes, every request for a permit by a local resident must be approved by the military—meaning that the military can deny it, even unjustly and with intentional arbitrariness—the locals must frequently apply to the military government through the wastonaires. Villagers from the Hebron area quoted me the following prices:

Arranging a building permit: 250–300 Jordanian dinars ($750–$900)

Arranging a business permit: 500–1,000 Jordanian dinars ($1,500–$3,000)

Arranging family reunification (the most coveted of permits): 3,000 Jordanian dinars ($9,000).

A terrorist cell was uncovered some years ago in a certain village, and a curfew was imposed for an unlimited period of time. For the village farmers, forbidden to go out to their fields, this meant in essence the loss of an entire year's crops. The villagers were powerless to do anything. The wastonaire in this particular place was the village elder, the mukhtar (a not uncommon combination). He demanded a thousand dinars from each family in order to arrange for the curfew to be lifted. Those with money paid and were allowed to leave the village immediately. Those without money remained restricted to the village for four entire weeks, and their crops withered.

These are extreme examples, but it is the common, everyday cases which are most infuriating. Generally, the unholy alliance between the regime and its agents means that Arabs are forced to pay large sums of money in order to receive what is, though they may not know it, theirs by right and according to law. The attitude of the locals to the wastonaires is mixed: they despise them, but they need them; they curse them, but are afraid to cross them.

I brought the subject up in conversations with officials in the civil adminstration. This was their comment:

"As to the wastonaire phenomenon—there is a lot of exaggeration. There are not many people who take bribes in order to arrange people's rights for them." As a matter of fact, one may assume that the wastonaires, gentle souls, will use any means to ensure that they remain a scarce commodity. The same "high-placed official" went on to say: "You have to understand that we are speaking here of a population not yet free of the customs of the Arab world. It is only natural for the civil administration to encourage people who contribute through their activity and influence to the community, in the sense of keeping things calm, which allows the economy to flourish and is therefore for the general good."

I appreciated his frankness.

Not long after that conversation, I saw an Arab in civilian clothes walking through Nablus with an impressive pistol prominently displayed on his waist. I asked a local who it was, and after some hesitation, he explained to me that this was a wastonaire. I went to the civil administration and asked if it supplies such people with arms. They said: "A permit to carry a weapon is granted only in the case where a person's life is in danger, and according to certain criteria which cannot be revealed. In any case, only a few dozen people have been given weapons."

The emergence of the wastonaires is not the only phenomenon to puncture the fabric of traditional local life: the status of the mukhtar has also greatly deteriorated as a result of Israeli rule. The security forces discovered that it is easier and more convenient to approach the local mukhtar with any local problem, and demand information and cooperation from him. The few mukhtars who refused to cooperate were cleverly dealt with by means of anonymous innuendo and humiliation, after which they could no longer function in their traditional role. Today the security forces use the mukhtars to guide them to the houses of terrorist suspects. Anyone who has served in the reserves in the territories knows that when he needs to carry out a midnight search in a given house in a crowded village, or in the heart of a refugee camp, the easiest way to do so is to go to the mukhtar's house, awaken him, and order him to lead the troops to the suspect's house. In this way the security forces have turned the mukhtars into collaborators. Anyone who chances into the office of one of the military governors on a day of a meeting with the mukhtars would think that he had barged unsuspecting into a strange meeting of a quaintly dressed board of directors of a large company. The atmosphere is one of calm, coffee, gossip, and flattering laughter. The mukhtars accept with suspect naturalness the fatherlike authority of the military governor. It may be that they believe that in doing so they better serve their interests and those of their villagers, or it may be their instinct for survival. In any case, one thing is clear: the institution of the mukhtar has been taken out of its natural context, and its content has been greatly distorted.

15

Like a Boy
with a Teddy Bear

"Abu Yussuf! Abu Yussuf!"

Night. Total stillness. A dog barks in one of the shut-up factories.

"Abu Yussuf!"

P., my companion this evening, stands together with me on a hot night and calls out at one of the factories in the industrial park in Holon, a suburb of Tel Aviv. Both of us feel as if someone is watching us. From in front? From behind us? From all sides, probably. Tens, maybe even hundreds of people hide out in the industrial park at night, laborers from the territories who sleep in Israel. Their presence within the Green Line is illegal, and if the police or border guards find them, they can expect imprisonment and, usually, beatings. It is for this reason that they now conceal themselves in their rooms and do not answer us.

A long time later, after heads peering out of top-floor windows had scouted us out, and after one window opened and suspicious voices wanted to know exactly who we were and what we were looking for, and after they were convinced that our intentions were good, we were allowed in. They told us they knew we weren't from the border guard because they always call either "Abdullah" or "Muhammad." A real lack of imagination.

We entered a large hall on the top floor of a large factory. I cannot give identifying details about the factory, or about the people I met, because that was a precondition of our conversation. When I quote them, they will appear only as "voices."

In the hall, divided by sheets of plywood into two spaces, are fifteen beds. It is very hot inside. The owner has given them an old fan about the size of those used in automobiles. The place is lit by a single neon lamp. Towels are hung on clotheslines which run the length of the hall. It is ten o'clock at night, and the laborers are getting ready for bed. Some wear only pants, some only underwear, because of the heat. Cigarette butts, candy wrappers, and old newspapers are strewn over the floor. They look P. and me over with exhausting suspicion. For now, they do not talk. Only their *ra'is*, the procurer who brought the workers to work in the factory, a young muscular man in an undershirt, is allowed to speak. He is responsible for them. He is the closest to the boss. He is the one who will decide how much they can criticize or speak their minds.

This silent examination of us takes almost half an hour. P., my companion, is an Israeli Arab—a self-described Marxist–Leninist who had been a laborer for many years and who now devotes his life to improving the lot of Arab workers. He tells our hosts that a new newspaper will soon appear in Israel, to be called *Iyar, May,* which will represent the workers and defend their rights. When he asks if they have never thought of organizing themselves together with other workers, those who sleep in the adjoining factories, for instance, in order to improve their situation, they smirk.

Voice: This is a prison. You say we should organize, but we are like living dead here. I work thirteen hours a day. I have two breaks, each one for half an hour. One at ten and one at two. I don't get paid for the breaks. I have to pay for food, too. The hardest part is working from two in the afternoon until eight. Your head explodes. After a day at work I don't even have the strength to think. I can't do anything but go to sleep.

Voice: I work every day from the morning until it is dark. On Friday afternoon I go out and see the sun. [Laughs.] And on Fridays, for some reason, there is always dust in the air, and no sun!

A black-and-white television sits on an iron shelf, with a distorted picture. It is hard to guess what it shows. The workers bought the television out of their own pockets, everyone chipping in. They bought an antenna as well and asked the boss to allow them to erect it on the factory roof in order to improve the quality of the picture. He refused. They sleep between piles of raw materials for the factory. Large mice run around, unafraid. The whole time we were there, we heard a constant, annoying sound; three days previously, the factory's alarm had gone out of order. Since then it has rung without stopping. Twenty-four hours a day, though the boss promised to bring someone to fix it.

Voice: I more or less live in Tel Aviv, but I haven't seen anything here except the machine in the factory. I graduated high school in Ramallah, and I have a three-month-old daughter. We named her Sabrin, which means patience. I had a son who died two days after he was born. I don't like the work. I work on a machine and it drives me crazy. Look at the clock a hundred times an hour. I go home once a week. I get there at five in the evening on Friday and go to sleep. I sleep until twelve on Saturday. Afterwards, I fix things at home and look at my daughter to see how she's grown. She still doesn't know me. It will probably take her a long time before she does. On Sunday at seven in the morning I'm already back at my machine. I don't have any choice: I support my brothers as well. I have a brother who is taking his high-school graduation exams now, and I have to keep working here.

The *ra'is* answers a question of mine: No, thank God, we're all friends here, we get along fine with each other. There aren't any problems and no tension.

Voice: My body is too busy fighting with itself to be able to fight with all the people here.

[Laughter.]

Voice: We earn about $95 a week. That's about a dollar and a quarter an hour. When we come up here in the evening we don't leave until morning. Even if we weren't afraid of the police and the border guard, I wouldn't go to a movie. How can I shell out ten dollars on a movie and a night out when I have to support my family back home? What would I tell them? That I went out to have fun?

Voice: To get a raise, I have to go to my boss and cry. Actually cry. Our boss starts sweating when we ask him for money. He doesn't pay social security on us and we don't get cost-of-living adjustments, and of course we don't get a pay slip. We are totally dependent on him. Whoever asks for too much gets kicked out. If he kicks me out, I'm done for.

The heat intensifies. Beads of sweat drip down my forehead. Clouds of dust rise from the mattresses and wool blankets at the slightest touch. In the corner of the hall is a small cell built of bare brick, in which there is a water pipe—the shower. There is no light in the shower. Pairs of underwear hang on a clothesline stretched across the room. Each worker showers once every two days, and is allowed to stay in the shower for a quarter of an hour. The kitchen is at the other end of the hall. There is a rust-eaten gas burner and a sink. The workers eat with tin implements. They buy and cook food for themselves. They had finished a standard supper just before I arrived: potatoes, lentils, onions, and tomatoes.

They sit facing me on the beds, tired, scratching themselves. A few of them look to me as if they are fourteen years old, but they insist that they are eighteen. When I ask what year they were born, they get confused and laugh. Someone is already sleeping, mouth gaping, on one bed. Yawns dance like black flames in an endless chain around the room. The younger men already stare mindlessly into space. I ask the one sitting next to me why he and his friends do not clean the place for themselves. It would be possible, after all, to improve the atmosphere a bit. He shrugs. Too tired. No one wants to. They live here for months and years. They slowly lose contact with their friends, and with themselves.

According to the data given me by David Nagar, the director of the Committee on Workers from the Territories of the Histadrut, the Israeli national labor union, some hundred thousand laborers from the territories now work in Israel. At least half of them are not registered with the national employment service, and therefore work in Israel illegally. They are unprotected against exploitation and injustice, and lack in effect any rights at all. The Histadrut, Mr. Nagar says, cannot search them out. That is the job of the police. The Histadrut has an interest in finding such workers, he noted, because in doing so it can protect Jewish workers from being crowded out by cheap labor. I asked why Histadrut representatives do not do the simple thing that I did, and go at night to industrial parks, find the workers, and force the factory owners to register them as the law requires and grant them their rights. That's the job of the police, he said.

In the meantime, the current situation continues. It would be possible to imagine a process by which the young man who leaves his traditional surroundings for the big city would develop—despite the harsh living conditions—and discover the world and himself as an individual, but the people I saw, and no doubt tens of thousands of others, are regressing. They have retreated into a demeaning, degenerate, inanimate form of existence.

Written on the plywood, between the obscene drawings:

"Important event! For the first time in the history of work, on Thursday, the last day of the week we sleep here, the food was not exhausted, and we ate supper, because something unexpected happened, and we received outside assistance from Brother 'Ali, who works in Kiryat Sharett, who brought us watermelons and cantaloupes and number-five peaches and plums."

*　*　*

Midnight. In a subterranean parking garage, under a well-known restaurant. Khaled and Fateh (the names have been changed at their request), nineteen years old. From Han Yunis in the Gaza Strip. They both have children. Khaled is divorced. His two daughters live with his mother, who is raising them. He and Fateh work as dishwashers.

Khaled (thick, kinky hair, talks quickly, in Hebrew, makes jokes at his own expense, nurses his cigarette in a slightly dramatic way, an entertainer looking for a chance to perform): I work here every day from 6:30 in the morning to twelve at night. [Fateh goes and brings me their punch cards, stamped by the clock.] At twelve, I finish working. Sometimes I don't see the sun for an entire day. Only when I go to throw out the garbage I can stand for a second and see that it's still there. Once every two weeks, when I have a vacation, I remember that there is a sky and wind and stars.

Fateh: If I were to go and ask for a permit to sleep in a real apartment in Israel, not here in the storeroom, your intelligence people would tell me that to get a permit I have to work as an informer for them. There are a lot of Arab criminals here, and some of them finished college! And they all take drugs. Why? Because when one of them finishes studying, the Shin Bet comes to him and says work for us, and he says no. So they begin pressuring him, and destroy him little by little. What does he have left? Drugs. He works all day like a slave, and at night, so as not to go crazy, he smokes.

Khaled: I bring up my children, and get older, and my children will also come and work for you and grow old, and their children, too. What most hurts me is that I feel as if my mind has already gone soft. I never thought

I'd end up like this. I spend my life in the *intihar* ["suicide"—their name for washing the large pots]. I have no life outside of work. Only dirty work. No one cares about my life, no one thinks that this also is a human being who wants to do something with himself.

Fateh: Our life is trash. Once a sewage pipe in the restaurant got stopped up. The boss told me to go down and open it. I told him, I can't, it disgusts me. He said, You stopped it up, and you'll open it up. I told him that I don't know how to do that sort of thing. That he should bring someone to do it. He said, You want me to bring a Jew for that? He forced me to go down there, way inside. When I came out, I was sick. I was in bed for a whole week. The boss didn't pay me for the days I was sick. Why should he pay? A week ago my leg was scalded by hot water. I worked for four hours and then the foot went. He docked me for the whole day.

Khaled: We're slowly going crazy here. We hit each other. It's from nerves. Who can we take it out on? Only on each other. And when I come home, once every two weeks, I take it out on the family, and they really don't deserve it.

Fateh: We're the lowest. Even the assistant cooks are Jews. I can't be an assistant cook? But if I ask the boss, he says, You're an Arab. You're fit for garbage and dishwashing. They won't even let me be a waiter. Only one who looks a little Jewish is allowed to work with the customers, and even he has to change his name to Moshe or Yossi. But if you look like an Arab, the Jews don't want to see you while they're eating.

Khaled: Every day I take out ten full cans of garbage and throw it in the city's bin upstairs. There is a service elevator next to the restaurant that lets you off right near the bin, but the boss won't let us use it. So I tie the cans to a rope, and the rope around my neck, and drag, and I've made up songs I sing when I drag the garbage, and when I wash dishes.

He shuts his eyes, sucks on his cigarette, and shakes his foot like a conductor tapping his stand with his wand, and warbles nasally:

"I entered a garden through the gate / The jasmine cried and the rose bowed its head / The lilies laughed and said—Here comes the poor boy / One day we will plant peaches / And one day figs / Love is only for the rich / And I am only a poor refugee . . .

"The evil man called to a noble poor man / Come, he told him, work for me. / Serve me like my servants do. / Cook, launder, clean my house. / The noble poor man said: / Better I should climb a deserted mountain, / That the owls and ravens eat me there, / Than to work for an evil and cruel man."

Khaled concludes his song. I wait for the last notes to echo in the large empty kitchen in which we sit, and I say cautiously: "But you work for him nevertheless."

And Khaled says: "Yes, what can I do."

It is already one in the morning. They do not want to go to sleep. Our interest has awakened them. They want us to stay. With sudden enthusiasm they announce that they will prepare a meal for us. They are not willing to take no for an answer. So, in the middle of the night, in a subterranean kitchen, they switch on the microwave and set us a table graced with all the delicacies of the restaurant. They pile more and more onto the table, steaks and salads and relishes and drinks, and press us to eat, and I, I must admit, dine with great enjoyment, and I feel that eating here is a way of getting back at

the boss, and at the garbage heap surrounding them up
to their necks.

"You aren't going to eat?"

"No"—they laugh—"we can't stand Jewish food.
Mayonnaise from a bottle! Fish and eggs together! Sometimes we take things from the refrigerator and prepare
them like Arabs do."

Khaled: Sometimes the boss tells us, Here is something
you are allowed to eat. It's always something that's been
in the refrigerator for a week, that no one else wanted.

They have worked here for two years. I ask them if
they can mention something good they have learned
from the Jews, something that they gained from their
life in the big city.

Khaled laughs. "I've learned only one thing here—to
wash dishes. And even that my mother taught me a long
time ago."

We finish our absurd midnight meal. Khaled sings
another song, maybe the beginnings of another blues
era, the Arab Worker Blues, and before we leave brings
us a little school notebook in which he writes down his
thoughts. A diary. I translate a section word for word:

"Confusion, thoughts, and sorrow, and dreams and
remorse. Like the life of a prisoner who has sentenced
himself to life in prison, shut all his days behind bars, behind electrified doors, in solitary confinement underground. Only by his watch can he know what the time is.
He does not see true light. Only neon light. Sometimes he
does not know if it is day outside, or night ..."

Last stop: the Levinsky teachers' college.

Two in the morning. By way of an unfrequented dirt
path off the road to the Tel Baruch beach, near the

country club at the northern entrance to Tel Aviv, we arrive at the back yard of the Levinsky teachers' college. The college is lit on all sides. There is work going on. Two boys come down to us. They do not have keys. They are shut up here each night, and in the morning someone comes to let them out. We talk to them through an iron net. They are not afraid to give their names: 'Ali and Samir from the Jabalia refugee camp in the Gaza Strip. The first is fifteen years old, and the second sixteen.

'Ali: "A cleaning contractor named Rafi brought us here. We've worked here every night for a month and a half. We come every day at six in the evening, when the Jews go, and leave at seven in the morning, before they arrive. Every night, we clean and mop all the rooms. There are maybe fifty rooms here, and we are by ourselves. Sometimes there is someone else with us, an Arab, and there is also an old guard, who is scared of everyone, including us."

Samir (dark-faced, with large eyes): "We work all week. Even on Friday nights. We get $375 a month. No pay slip. No social security. We finish work at seven in the morning, and sleep in an apartment the contractor rented for all his workers. All kinds sleep there. We buy food ourselves. Don't cook. We eat hummus and salad. We're in the apartment until the evening, and then we come back here. We mop until four in the morning, and then we are tired and go to sleep a little. We put three chairs together in the hallway and sleep on them."

I write. The fence dividing us casts a barred shadow on the paper. Next week is Israel's thirty-ninth Independence Day, and a flag on a nearby streetlight already waves and cracks in the wind. The two stand facing me, small, thin, and drowsy. Their exhaustion makes them look even more juvenile. The last of the partyers are returning from the Tel Aviv nightclubs to their homes in Herzlia, Netanya, and Haifa. Israel sleeps. On the nearby Tel Baruch road, cars honk at the prostitutes. When I ask them about the prostitutes, they are very confused. Better to jerk off, they explain seriously, than to get syphilis or that new thing.

"All this is yours for now?" I ask, indicating the building. They boast: "We are responsible for everything here. We can turn on all the televisions and the VCRs. We can eat anything in the kitchen, make telephone calls to anywhere, but we don't know anyone we can call."

That, too, is one of the absurd parts of the situation: wherever they go, people are suspicious of these Arab workers, and search them, restrict their movement, and make their lives miserable, but on the other hand, there are long hours every day, all night, in which they get the keys to everything from us.

"How often do you see your parents?"

"We go home once a month. For the weekend. We visit family, friends. Sleep at night.

"My friends go to school. I couldn't go to school, because things are hard at home. I bring all the money I earn to my father. I put a little aside for myself that he doesn't know about. I miss my mother most of all. My mother is worth the whole world."

I ask them if they know what the place they work in is. It's like a school, they say, a sort of university or college. Have they ever seen the students who study here? No. We always leave before they come. I light them cigarettes through the fence, and they return to the large building, Samir taller and 'Ali slightly bent over behind him, dragging their feet inch by inch up the stairs. Like a boy with a teddy bear trudging his way to bed.

16

The Terrorist's

Father

Mohammed Ali Al-Kal'ilah is a man of forty-nine, tall and of noble bearing. He was born in the village of Samu'a, twenty kilometers south of Hebron. The village has a population of ten thousand, all of them Moslems who earn their livelihoods from farming and from the large stone quarries next to the village. They send the cut stones to Jordan, and someone once said that this, too, is a way of returning the territories to that country.

The security forces arrested Mohammed Ali Al-Kal'ilah in June 1985. He worked as a room attendant in a Dead Sea hotel and was taken from there to a prison in Hebron and placed in a cell. He told me his story in Hebrew.

"A few guys came to me, as if they wanted to beat me up, and said, You are a dog and a son of a dog, and I said, What for? They said, You don't know why we brought you here? Where is your son? I said, My son was home with me about three weeks ago, and afterwards, he went back to his house in Ramallah. He has a house there where he lives with his wife and children. They said, No, no. Tell us where he is now."

The son, Ali Mohammed Al-Shehade Al-Kal'ilah, left his father's house in Samu'a when he was eighteen years old and rented a house in Ramallah. He lived there with his wife—who was a teacher—and with his three children—'Afaf, Mohammed, and 'Amar.

"They said, We want your son, and only you know where he is. I said, I don't know. They said, You are a whore and a son of a whore and a dog. They came to beat me, and someone said, 'Don't beat him, he'll tell everything soon. I said, I don't know anything. They said, We'll bring your wife here and we'll fuck her in front of you. This went on for almost a week, only talk, without beatings at all.

"After that, they said suddenly, Now go, bring your wife, and your son's wife, and sit here, in the office of the *mukhabarat*, the intelligence service, in Hebron, every day from seven in the morning to seven in the evening. So I brought them, and there was also my son's baby, and officers pass us the whole time and spit on us and say, Tfu! you are dogs and the sons of dogs, and every day they would leave us there until nine at night, and every day we had to take a taxi, and when we came home at night, the *mukhabarat* would come again, at four in the morning, and enter the house, and pull everything out of the closets, wake up the children, and they would bring big dogs with them and say, We want your children to see the dogs and go crazy from fear of them.

"After that, the daily detention in Hebron ended, but the *mukhabarat* would still come to search the house every night. And after about three months I went again to the hotel at the Dead Sea to work, and I heard on television that the army had a battle with some people near Hebron, killed four and captured one wounded, and my wife called me on the telephone and said to come back, and I went and I saw my house bulldozed, not one stone left on another."

Why were they searching for your son? What had he done?

"They say he killed Israelis. I don't know. He never said anything."

You really don't know? Even now you don't know?

"I don't know! I didn't even get along with him. He never spoke to me."

This is the story: The son, Ali, was arrested in April 1978, accused of membership in the Fatah, and released. He claimed that he had been freed on the basis of a certain bargain, and he apparently did not live up to it. He was arrested again in 1979, accused of the original crime, and sentenced to four months in prison, with another half year suspended.

From the moment he was released, he was a marked man: on the one hand, the security forces watched his every step, and on the other hand, his former friends tormented him, accusing him of collaborating with the enemy. No one spoke to him. He was a pariah. A person who met him during that time testified that he seemed as if he had gone mad. He lived like a hunted beast, and sensed that every passing moment brought his end that much closer. It may be that for some the occupation, with its cruel demands, is a challenge which hardens their souls and pride; but there are, without a doubt, many more who, caught between the conqueror and the conquered, lose their humanity.

In order to counter the accusations of his friends, the young man went out to the mountains and made contact

with a particularly deadly gang of terrorists, a gang which
a year previously had murdered a Jew in Ramallah.

Ali Al-Shehade Al-Kal'ilah took part in the gang's
horrifying murders of two couples, one in a forest near
the town of Beit Shemesh (within the 1967 boundaries
of Israel), and another not far away, near the settlement
of Mavo Beitar, in the West Bank.

When I learned, a week after my conversation with
the father, what his son had actually done, I felt that I
didn't want to hear the rest of the story from the father.
I remembered the innocent, naive, and optimistic faces
of the murdered couples, and I could not find in myself
any sympathy at all for Ali Al-Kal'ilah's father, la-
menting his son and demanding that he be allowed to
rebuild his destroyed house.

I refused to even think about him for three weeks.
The deed was like an open, coagulating wound. I thought:
So they knocked down his house, big deal! I reserve my
sympathy for the real victims, for his son's victims. I
refused to go back to see him.

But after three weeks, during which I met so many
Arabs and Jews, dogmatically miserable and some unaware of how miserable they are, I sank deeper and
deeper into frustration and melancholy, and the futility
of the unbreakable prison of circumstance, without a
solution and without an outlet, only continual pain, an
ongoing and spreading terror. I then understood that I
had to go back to Mohammed Ali Al-Kal'ilah; to go
back to him precisely because of the repulsion and repugnance I felt, and hear his story to the end, because
it is a story that repeats itself in a thousand and one
variations, the hard and evil story in which there are no

victors, and in which no one is in the right, only death and destruction and people who are bound to their fate with a curse.

Mohammed Ali Al-Kal'ilah is a tall, mustached man, a man with presence. Swollen, purple bags under his eyes. He had a four-room house and a large garden in Samu'a. In the garden he grew figs, grapes, olives, and vegetables. The rooms were carpeted with rugs his wife wove with her own hands. It took her four months to make each rug.

One morning, soldiers came to the house and notified her that she had fifteen minutes to get all her belongings and her daughters out of the house, after which the house would be leveled. Sometimes, when I hear about the destruction of houses in the West Bank, I wonder what I would remove from my house during that quarter hour—the basic necessities, I suppose: bed linens and cooking utensils. But what about the photograph albums? And my manuscript? And books? And old letters? How much can you get out in a frenzied fifteen minutes?

Al-Kal'ilah's wife took mattresses and blankets, plates and a gas burner, and a suitcase full of clothes into which she had the presence of mind to shove the family photo album. She and her two daughters, Ibtasam and Noel, stood there and cried. The soldiers knocked down the house and spread its stones over the entire garden. The head of the family arrived after the destruction. A neighbor offered the family accommodations in a single room in his house. As Mohammed Al-Kal'ilah stood by the ruins of his house, security personnel approached him once more. "They told me, Come, you son-of-a-bitch, come with us now. I said, What more do you want from me? He said, We killed your son. I said, Fine, you're strong, you can kill us all. I'm only one man and you are a government. They handcuffed me and took me for interrogation in Hebron. I said, I don't have anything to tell you, I haven't seen my son for a long time. They showed me my son's identity card covered with blood, and said, Look, this is his blood. Now tell us where he was during the months when we didn't know where he was.

"I said, I don't know. They don't believe me. And I was like a dead man, because my son had been killed, my house had been destroyed, and at work they told me not to come back. What do I have left, what?

"They interrogated me. Beat me with their hands all over my body and threw me hard against the wall. Afterwards, I would sit in a chair—and they would come suddenly from behind and throw me over. The interrogator would sit across from me in a high chair. He would present the sole of his army boot to me, and then press down on my balls hard and harder, and spit on me from above, from head to foot, and when he had no more spit he would go drink a cup of coffee and come back and spit some more.

"Later, they put me on trial and gave me four months in jail, because they said I helped my son hide in my house, but I didn't help him, he didn't hide in my house, because he had his own house in Ramallah, and even the *mukhabarat* knew he had not been with me for years, and even if he murdered all the Israelis, he is the only one responsible for what he did. Why did they knock down my house? Why did they destroy my body in the interrogations after he died? Who does it help that they kill me, too? Why do they have to do that?"

In the Emergency Defense Regulations of 1945 (promulgated by the King in his Privy Council), part 12, section 119, it says: "A military commander may issue an order confiscating for the government of Israel any house, building, or land, if there is reason to believe that any firearm was illegally fired from it, or from which were illegally thrown, detonated, exploded, or shot in any other way a bomb, hand grenade, or any other explosive or inflammable device, or any house, building, or land situated in any area, city, village, neighborhood, or street, in which it has been discovered that the inhabitants, or some of them, violated, or tried to violate, or assisted violators, or were accomplices after the fact to the violation of these regulations, violations involving violence or threats of violence or any violation judged in a military court; with the confiscation of the house or building or land as stated above, the commander may destroy the house or building or anything within the house . . ."

The wording of the regulations allows, in fact, the destruction of any structure in any village or city in which one resident has committed any security violation; the commander may order that the house be destroyed, confiscated, or sealed without having to give any notification, and without charging the owner of the house with any crime.

"Now they won't allow me to build myself a new house. They say, Someone like you can't get a permit. We now live in a rented house, two rooms without a kitchen and without a bathroom. Eight people together with my wife and my son's children, and we cook everything in the bedroom. They made us into animals. Now tell me what law you have that doesn't let a man build a house for himself? And not only that—you killed a man, why don't you give him to his parents? Why don't you tell them where he is buried? What more do you want? Are you afraid of his body? Let us know at least that he has a grave. Even if he is a murderer, he is still our son."

Attorney Leah Tsemel, who has taken on Al-Kal'ilah's case, has submitted uncountable petitions to the authorities, and asked why his house was destroyed. On January 12, 1987, the laconic answer arrived: "The petitioner's son resided in the destroyed house." In March of this year, Tsemel appealed to the High Court of Justice. The hearing on the petition has not yet taken place.

I have told the story as it was told to me. One's heart does not go out to Mohammed Al-Kal'ilah, who raised such a son. But perhaps one must take a rational, principled stand here precisely because he arouses no sympathy. It is a difficult thing to do, nerve-racking to the hearer of the story. To the entire Israeli ethos. It is precisely the exceptional, repugnant cases like these which are the real forge of a moral and human code of behavior. To display wide-hearted humanism even in such cases, and reduce somewhat the hate and bitterness.

I did not, however, tell this story for any purpose. If I had a goal in mind, I could have chosen a much less ambiguous incident. There is no lack of them. I chose this story because it is a sort of bitter microcosm of the big story—of two nations' life together. One that brings to life the simple misery in which we live.

Attorney Leah Tsemel is still trying to get the terrorist's body. "I have a few bodies like that I haven't gotten yet," she says, as a sort of grotesque conclusion to the whole story. There is a cemetery near Jericho for terrorists, and for prisoners who died in hunger strikes from improper forced feedings. Mohammed Ali Al-Kal'ilah goes every day to see the ruins of his house. I cannot even begin to measure the sorrow of the families of the murdered. I know that a family which has lost a dear one in such a way has no life. I think of the young, full lives which were cut off. I do not know if the families of the victims find any comfort in fostering hatred of the murderer, his family, his nation. How can we judge them if that is how they feel? The murderer's father said to me: "If my son murdered, kill him. Kill him immediately! But why have you destroyed my entire life? Why have you made me and my family into beasts? I still have power in my hands"—he clenched his fist for me and trembled—"I could kill a million times the man who ordered my house destroyed. Did I ever do anything like that? Did I ever think like that before? I only wanted to live. Now they have made me like that, too. They have turned me into a murderer."

I asked him how he supports his family now, after he was fired. At first, he did not want to answer. Afterwards, he said he had become a beggar. He goes from village to village and pleads for money. Not in Samu'a. He is ashamed to go there. Sometimes he goes to a village and sits in the street, and someone he knows passes. Both of them turn their heads in shame.

17

Last Night There Was an Inferno Here

The West Bank was a storm during the entire month before the attack at Alfei Menashe. There were daily demonstrations and arrests, stone throwings and tire burnings. Three thousand security prisoners were in the midst of a hunger strike in the military jails. The entire population was restive over the strike. Disaster was in the air, inescapable; whoever traveled the West Bank roads at that time felt it. One Friday, as I exited the village of Dura, an explosive device went off there; a week later, as I returned from Kfar Adumim, stones were thrown at my car. On our way to Nablus, the Israeli cabdriver took a large, black-and-white checked kaffi-yeh, the traditional Arab headdress, out of his glove compartment and spread it conspicuously over his dash-board. To fool the enemy, he said, so that they stop to think before they start throwing stones.

The disaster occurred on the Saturday night before Passover. The Moses family was traveling in its car from the settlement Alfei Menashe to neighboring Kfar Saba. As they left the settlement, a Molotov cocktail was thrown at the car, apparently from an orange grove along the road. The car burst into flames. The father, his clothes on fire, succeeded in getting his children out of the car. The mother, Ofra, thirty-five years old, five months pregnant, was trapped and perished. The survivors are still suffering from serious burns: the father, sons Adi and Nir, and the son of friends, Yosef Hillel. Five-year-old Tal died in July.

The morning after the attack, three military cars are parked alongside the road to the settlement. Senior officers survey the area through dark sunglasses. They converse in post-disaster low voices. On the road, an ugly black stain, composed of the remains of a burnt tire and a timid wreath of three flowers in the middle of the spot.

The businesslike presence of serious-faced security men fills the area. Roadblocks, searches, the crackle of walkie-talkies, a patrol plane flying above. A curfew has been declared in the nearby Arab city of Qalqilia, and in the surrounding villages. Two gray army bulldozers knock down the first rows of trees in the orange groves on both sides of the road. In one of them, apparently, the thrower of the Molotov cocktail lay in wait. As of this writing, he has yet to be caught.

It is possible, on the basis of past experience, to sketch his portrait. It is possible to re-create the words those who sent him poured into his heart in order to seal it, so that it might serve as a deadly, blind instrument. In his friends' eyes, he will from this point on be a hero. A freedom fighter. The situation is a mint casting human coins with opposite legends imprinted on their two sides. But the contradicting legends do not change the fact that between them—freedom fighter or terrorist; ours or theirs—can be found the dark, hidden raw material: a murderer.

This morning the air is perfumed by the flowering orange groves, and the land's breath awakens the abundance of springtime and the exorbitant profusion of nature. The pale roots of the orange trees break through the wounded ground, and green oranges still roll earthward, coming to rest on a carpet of wildflowers.

Four hundred and fifty families live in Alfei Menashe. Three and a half years ago they came to the bald, boulder-crowned mountain. Rows of houses are stuck in a semicircle on the side of the hill, and from far off, in the glare of the sun, they look like the sparkling hooks of a net thrown over the neck of a huge gray whale.

Close up, one sees that the whale has surrendered: roads and public parks, playgrounds, houses surrounded by green, a shopping center for morning chats and cultural evenings, and in the schoolyard boys play soccer.

The settlement Alfei Menashe is located very close to Kfar Saba and looks much like one of the neighborhoods of private houses which surround, for instance, Jerusalem. "We are, after all, included in the Alon Plan," say the residents, surprised, referring to the compromise borders proposed by then Foreign Minister Yigael Alon in 1976, under which Israel would absorb parts of the West Bank. "We aren't settlers at all!" As if they don't understand how the terrorists could mistake them for such—how did they not understand that they are included within the consensus?

The residents of Alfei Menashe do reside, as they say, within the area about which there is general agreement. They are like tens of thousands of other Israelis who now live over the Green Line for reasons of convenience and quality of life, rather than as a matter of ideology. Another practical nibble at the moral problem, another step toward surrounding the immoral with the amoral. In ten more years, if the present situation continues, it will become clear that the motherly, broad down blanket of the consensus is actually made of rubber, and there will always be those who will not stop stretching it more and more, from five minutes from Kfar Saba to a stone's throw from Sidon.

At night there was an inferno here. After the attack the residents of Alfei Menashe and of other settlements gathered to take revenge. First they cut down two trees in the nearby orange grove, "to symbolize the cutting down of an Israeli family," and afterwards, while the smoking car still lay on the road, they entered the nearby Arab city of Qalqilia. In their words, they "burned four piles of weeds." The press reported burning fields and broken windows in hundreds of cars and homes, and the frightening of the inhabitants of Qalqilia and a nearby village, Hablah.

Shaul Hai from Alfei Menashe took part in those actions. "What happened? What's the big deal? Did we kill anyone? Did we take an eye for an eye? Did we even slap an Arab in the face? If you were to go to Qalqilia today, you would see the truth. I'm a moderate type, I swear, but when I see something like that—a whole family . . ." He fell silent, biting his lip. "I ask the bleeding hearts, those who are now shouting that we took the law into our own hands, what have they done to prevent this situation? What have you done, what?"

And what happened in Qalqilia? And what did you do in Hablah?

"Settlers from Karnei Shomron and Kdumim went there. The army—which always fights us instead of the terrorists—stopped their cars, so they got out and went on by foot, over the fields. They only went into the city and into Hablah and burned piles of weeds, and afterwards I read in the newspaper about burning fields in Qalqilia! What would they do to those Arabs in a case like that in Russia? Bang bang bang bang bang! To the wall, no questions asked! No one would open his mouth! I'm telling you—good for those guys who gave it to the Arabs—they really know how to put things straight. You can't put out a fire with polite talk!" He leaves me, boiling with anger, and I don't know which fire he was talking about: The car? The desire for revenge? The large barrel of gunpowder?

I try to imagine those moments last night, in Kdumim: the telephone in the settlement's office rings. "There has been an attack. One or more dead. Not clear how many. Have to notify. Have to do something." The whisper turns into a rumble. People run quickly, grimly, from house to house. The air thickens as everyone becomes part of a taut web of nerves. The news passes silently from person to person. From settlement to settlement. The men get in their cars (which immediately become "transports"). At the gate, someone ducks his head into the car and says in a hushed voice that he just now talked with a leading figure in Gush Emunim and he will be there, too. That grants an unspoken official seal of approval. I imagine that they did not talk much in the car about what was about to happen. The people already know that there will be an investigation, because that's how the authorities work, that no one here will actually give the order. So that no one person will be culpable.

In this way a sort of collective, agreed-upon distance from the decision is created. They allow the violence to pulsate in its raw form, shapeless, in the fear and the hope that it will work itself, direct the hands and blind the eyes and hearts, and force them to act in one pre-determined way.

Do I not already know all the heroes of this tragedy? The murderous terrorist, whose brothers in hatred I have met so many times in Nablus, in Hebron, in Deheisha; and those who set out for revenge, to correct a crime with an injustice, the determined, history-conscious people from Ofra, from Kfar Adumim; and the poor family itself, the children, the parents, and the innocent inhabitants of Qalqilia, taking cover in their houses in fright, listening to the approaching footsteps?

I knew them all, and I could speak with all of them, as well as find similarities and sympathy between us. But now every eye is bloodshot, they are all possessed, the slaves of a single power, tyrannical and cruel, leading them, blinded, one into the other.

I enter Qalqilia. It is my first time in a city under curfew. It is strange to pace through complete stillness, when every step sounds as if it breaks the surface of a frozen puddle. Everything is locked up—the stores and the houses. Human footsteps no longer sound in the street. And spring bursts into this emptiness with all its might, flowing like a drunken crowd through the empty streets and alleys, its butterflies, the colors and perfumes of its flowers, and for a moment it is possible to err and wonder whether the city has only been drugged by the abundant, sensuous perfume, addicted to it, dizzy and loose-limbed like Jericho.

A pretty city, Qalqilia, fair to the eye. Well kept. Roses flower in enclosures along the main boulevard. There are no signs of violence. I do not see broken windows or the remains of a fire, even though the settlers themselves said they came here as a great and angry group.

Suddenly a boy leaps from the doorway of a house in a narrow alley and runs to the road. Hey, boy, don't you know there's a curfew? Yes, yes, I know, but I slept at night at my aunt's house, and I want to go home, and not only that, I'm not a boy, I'm a girl!

You're a girl?

"Yes!"

She is truly insulted.

Fine, fine. Excuse me that I didn't notice. But your hair is very short.

"Yes, but I'm wearing earrings!"

And she presents the tiny earrings, sparkling in her earlobes, for my inspection. No doubt about it—a girl.

I apologize once more. Her name is Samah, and she is nine years old. She is not afraid to run, because the army isn't in this side street, and not only that, they won't do anything to her, because she is little.

Do you know what happened here at night?

Her fresh, mischievous face locks. Don't know. Didn't hear anything.

Were you afraid?

Yes, but only because her aunt cried all night. Now she has to run.

I follow her with my eyes as she crosses the street. She looks both ways, and afterwards, speedily, like a trained fighter, like a hare crossing an open field, she rushes, slightly bowed, and disappears. What life teaches.

Now I begin making out heads peeking from roofs,

from the balcony railings, from the half-closed blinds. The alley next to the Shalom Café is closed at present, and I exchange a few words with a family hiding behind a slightly open iron gate. They did not hear anything; at night there were cries and shots and they smelled smoke. The Jews' cars sped past, honking. Then the army came, and the inhabitants calmed down, because the army is less dangerous than the *mustawtanin*, the settlers; soldiers passed and announced over loudspeakers that there would be a curfew. Until when? Don't know. Maybe one day, maybe two. Until further notice. They did not sleep all night out of fear. There is also a problem—Grandmother is in bed upstairs and she has pains in her chest, maybe it's her heart, she is crying from the pain, and they cannot bring a doctor.

I ask if they know what happened yesterday on the road by Alfei Menashe. No. They don't know. They only heard that the Jews tore things apart. "Someone burned a family with small children on the road. They killed a woman," I say. Once again I find myself facing an expression emptying itself of all emotion, like a door slammed in my face. "We don't know anything. We haven't heard anything."

On the main street, I am surprised to see televisions, refrigerators, and ovens on the sidewalk, outside a closed store. Across the street, furniture: armchairs, beds, and mattresses. Two soldiers call me over and ask who I am. In those places where the storekeepers did not manage to get their merchandise into the store before having to lock up, the army has stationed guards to prevent plundering. This mixture of violence and consideration, of brutality and basic humanity is what makes everything hard to deal with and hard to understand. It is even harder for those who do the work themselves. Is this an army of occupation, or a police force protecting citizens from their own fellow nationals? What does a young soldier (maybe a farmer's son) feel when he has to cut down young trees? What does an Arab feel as he labors on the construction site of a new settlement on the hill overlooking his village? What kind of occupying army can it be whose soldiers did not rape a single woman from among its surrendering enemies? What does the student reservist, who studies together with Arabs at the Hebrew University, feel when he suddenly has to shoot into a crown of demonstrators at An-Najah University in Nablus?

Another question: Into what reality are children to be educated? How fuzzy can the lesson I give to my sons be? Maybe I do them an injustice when I bring them up with certain values and do not prepare them for the brutal life we live here?

And a last question: Is the feeling that the situation cannot possibly continue forever really a reasonable guarantee that it will eventually change?

The secretariat of Gush Emunim and the heads of the Jewish settlements in the West Bank and Gaza Strip meet in the gymnasium of the school in Alfei Menashe. They are all here, those whose names you see in the newspapers, and many of their friends. They damn the army, the Chief of Staff, the Minister of Defense, and the entire government with fire and brimstone. They sit around tables in the gym, between ladders and vaulting horses, their faces red with fury, fingering their pistols. They know that at such moments it is easy for an unsure government, overwhelmed with guilt, to give in to their demands, and they strike the iron while it's hot. You can understand their motives, but they are repellent. Most of the residents of Alfei Menashe that I spoke to wanted nothing to do with this political convention, exploiting their sorrow for its own purposes—most of them boycotted it.

Hooliganism echoes in everything the leaders of Gush Emunim say. A smooth, sharp hooliganism, but hooliganism nonetheless. With television cameras in the gymnasium, every speaker makes sure to give lip service to "the need to work within the law," but they pronounce the words like someone spitting a rotten piece of apple from his mouth.

Rav Levinger, leader of the Jewish settlement in Hebron, his beard stiff and wiry, his face red, calls the Minister of Defense a murderer. His hands spilled this blood. Levinger hints that another Jewish underground will arise. It will arise because of the government's failures. "They decided that there would not be another underground, and I accepted the decision," he declares and hints. He accepted but did not agree. "But today we once again face a situation in which the Ministry of Defense has made us fair game, and the Ministry of Defense bears, after all, the major share of the guilt for the last underground." Those were his words. Maybe one of the young people of Gush Emunim understood the hint the Rav dangled before them, and afterwards the people of Gush Emunim will be shocked and say that their entire system of education opposes violence.

"If we allow ourselves to get used to stone throwing," Levinger seethed, "we will get used to funerals. One funeral and another and another. Blood and more blood and more blood!" His finger jabs the air as if he were debating a passage of Talmud. His head bobs constantly, as if drawing something out of the depths of his being, as if he has drilled through his soul to its primal layer, even deeper and wilder, where lies all the sediment of Jewish suffering and an incomparably dark thirst for revenge. And now he straightens his neck and sputters death. We need a death penalty! Death penalty! Why are you afraid of the death penalty? In the United States they execute lots of people!"

Beside the preacher of death, Daniella Weiss, Secretary-General of Gush Emunim, nods and her eyes sparkle, two rings of red raised on her cheeks, but it seems to me it is not the spring that is bringing out this bloom. She repeats his words, her eyes hanging on his lips, her lips moving, as if she is the only one who knows how to read his words, death penalty! It is a short distance from seeing these two move opposite each other in the stylized movements of a sacrificial revenge ceremony.

Elyakim Ha-etzni, a Kiryat Arba leader, stands and froths before the assembly, but his voice is so high that the echoes bouncing off the walls of the gymnasium crash into each other and it is very hard to hear what he is saying. It is almost certainly fascinating—it seems that he has prepared a list of steps the authorities must take against PLO activists in the territories, and maybe against anyone who has ambitions which clash with Ha-etzni's. I make out the words "expulsion," "closure," "imprisonment," "death penalty," "destruction," and for a short, mad moment I see Ha-etzni prancing happily through a West Bank completely emptied of people.

Someone else rises to speak. A resident of Alfei Menashe, a lieutenant colonel in the standing army, large-bodied and with a sympathetic face, the face of a golden boy of the land of Israel, and as his speech takes off, his face becomes more serious and harsh, and he concludes by promising that he himself, and all residents of the settlement, will deal with the Arab villages in the area "with all the means at our disposal." "We will go in there like commandos!" he roars, his finger waving in the air. The journalists take it all down.

Then the funeral. Alfei Menashe still does not have a cemetery, so Ofra was buried in Segula. Two soldiers who fell in the Lebanese War are also buried there. Somber and bitter. The crowd treads silently. The husband and the children are still fighting for their lives in the hospital. Meir Kahane arrives. He frequents burials. He strides, surrounded by a few strange, tense young men, both drawing and repelling everyone's glances, like an embarrassing subconscious failing.

We pace along the cemetery paths, and Haim Korfu, Minister of Transportation and the government's flesh-and-blood representative, drives among us in his Volvo. To my left I hear Ha-etzni explaining to someone how Israeli peace initiatives of the past and present have only caused more Jewish deaths: "When I heard Peres's idea of an international peace conference, I immediately knew there would be more victims." I peer at him, and try to figure out where he plugs in the device that allows him to make such logical contortions—and wonder whether the misfunction is mine.

The government's representative speaks by the grave: "Just as the two soldiers who fell yesterday died in defense of the safety of the Galilee, you, Ofra, fell in defense of the safety of Jerusalem."

I find it hard to believe my ears: "You, Ofra, are our

soldier . . . We established settlements in order to make
Judea and Samaria safer . . ." These words seem so
foreign to the pain, and to the facts. "The settlements
are a guarantee against the Palestinian state of those
who hate us!" Korfu declares, and someone shouts at
him: "You are Peres's whores, all of you!" He is silenced
by those who stand around him. Relatives sob. They
almost certainly do not take in Korfu's words. Like standard words of greeting and curses. I hope they do not
hear it. What can they feel when their dead loved one
turns into the instrument of a cynical political game?
Why does there have to be a government representative
at such a tragic event? Is death also the government's
domain? Do the living also partake in this same hollow
protocol? Why do politicians not know how to make
themselves scarce, and shamefacedly withdraw from the
place of the pain and sorrow which they, in their im-
potence, have a part in causing?

I listen to the government representative and begin to
understand. There is no guarantee that what has to be
done here to prevent more and more suffering will actually be done. Most of the tragedies which have befallen
nations happened because of the mistakes those peoples
made. There is a no-man's-land, a dead place, dividing
personal pain, a man and his feelings, from the place in
which things are decided and the agreements and party
manifestos and official eulogies are drafted. "The PLO
wants to cut us off at the roots, but we will do the same
to them!" Korfu concludes the official prayer of the government representative at the cemetery.

The funeral has ended, it was announced. Then there
was total stillness. The crowd waited as if for some sign,
for an event that would carry off all its emotions in a

storm. Violence waited above like a torch sputtering in
the wind. The air was filled for a moment with the
flatulent whisper "Kahane." Then the tension subsided.
The crowd began to disperse. Korfu sailed off in his car,
and the television crew folded up its equipment.
The sun was covered by a slight cloud, shimmering
through it, as if covered by a handkerchief. Ofra Moses's
close friends and relatives quietly approached the grave.
Now they were alone, without politicians and functionaries and merchants of tragedy. The close friends gathered into a tight group, embracing and solid in their pain
around the small, long mound of earth, and tightened
their circle more and more, gazing inconsolable and un-
believing at the new scar on the ground.

18

The First
Twenty Years

I belong to the generation that celebrated its bar mitz-
vah during the Six-Day War. Then, in 1967, the surging
energy of our adolescent hormones was coupled with
the intoxication gripping the entire country; the con-
quest, the confident penetration of the enemy's land, his
complete surrender, breaking the taboo of the border,
imperiously striding through the narrow streets of cities
until now forbidden, and the smells, the primal view,
and that same erotic tingle latent in every first meeting
between conqueror and conquered—ah, what a sensuous explosion of all the pent-up desire that was in us!
And on a grand scale! With the entire country!

We were thirteen years old, and we reached maturity
in a collective rite of passage together with the adults.
Secret desires and fears broke out into the sunlight and
became sensible. Only a month before, in May, we had
watched a military parade of the Israeli Defense Forces
in the streets of Jerusalem: because of the cease-fire
agreement with Jordan, armor and aircraft could not be
brought into the city, and so the representatives of those

forces had to be satisfied with displaying cardboard cut-outs of planes and tanks. What poor proxies they were!

Afterwards, everything happened.

And in twenty years, everything happens, and it is as if nothing happens at all.

Seven years ago, I felt I had to write something about the occupation. I could not understand how an entire nation like mine, an enlightened nation by all accounts, is able to train itself to live as a conqueror without making its own life wretched. What happened to us? How were they able to pass their values on to me during these years? For two years I sat and worked out those thoughts and dilemmas of mine. I wrote a novel, *The Smile of the Lamb*, and the more I wrote, the more I understood that the occupation is a continuing and stubborn test for both sides trapped in it. It is the sphinx lying at the entrance to each of us, demanding that we give a clear answer. That we take a stand and make a decision. Or at least relate. The book was a sort of answer to the riddle of my sphinx.

Years passed, and I discovered that one does not have to battle that sphinx. That you can go mad if you allow it to torture you with questions day and night. And there were other matters, and other things to write about and do. Because there are other sphinxes as well.

So I also became an artist of sublimation. I found myself developing the same voluntary suspension of questions about ethics and occupation. I did not visit the territories; I did not even go to Old Jerusalem. Because I felt the hatred of the people there, but mostly because I cannot tolerate relations that are not on an equal basis. Like so many others, I began to think of that kidney-shaped expanse of land, the West Bank, as an organ transplanted into my body against my wishes, and about which soon, when I had time, I would come to some sort of conclusion and decision. Of course, that transplanted organ continued to produce antibodies in my consciousness. I also knew how to declaim the familiar words meant to satisfy old sphinxes: it cannot go on this way, the occupation corrupts us, we have created a system of masters and slaves, and so on. But the furnace which forged those words went out and cooled long ago, and I did not want to feel it.

I took on this seven-week journey through the West Bank at the suggestion of *Koteret Rashit*, an Israeli news-weekly, because I understand that my sphinx had become a spayed cat purring contentedly at my feet. Because the worn sentences that I used like so many other people, though true, seemed now to be something else: like the walls of a penitentiary that I built around a reality I do not want to know; like jailers I stationed in order to protect myself from a gray world now repugnant to me. Suddenly I discovered that some jailers and criminals create—after years of living together and becoming accustomed to each other—unholy alliances. But I am in great danger from this, too, so I wanted to go to the places which most haunted me. Into the heart of the harsh clash between Jew and Arab. To see things with my own eyes in order to write about them. At first I thought they were not so terrible. Maybe only a mountain shadow which seems to us to be a mountain. If so, it must be told. And if not, even more so. After sharing my experience, the reader may decide to stand by his previous opinions, but he will have to take note of the price he pays, and what he has until now been prepared to ignore.

In another thirteen years there will be two million Arabs under Israeli rule in the West Bank and Gaza Strip. In 2010 their number will equal ours.

There are those who say it is possible to continue on in this way for years. That over the years the "fabric of life" (mutual acquaintance, economic links, and so on) will overcome enmity. That is idiocy, and reality proves it even now. As long as the present "fabric of life" continues, it is wrapped around an iron fist of hate and revenge.

The argument based on the "fabric of life," which now seems sober, pragmatic, almost businesslike, is a very dangerous argument for us, the Israelis. It turns the matter of the territories from an immoral matter into an amoral matter. It corrupts and anesthetizes us. One day we will wake up to a bitter surprise.

I want to go off on a tangent and tell a little story about this "fabric of life."

An Arab woman cleans the stairwell at the housing project in which I live. Her name is Amuna, and she lives in Ramallah. I talk to her from time to time. A three-year-old boy, the son of one of the neighbors, used to seeing her bent over a pail of water, heard us talking and was surprised—I saw it on his face. He asked her name and I told him. Afterwards, he asked what we had talked about in Arabic, and I explained. He thought a minute and said: "Amuna is a little bit a person and a little bit a dog, right?" I asked him why he said that. He explained: "She is a little bit a dog, because she always walks on all fours. And she is also a little bit a person, because she knows how to talk."

End of story.

So what will be?

I can only guess, and be aided by what I know—not about the situation, but about people.

I have a bad feeling: I am afraid that the current situation will continue exactly as it is for another ten or twenty years. There is one excellent guarantee of that—human idiocy and the desire not to see the approaching danger. But I am also sure that the moment will come when we will be forced to do something, and it may well be that our position then will be much less favorable than it is now.

It is not a question of who is right, we or they, right or left. It is a question of facts and numbers, and a few other things beyond facts and numbers, things in the fuzzy area between dogs and people. Whoever does not agree to speculate in this way about the future need only glance backward. The history of the world proves that the situation we preserve here cannot last for long. And if it lasts, it will exact a deadly price.

When I left on this journey, I decided not to talk with Jewish or Arab politicians or officials. Their positions are well known to the point of weariness. I wanted to meet the people who are themselves the real players in the drama, those who pay first the price of their actions and failures, courage, cowardliness, corruption, nobility. I quickly understood that we all pay the price, but not all of us know it.

We have lived for twenty years in a false and artificial situation, based on illusions, on a teetering center of gravity between hate and fear, in a desert void of emotion and consciousness, and the passing time turns slowly into a separate, forbidding entity hanging above us like a suffocating layer of yellow dust. From this point of view, nothing matches the occupation as a great personal challenge. As a personal crossroads demanding action and thought. Sometimes you can gain in this way—for a split second—real mountain air.

Albert Camus said that this passage from speech to moral action has a name. "To become human." During the last weeks, and seeing what I saw, I wondered more than once how many times during the last twenty years I had been worthy of being called human, and how many people among the millions participating in this drama are worthy of it.

afterword

David Grossman

April 2002

"So many things have happened since *The Yellow Wind* was published, and so little has changed."

So I began the introduction to the 1998 edition of this book. Can I write the same thing today?

A lot has happened over the past four years. Thousands of Palestinians and hundreds of Israelis have been killed and injured in hostilities, the Camp David peace talks failed, and Israeli governments have risen and fallen because of the conflict with the Palestinians. The second Intifada began, and with it came a wave of Palestinian suicide bombers, a human weapon without precedent in the history of war and, not long before I sat down to write this, Israel, under the leadership of Ariel Sharon, launched an offensive aimed at "destroying the infrastructure of terrorism," and perhaps at shattering the Palestinian Authority.

Yet so little has changed. The occupation continues, the Palestinians suffocate inside the "closures" and "cordons" imposed by Israel, humiliated and pushed deeper and deeper into the abyss of despair. On the

other side, Israel's citizens live in unrelenting fear, too
frightened to leave their homes because of the suicide
bombers who murder them indiscriminately. Israelis
believe that at Camp David their former Prime Minister,
Ehud Barak, made the Palestinians the boldest and most
generous offer possible, and that it was violently
rejected. The Palestinians are certain that the offer was
intended to entrench the occupation. The two sides continue to blame each other for their deteriorating relationship, and to accuse each other of being insensitive to
the plight and the fears of the opposing side.

Nevertheless, something profound and fundamental
has changed. Enmity and despair are now paralyzing
both peoples with a force beyond anything in memory.
More than a hundred years of reciprocal violence has
now brought to the surface primal hatreds containing
racial and especially religious elements, and the terms
being used by the two sides are more total and apocalyptic than they have been before. The hope of a pragmatic political solution seems more feeble now than
ever. The Palestinians feel they have been betrayed by
the entire world, as their dream of a free country, a
homeland, grows ever more distant. The Israelis, most
of whom believed that they had somehow been extri-
cated from the tragedy of Jewish fate, now sense that
same tragedy closing in on them once again like an
ancient curse, preventing them from ever enjoying the
Promised Land, even though they have been living there
for fifty-four years.

It's very easy to say that those who believed there was
no possibility of peace were right. That the extremist
nationalists on both sides have been proved correct in

their opposition to the Oslo process, which they argued would lead to catastrophe. But it would not be an accurate assessment of the situation.

Those skeptics did not make do with simply expressing their opposition. They took action, and did all that they could to ensure that the dialogue would implode, and their ominous predictions would be fulfilled. It was Israel's extremists who planted their settlements precisely in the places that would make any solution based on Israeli withdrawal nearly impossible. Since the Oslo agreement was signed, the number of settlers in the West Bank and Gaza Strip has been doubled. It was Ariel Sharon who, in September 2000, went up to the Temple Mount. While that act ensured his election as Prime Minister, it also provided the spark for Arafat to ignite this incendiary region.

It was the Palestinians, including senior leaders of the PLO among them, who encouraged acts of terrorism against Israelis—all Israelis, without exception—and more than once did so precisely at those moments when it seemed that a compromise agreement might be possible. Palestinian leaders and politicians—including Yassir Arafat himself—encouraged and glorified the suicide-murderers whose deeds injected an aspect of "holy war" into the conflict with such dire consequences. At almost every point of decision, the leaders and peoples on both sides chose the way of more violence and less dialogue, the way to which they have been accustomed for generations, for which, the evidence is, they are preprogrammed.

And so, within the hermetically sealed bubble of "the situation," only the warped logic of violence and hatred applies. Each side can justify its actions and crimes by referring to the actions and crimes of the other side. If Israel continues its occupation, the Palestinians feel they have the right to choose the most effective weapon they have—the weapon of terrorism against Israeli civilians. With that as a given, Israel believes it has the right to hit back at those who initiate and support that terror. But then, of course, the Palestinians despair even more, and commit ever more extreme acts. Each action has a logical explanation and justification within the bubble, but all of us, Israeli and Palestinian, suffocate within.

The process is rapid and depressing: as violence increases, fewer people believe in the effectiveness of dialogue, and even fewer in the possibility of coexistence. Each day one can see how increasing numbers of moderates are coopted by the extremists, becoming persuaded that there is no other way to resolve the conflict except by violence, and that the other side "understands only force."

Talk of conciliation, of understanding the tragedy of the other side, or—dare I say it—the justice on the other side—is now perceived, in both societies, as tantamount to treason. Words, hopes, temperate ideas have meager strength when the daily reality is so brutal, and when people are literally being blown apart.

In moments of despair I remind myself that it may well be impossible to resolve such a violent and complex conflict with a single, bold move and in a relatively short time. More interim stages may be needed, periods of regression and of progress as both sides slowly lose their illusions. Perhaps we are now in the midst of one of those interim stages, one in which both sides will eventually become aware of the limits of their strength, and of the limits to the concessions that the other side is able to make. Who knows? Perhaps a part of the bloody violence we are directing at each other comes out of our frustration at the painful concessions that we already know are inevitable?

I wish to dedicate this edition of *The Yellow Wind*— once again—to those who still believe that peace between the Palestinians and Israelis is possible. Yes, they are fewer than before, and their actions seem like an attempt to carry a lit candle through a raging storm. Yet, despite this, their perseverance is what keeps alive the alternative to an otherwise general paralysis and lethal despair. It is what reminds us that there is no divine decree that states that Israelis and Palestinians must forever kill, and be killed by, each other.

In the end, when the two sides exhaust each other, or when solution is imposed from the outside, we will all return, once more, to the negotiating table. Somewhere in the future we will arrive at the single possible solution that can ensure the lives of both sides. When that happens there will be two independent sovereign states here, side by side, Israel and Palestine. A border will separate them, not an iron wall of continuing hatred and mutual ignorance. A *border* between two neighboring countries.

And within their borders each country will finally create its own identity, which will not be defined in terms of the conflict, and of the enemy, but by turning to its own culture, heritage, values, and intimate life, which the conflict has confiscated and nationalized.

With this new identity, if we enjoy enough years of stability and security, the citizens of Israel and Palestine will be able to gaze on the acts they have committed against each other in their century of animosity, and recognize the crimes and atrocities. To expose themselves finally to the suffering they have caused and, perhaps, even to request forgiveness.

At the present moment it is difficult to believe that this can ever happen. The very fact of writing these words, of expressing a hope of any sort, already threatens to crack the hard protective membrane each of us has now generated to ward off hurt, and to prevent us *feeling* too much. All of us, Israelis and Palestinians, live our lives like the walking dead. All of us have become accustomed, over the years, to living a parallel life to the one we were meant to live. Yet despite this, if we do not remind ourselves that a better future is possible we may never find the strength we will all need to get there.

Translated by Haim Watzman

Gratitude & Kindness

A Modern Parent's Guide to Raising Children
in an Era of Entitlement

Dr. Carla Fry & Dr. Lisa Ferrari
REGISTERED PSYCHOLOGISTS

Dedication

This book is dedicated to the numerous clients that we have worked with over the years. They lit our fire to put words to paper to share what we know about this entitlement phenomenon that is infecting our communities and families as we speak.

Acknowledgments

We give thanks to our remarkable families for their flexibility, understanding, and patience. Five a.m. editing sessions, missed dinners, and postponed movie nights were forgiven and understood. They have inspired us with their words and their deeds, which helped to make this book the thriving beast that it is. Our families inspire our awe.

Contents

Note by the Authors

If this book looks shiny and new at the end of your read of it, we have failed you. If this book has dog ears, three shades of highlighter pen marking up the chapters, notes in the margins, sticky notes on every third page, coffee stains, asterisks, bookmarks, and muffin crumbs stuck deep in the spine, we will have served you well.

Please read this book thinking about action, interaction, change, and movement. We would like to sit down with every one of you to discuss in person your trials and triumphs down the pathway of encouraging gratitude and kindness with your children and sidestepping the pitfalls of unwittingly encouraging entitlement. But alas, providing you with our best knowledge, tips, and how tos in the following pages will have to do.

Please do not be a passive recipient of information as you move through the chapters. When the mood strikes you, do the exercises, make lists, text tips to yourself to remind you to stay on track, and talk to your friends, your spouse, and your kids.

We are grateful to the many families and individuals who have provided heartfelt inspiration, have shared their joys and pains with us as we have gathered our data and clinical impressions and combed over the research of our peers to bring you this book.

We are grateful to you for picking up this book and considering some kind of change—even though we have not met you. Every ounce of change that each of us makes in this area affects our local, national, and international communities.

~ **Dr. Carla Fry & Dr. Lisa Ferrari**

Preface

You have picked up this book, which means that you have a real commitment to your family and an earnest desire to do what is right for your children or for children you care about. The good news is that you are now further transforming yourself to become a more active part of the positive change movement in our local, regional, and global society.

Positive Psychology, a scientific area of psychology founded by Martin Seligman, is gaining in momentum and covers the study of positive emotions, engagement in activities, virtuous personal characteristics, and the search for paths to meaning and deeper fulfillment in life.[1] As the scientific basis for this book, it will help equip parents with specialized knowledge and tools that will help them to make the good changes they want to make in the lives of their children.

This book has been designed to address the cultural phenomenon of entitlement, and how we transform it from the norm to the exception by adjusting the way we talk, think, and act in front of our children. Entitlement has snuck its way into society like an unwanted party guest. We are here to show you how it got in—and how we can kick it back out. It is not up to our children. It is up to us.

As a parent, you know that you can only do what you can and, you are already likely doing lots of things to be proud of—as parents, leaders, and teachers. This guide should make it easier for you to take the next step on your parenting journey.

---

1. Positive Psychology: Harnessing the power of happiness, mindfulness, and personal strength, Harvard Health Publications, 2013.

We are clinical psychologists who work with groundbreaking Positive Psychology methods and techniques with families and individuals. Our practice specializes in pediatrics, mental health, families, divorce adjustment and medical psychology. We are the co-founders of Real Parenting Lab, an enterprise consisting of multimedia and e-health research and services targeted at bringing positive change how tos to all.

As you read this book, you will become more aware of the realities of the trends in modern parenting and will learn how easily a child can be unwittingly encouraged to be ungrateful and uncaring in today's world. Best of all, you will be shown how to positively adjust these behaviors and attitudes based on solid clinical research and advice.

We have joined forces due to our shared passion, our commitment to children and families, and our growing interest in fostering kindness and gratitude in children. We have formed a practice based on cultivating resilience—the ability to bounce back from life's challenges—with individuals and families. After many long hours talking to teens, kids, and parents; comparing our clinical notes; engaging in our own research; and poring over the current research of our colleagues, this is what we are excited to share with you.

1

Why Do We Care about Gratitude & Kindness?

"As we express our gratitude, we must never forget that the highest appreciation is not to utter words, but to live by them."

[JOHN F. KENNEDY]

We have wondered about the answer to this question as well. We have spent days, weeks, and months massaging the data, doing our own research, and processing the rich experiences uncovered in our psychology practice.

Every day parents come to us panic-stricken that their choices may be messing up their family, and wanting to prevent unhappy, unsuccessful, rude children.

We know what parents want. We know what they are fearful of. What they find themselves not knowing sometimes is how to achieve what they want for their children.

When parents are focused on the physical health of their child, they turn to their medical doctor for advice. Parents can be easily reassured and relieved when their medical doctor tells them that to have a healthy child they need to get their child to bed on time, get him or her the flu shot, feed him or her balanced meals, and give him or her vitamins. You do these things because you understand the clear health benefits, and as a responsible parent, you want to take action. Most of you that are reading this book are doing these kinds of things every day. You incorporate these steps in your routine for the short- and long-term health benefits for your child.

We know that parents are desperate to do all that they can to avoid "screwing up" their children.

Now, what if the psychological doctors told you that all you need to do to have happy, successful, kind children, is to incorporate a few amazingly simple concepts to gain powerfully positive results?

We know that as motivated, caring parents keen to do the right thing —with this book in hand—you will do all that needs to be done. We are going to show you how.

In short, the amazingly simple concepts we refer to that have such a powerful impact are: gratitude and kindness.

We care because gratitude and kindness can increase a child's happiness, decrease their stress, increase their ability to reach their goals, and allow them to have more caring friendships and social connections.

We have come to the conclusion that this is worth caring about. Okay, here we go...

Notes from the Real Parenting Lab about Gratitude and Kindness

We held a small group meeting with parents and children who wanted to learn more about gratitude and kindness. It was soon clear that each and every one of them came into the meeting pointing the finger at the other for NOT having enough of these two traits.

The parents agreed that the children were in serious need of a more in-depth understanding of what it meant to be grateful and kind. They complained almost immediately: *"My children don't appreciate what I do for them,"* and, *"They don't know the sacrifices we've made to give them everything they have."*

The children were having none of it. *"She doesn't understand me at all,"* one of the children said. *"Even if I do say 'Thank you', my mom says my tone shows that I'm not really thankful. Nothing I do is ever good enough for my parents, so why bother?"*

The good news is, the parents and children had something in common—both agreed that things had to change. Both parents and children felt undervalued or underappreciated, but they were simply thinking about the situation purely from their own perspective. It was fascinating to see how miscommunication and blame seemed to be the final step in communication for these families. We executed a simple exercise called **Family Gratitude Dialogue** *(see Appendix 3)* that involved both sides detailing what they were most grateful for. The children spoke about their parents, and the parents spoke about their children.

By the end of the group meeting, we had shown the parents how important it is to live and model these behaviors if they want their children to be more grateful and more kind. The parents were able to make a connection between everyday opportunities to facilitate acts of kindness. For instance, one child commented, *"Sometimes when I ask if I can help mom, she says she'll do it herself quicker, then she complains later that I never help and that I'm selfish."* The parents began to understand that it is not so much about blaming their children for being self-centered, but much more about showing them how to *not be.*

Authenticity and Consistency

Positive Psychology offers up some of the most cutting edge research about human happiness today. Do not be fooled, however, by its seeming simplicity. Resilience and gratitude are far from new concepts, but we know now how to maximize these experiences and, conversely, how to miss maximizing them, too. How we demonstrate our gratitude makes the difference between whether we end up boosting our happiness or not.

More than simple emotions or attitudes, being kind and grateful are ways of being that philosophically make everything better in your life, according to researcher Robert Emmons, University of California Davis. He's one of the world's most published and respected social scientists. While studying the effects of gratitude, Emmons and his colleague, McCullough, concluded: *"The ability to notice, appreciate, and savor the elements of one's life has been viewed as a crucial element of well-being."*[2]

2. Emmons, R.A., & McCullough, M.E., (2003). Counting Blessings Versus Burdens: An Experimental Investigation of Gratitude and Subjective Well Being in Daily Life. *Journal of Personality and Social Psychology, 54 (1),* 377-389.

Parents we have worked with have told us that they are grateful to us for pointing out to them that there are often two ways of *being*: how we are at home, and how we are when we are in social situations. It is very important that we parents are authentic and consistent in showing gratitude in both situations.

What does a parent who authentically thanks family members for each small effort model when they are at a restaurant or shop and act without gratitude to their server or, vice versa, when a parent takes great effort to tip and thank, waiters, cashiers and the soccer coach, but almost never shows appreciation to their family at home?

Here is the first of many self-reflections we want you to consider as you read this book:

- **Does your private and public self match up with regard to being grateful?**
- **Are you consistent?**
- **Is what you practice at home the same as that which you practice outside the home?**

The family home is the teaching ground for children. As parents, we are very influential in the lives of our children. Our behavior directly influences them, and when we are not authentic and consistent, we cause confusion. It is essential that we have an awareness of the mixed messages we can send to our children. Preaching, versus practicing the value of gratitude in different situations shows that we are not being authentic and consistent. Through the years in our practice, it has become increasingly clear to us that children watch the behavior of their parents, but rarely listen to their lectures and pep talks.

Children can spot our lack of authenticity with eagle eyes, and they will not swallow our message if we are not real and consistent in how we act.

What Are You Teaching Your Children?

There's a perplexing phenomenon that occurs in parenting psychology that goes something like this: All the things you think you are teaching your children, you are NOT teaching them—and all the things you do not think you are teaching them, you actually are.

This is the reality of raising children: We parents are often not truly mindful of the lessons that we pass on, so a lot of bad habits are unfortunately easily learned along the way. We are sure you have probably heard the sayings, *"Say what you mean and mean what you say"* and *"If you want your children to do it, you must do it first."* We do not always live by these words of wisdom of past generations, but when it comes to kindness and gratitude, we must. We have to be grateful—genuinely grateful—if we want our children to be grateful too. Otherwise, children will learn to parrot the words and will never really understand what it means to live with gratitude.

When your child is at a friend's house and is given lunch by his friend's mother, hopefully he will say "thank you", but will he mean it? Has he mumbled the powerful words under his breath while looking at his broccoli, or recited it like a robot? Has he used eye contact and voice tone to:

- **Demonstrate appreciation for being invited into the family home?**
- **Show appreciation that they shared their family meal with him?**

We know, through Positive Psychology research and thought, that if your child is at a friend's house for lunch, and if he has respect for other people and appreciation for the friend's family, he may have said his "thank you" with true gratitude.

To continuously feed these important traits, our children need to experience what it is like to be grateful and kind so that it becomes part of their belief system. Speaking is only a small percentage of communication. As perceptive, insightful human beings, our children will pick up on the other forms of communication we may be underappreciative of, or clueless about, including the fact that our actions speak for us.

For example, they will see how we react to situations where gratitude can either be embraced or overlooked. If we ignore it, so will they. Not taking the way we speak to other people into account is a mistake. When thinking about what we are showing —and therefore teaching—our children about gratitude, we need to pay attention to our facial expressions, gestures, body language, paralinguistics (tone, pitch, inflection), and eye contact.

It is nearly impossible for us to hide the way we really feel about gratitude and kindness, which is why change needs to begin with us first. For example, if your children see you being over-the-top grateful to the neighbor for cutting part of your lawn but taking for granted their own efforts to tidy their room because you were busy checking emails and packing lunches, they are going to believe that this is the right way to behave. Unknowingly, you have just passed on poor behavior and the following confusing messages:

1. **Treat family with little-to-no gratitude.**
2. **Display fake, non-authentic gratitude to non-family.**
3. **Gratitude is not valuable.**

Yikes! Not what you would have thought you were teaching, right?. Don't worry: there is much that can be done to right all such inadvertent teachings and fumbled opportunities to teach gratitude the right way. There is almost always a second chance. First, let us look further in to what gratitude is, and what it is not.

What is Gratitude?

You already know that gratitude is a way of *being*. Robert Emmons[3] says that it is made up of two components. These components must be understood so that they can be applied.

The first is that gratitude is an affirmation of goodness. By being grateful, we affirm that there are good things in the world that we have received. The second is that we recognize that the source for this goodness is outside ourselves.

We can be grateful for tangible and intangible things, for big things and small things. That green traffic light when you are late for a meeting, that time your daughter packed her own toys away, and the fact that you have two functioning eyes or ears are all things worth feeling gratitude for. This signature strength of noticing the good, experiencing thankfulness and, in some cases, expressing gratitude as Positive Psychology emphasizes, will help our children lead happier lives.

GRATITUDE TIP Gratitude is the thankful appreciation of what you receive in life as you acknowledge the goodness around you. It will help our children realize that goodness lies partially outside themselves, and it will connect them with something larger than the individual experience—be it nature, spirituality, or connection to others.

---

3. Emmons, R.A. (2007). *Thanks! How the Science of Gratitude Can Make You Happier*, Houghton Mifflin Company.

Emmons and McCullough examined the impact of keeping a gratitude journal in their 2003 study. After 10 weeks, the group that focused on being grateful was more optimistic about their lives, less stressed, less depressed, and even visited the doctor less in that time. Turns out a "thank you" a day keeps the doctor away!

Our culture seems to have trained us to always reach for something new, something better. However, the practice of gratitude is a great way to really help us stop and appreciate what we already have. If we are not grateful for what we have now, chances are that when we get something new, we will not be truly grateful for the new thing for longer than it takes to send a text message.

What Is Kindness?

In Positive Psychology, it is important to focus on creating positive emotions by activating key strengths. It is no secret that when children feel grateful, they behave in a kind manner. That is why, where there is gratitude, there is kindness. The two work as a unit. It is rare to have one without the other.

It has been proven that kindness makes people happier. A study was conducted involving researchers at Harvard Business School and the University of British Columbia.[4] They found that when people spent money on others, they felt happier, and that made them more likely to focus on making others happy in the future.

This is the positive feedback loop between kindness and happiness. Performing kind deeds for others does make you happier. But just telling your children to be kind does not make them more compassionate people. You need to cultivate conditions for compassion, so that your children can experience these emotions on their own.

---

4. Dunn, E. & Norton, M. (2013). *Happy Money: The Science of Smarter Spending*. New York: Free Press Simon & Schuster.

Children need to be given opportunities to practice kindness, in order to experience the pleasure it generates. Gratitude is a great way to get your children to open up and allow them to experience the world in a positive light.

Social reciprocity theory[5] states that we treat others as we are treated. If someone is nice to your children, they will tend to be nice back. If someone is rude, mean, or unkind to your children, they will almost always respond with a similar behavior. Your goal is to practice kindness so that you increase the likelihood that your children return the kindness and pass it forward.

KINDNESS TIP Kindness can be defined as the act of being good, charitable, pleasant, and considerate of others. When you practice kindness, it becomes easier to be filled with gratitude. Likewise, when you practice gratitude, it becomes easier to be filled with kindness. Both have remarkable effects on happiness.

When your child is able to treat the rude, mean child with kindness or compassion, it is a step toward changing the world. But first they need to be shown, by you, that kindness is an essential part of life. It will be important to practice genuine gratitude and kindness in order to show your children meaningful ways to relate to others.

---

5. Falk, A. & Fischbacher, U. (2006). A Theory of Reciprocity. *Games and Economic Behavior, 54 (2)*, 293-315.

Why These Two Social Skills Are Important

As we have already mentioned, gratitude and kindness are instrumental to the future happiness of your children: Grandmothers have always known it, and modern science has proven it. Kind deeds for others make us happier people, and the happier we are, the more likely we are to perform kind acts.

A child who is grateful and kind early in life is given a rock star advantage in all things. By cultivating gratitude in your children, you simultaneously cultivate kindness.

Grateful Children = Kind Children.

When you are able to relish positive experiences and enjoy and appreciate the things that you already have, it lowers stress levels and significantly increases your happiness. Martin Seligman[6] studied the implications of Positive Psychology with 411 research participants. He instructed them to deliver a letter of gratitude to people in their lives they had never thanked before.

There was instantly a huge increase in their happiness scores and a major decrease in their depression scores. The benefits of this lasted for about a month—pretty significant in our opinion. It's clear we can encourage kindness with such a simple **gratitude action** and, that combined, the elements of kindness and gratitude make a potent recipe for happiness.

Gratitude and kindness also give us a huge social advantage. When your children practice these strengths, they become aware and conscious of other people's feelings, which results in positive social adjustment as they grow up.

---

6. Seligman, M.E.P., Steen, T.A., Park, N.P., & Peterson, C. (2005). Positive psychology progress: Empirical validation of interventions. *American Psychologist, 60,* 410-421.

As your children become internally motivated to care for others, they will develop their own tendencies toward compassion and other social behaviors that will help them connect with other people in powerful ways. Social connections and good relationships are essential for a happy life.

GRATITUDE ACTION To experience the wonderful effects of gratitude, write a gratitude letter to someone in your life to whom you cannot deliver the letter - someone who has passed away, perhaps. Take this opportunity to appreciate their kindness. Some of you may ask "what's the point of this gratitude action if you don't send the letter?". Research shows that you do not have to deliver the gratitude letters for them to have a positive effect on your social, physical or emotional well-being.

In fact, the simple answer is that the intention, appreciation and gratitude action of the grateful person doesn't require recognition or appreciation for what they have done to have the positive effect. This is about the grateful person's own increased life satisfaction, optimism, joy, pleasure, and better sleep and improved immune system.[7] It also helps children to be resilient, compassionate, and forgiving.

---

7. Seligman, M.E.P. (2002). *Authentic Happiness: Using the New Positive Psychology to Realize Your Potential for Lasting Fulfillment*, New York: Free Press Simon & Schuster.

The Entitled Child Today

Why are there so many children that feel entitled instead of grateful? Consistently in our workshops, there are an overwhelming majority of parents who state that their children and their communities are increasingly impacted by entitlement. Some are calling this an epidemic, and we find ourselves regularly being begged for help.

The entitled soul feels that they are owed advantages, friendship and rewards just because they are alive. These children get into more trouble at school. They are notoriously impatient, have low motivation, are demanding, and are described by others as "whiny" and "high maintenance." They tend to be hesitant to accept the consequences of their actions and almost never take a "NO" from others eloquently or with graciousness.

To the modern parent, this can cause endless worries, not to mention the dreaded parental guilt: "Did I spoil my child?" "Where did I go wrong?" "It is all my fault..."

An entitled child is a child crying out for help—but that might not be obvious to them or to their parents. The help they are crying out for is linked to their own inability to regulate feelings such as sadness, stress, fear, anger, boredom, inadequacy, loneliness and rejection. A child who acts entitled is seeking stuff or special privileges as a means of distracting or deflecting from these uncomfortable feelings. Giving them the things they are demanding is not truly what they are looking for from their parents. It's what it sounds like, but that's not what it is. We encourage you to be more curious about what your child's emotional state actually is. Cater to the emotional needs that may be fueling entitled behavior. Pull back from indulging in the material demands and granting privileges.

If you are reading this because your children lean more easily toward being entitled than grateful, not to worry. This is why we wrote the book—and why we want to spread the word to everyone, whether they have children or not. As Western culture spreads globally, it supports children and youth in always wanting more, and our children will expect that from everyone if nothing changes. Generation Y has a reputation as being narcissistic, ungrateful and entitled, expecting jobs, university placements, high salaries, and families and friends that give, give, give.

If your children are turning into these not-so-grateful members of society, you can still do something about it. Entitled children grow up to have a hard time at work, in social situations, and in life in general. You can prevent that by learning how to implement gratitude and kindness in all of your lives now.

 ## Exercise: The Parenting Values Checklist

Do you know what your parenting values are? Many parents wing it when it comes to raising their children. They have a sense of the values they would like their children to have, but they have not mindfully taken the time to actually sit and reflect and make note of them.

Listing the values that you would like your children to have will allow you to parent your children according to these values in a more coherent manner. Before you take a closer look at how to enhance gratitude and kindness in your home, you need a clear vision of what you value and what you are hoping to support in terms of future qualities and strengths in your children.

1. **Check the qualities / values that you envision for your children:**

	Happiness		Inquisitive / Curious
	Success		High Self-Esteem
	Assertive		Honest
	Leader		Respectful
	Emotionally Connected		Grateful
	Kind		Unique
	Financially Successful		Persistent
	Adventurous		Good Sense of Humor
	Positive Attitude		Family Centered
	Passionate		Love of Learning
	Forgiving		Many Friendship
	Generous		Motivated
	Empathic		Spiritual
	Risk Taker		Hard Working
	Disciplined		Justice Focused
	Loving		Affectionate
	Compassionate		Creative
	Self-Centered		Impatient / Demanding
	Entitled		Greedy

2. **Now go back and circle the top six that are the most important to you.**
3. **Go back one more time and put a star by those that you believe you are already doing a lot to support.**

Okay, chances are you did not check off any of the last four qualities, nor did you fill in the blank spaces with qualities such as angry, bossy, whiny, or rude. But, if you have given-in to a child who asks for something in a rude or impatient manner, you are supporting the growth of these qualities *not* the growth of positive qualities such as assertiveness or motivation. We say this because, if you are like most of us, you may have tried to reassure yourself that you are supporting positive qualities to get yourself off the hook when reflecting on your parenting successes and failures. But the truth is—when you don't challenge rude behavior, you support and encourage it instead.

Your parenting values checklist should be unique: If you have values that are not on this chart, add them in. Every family is different—what works for one does not necessarily work for another.

Our hope is that once you have completed your checklist, you will be able to see which qualities you would like to boost to enhance your family's well-being.

The Development of Gratitude

What we expect from our three-year-old in terms of appreciation and gratitude is clearly different than what we expect from our 17-year-old. What is reasonable to expect, and what must be expected, needs to be viewed in terms of development of the child through each of the ages and stages of development. In this next section, we describe the typical thoughts of children at developmental stages and the Positive Gratitude Behavior that can be expected at that age using the revolutionary cognitive development research of Jean Piaget.[8] *(Prior to Piaget, psychologists basically thought children were just less smart versions of adults.)*

---

8. Piaget, J. (1952). *The Origins of Intelligence in Children.* International Universities Press Inc.

Piaget's Stage of Development Age	Typical Thoughts & Actions	Typical Positive Gratitude Behavior*
Sensorimotor 0–2	Young child builds an understanding of the world by coordinating information from the five senses with movement of his/her body	Common actions when an infant or toddler's needs are being met can be demonstrated by non-verbal cues of gratitude, such as: • Eye contact • Smile • Baby sign language for thank you • "Thank you" connected to same, once child is speaking
Preoperational 2–7	Children begin to use language and pictures and symbols but make decisions based on their "gut instinct" and are self-centered.	Children learn the **"family currency"**** that they can exchange, helping set or clear the dinner table for the food they eat, or that they can exchange a "Thank you" for being driven to a special event.
Concrete Operational 7–11	Children begin to solve problems more logically, but understanding of their world is still simple. They respond well to clear expectations.	At this stage, we can expect the following gratitude behavior: • Children respond well to consistent rules about gratitude behavior (eye contact, kind tone of voice, "thank you"). • The child understands that asking for things does not always get a "yes" from the parent. • The asking is done with respectful voice, words, and body language.

continued on next page

	Adolescent thinking is more complex and abstract at this stage. They can make predictions and come to conclusions about complicated things.	An adolescent is able to predict, imagine, assume the emotions of others, and appreciate the effort of the giver and give back with: • Words • Actions • Emotional connection
Formal Operations 11 +		

*adapted from Piaget's original theory
**see Chapter 3, page 62 for more on Family Currency

The goal, of course, is to get our children through each of these stages by introducing the values and actions as they are ready for them. Gratitude and kindness can be taught from infancy and are best grown by consistency of modeling and coaching through all the later stages of development. It is easiest on our children and on us if we start early, but it is never too late to dig in to teaching our children gratitude lessons and habits. We humans are adaptable and resilient, and can almost always learn and grow.

Points to Remember, Actions to Take

In this section of each chapter, we do a quick review, highlighting the key takeaways you will need to familiarize yourself with as you go along.

• **Key 1: Children learn by what you DO in and out of the home.** They witness how you respond to gratitude and kindness—and are learning directly from that. This directly affects how they feel about the world, themselves, and other people, changing their perspectives in very real ways.

- **Key 2: Adjust your parenting style.** It is possible that some of the things you think you are teaching your children, you are NOT teaching them—and the things you do not think you are teaching them, you actually are. Gratitude and kindness are a way of being. They are not just words or actions.

- **Key 3: What is gratitude?** Gratitude is an affirmation of goodness. By being grateful, we affirm that there are good things in the world that we have received. Gratitude is also the recognition that the source for this goodness is outside ourselves.

- **Key 4: What is kindness?** Neuroscience tells us the experience of kindness changes the brain. It is only learned when it is used; you need to offer your children opportunities to both give and receive kindness.

- **Key 5: Why are gratitude and kindness important?** Gratitude and kindness lead to an abundance of life satisfaction, optimism, joy, pleasure, improved sleep, and a better immune system. They create children that are resilient, compassionate, and forgiving. Science has proven this with extensive testing and research.

- **Key 6: Entitled children are difficult children.** These children get into more trouble at school. They are notoriously impatient, have low motivation, are demanding, and are described by others as "whiny" and "high maintenance." They tend to be hesitant to accept the consequences of their actions.

2

The Glass Half Full

"A grateful outlook does not require a life full of material comforts but rather an interior attitude of thankfulness regardless of life circumstances."

[ROBERT A. EMMONS & CHARLES M. SHELTON]

The experience of gratefulness is very complex. We cannot even move forward in talking any further about gratitude at all without taking our hats off to the amazing early work of Baumgarten-Tramer in 1938.

Some of us may think gratitude is simply being polite and saying "thank you", but more than 75 years ago Baumgarten-Tramer[9] was already pushing the limits of what makes up gratitude:

1. **There is the experience of receiving a gift or kindness.**

2. **There is goodwill directed towards the giver with a response such as, "Thank you."**

3. **Then there is the social part: there is a positive noticing of the person that helped.**

4. **One can immediately feel a combination of feelings, such as delight and the desire to give back.**

5. **This can sometimes end up with us feeling like we have an obligation to the person who did the giving.**

So this gratitude business is more complicated than it first appears. That's okay. Let's dig into it further and see where your family's true gratitude sits on the scale.

TAKE ACTION Create your parent values checklist to ensure what you have been teaching your children is want you want to be teaching your children. As we say to clients in our office: Walk your talk!

9. Baumgarten-Tramer, F. (1938). Gratefulness in Children and Young People. *Journal of Genetic Psychology, 53,* 53-66.

Notes from the Real Parenting Lab about the Difference between "Thank You" and Gratitude

We spoke at length with a mother who came to see us about her 11-year-old daughter. She exploded with many of the same complaints that other parents rant about, reciting a long list of situations where her daughter insisted that her mother cater to her every whim. And the demands were always delivered with no consideration for her mother whatsoever.

The mother shared with great frustration:

"Is it asking too much for my child to say 'thank-you' and actually mean it once in a while? Can't I expect that at her age she could use some of the manners that I have been pulling my hair out trying to teach her for the past five years?"

Sound familiar? It is normal for parents to want their children to truly appreciate all that they do for them, but how do we teach our children the difference between speaking the words "thank you" and actually feeling grateful?

We noticed a disconnect here between what the mother asked for (a "thank you") and what she really wanted from her daughter, which was true appreciation and feelings of gratitude.

Sometimes we parents have difficulty clearly communicating what we really want from our children.

A Closer Look at Gratitude

A concept such as gratitude is challenging to define because it means different things to different people. What is certain is that gratitude leads to happiness, mood improvements, increased work performance, and better physiological health. That is why we are going to take some time to explore the layers involved in defining gratitude.

When you think of the word "gratitude," you imagine someone receiving a present and saying "thank you" for it. But how often do they mean it? Gratitude is not a word. It is more than an action. It is a state of being. Grateful people will more easily acknowledge the time, effort, and money spent on the gift and realize internally that the person cares about them and wants them to be happy.

Here are some concepts surrounding gratitude to think about:

- **Gratitude fuels social emotion and makes you aware of positive benefits that have come from an outside source, even though they were not earned or deserved.**

- **Gratitude motivates people to repay their benefactors and pay it forward. Gratitude is therefore an adaptation for reciprocal altruism and has played a unique role in human social evolution.[10]**

- **Gratitude is an emotion expressing appreciation for what one has. Instead of always wanting more, you are able to consider what you have and feel lucky to have it.**

- **Gratitude is an affirmation that there are good things in your life and people who love you, who will give you good things.**

---

10. McCullough, M., Emmons, R. and Tsang, J. (2002). The Grateful Disposition: A conceptual and empirical topography. *Journal of Personality and Social Psychology, 82(1)*, 112-127.

- Gratitude can be taught in schools—if the teachers establish positive personal relationships with the children. Feeling connected in school can help children feel grateful for the environment they are in. Just ask your child the difference between her favorite teacher and her least favorite. Chances are, the best teacher stands out for giving the job one hundred per cent, and the children really appreciate that.

- Gratitude has the power to heal, energize, and change your life. It can turn contentious families around, stop constant fighting between siblings, and greatly improve the mindset of the child.

A Child's Perspective on Gratitude

Children's ability to appreciate and understand gratitude is very different through the ages and stages of their development. Also, children and adolescents express that gratitude quite differently. Baumgarten-Tramer's chart[11] on types of gratitude at the different stages may help you to understand what to expect from your own child:

---

11. Baumgarten-Tramer, F. (1938). Gratefulness in Children and Young People. *Journal of Genetic Psychology, 53*, 53-66.

Types of Gratitude	What does it look like?	Who does it?
Verbal	"Thank you."	Small children use this one most often, but 7-15year-olds use it equally.
Concrete	Child repays with something that matters to the child (but not necessarily valuable for the giver).	Most often 8-year-olds do this, and it is rarely seen in 12-15-year-olds.
Connective	Relationship with the giver, where something of value is given or an expression of feelings is made toward the giver	Older than 11 years of age and is seen most often in 12-year-olds.
Finalistic	Repayment of a favor with something that also helps the teen get what they want ("If you give me an opportunity with this job, I promise I will be punctual and will work hard").	Seen most in 14-year-olds.

Appreciation and Gratitude

Counting one's blessings can rapidly increase positive emotions, health, and even individual self-worth.

This is why the appreciation aspect of gratitude is so fundamental to children. If a child is able to regularly savor a positive experience,[12] it leads to being able to cope with stressful life circumstances more easily.

12. McCullough, M. E., Tsang, J.A., and Emmons, R. A. (2004). Gratitude in intermediate affective terrain: Links of grateful moods to individual differences and daily emotional experience. *Journal of Personality and Social Psychology, 86,* 295–309.

Pretty simple, right? Children that really appreciate the good in their lives are less stressed.

What we know from the research is that a singular experience of gratitude can increase the fulfillment at that moment, but the regular conscious appreciation of what is good, leads to better mood, better health, and better sleep.

GRATITUDE ACTION Spend some time with your child, and notice how he or she appreciates daily experiences. When the opportunity arises, ask your child why he or she appreciates these things. Being mindful of this can bring your child closer to understanding the importance of gratitude in daily life.

Appreciating something or someone almost always leads to a closer relationship between people. This can be an essential part of connecting with, and nurturing, family and friendships. It is likely that your child's best friend became his or her best friend because they appreciated each other.

How to Turn Gratitude into Action

Effective Gratitude Talk for parents does not mean endlessly voicing, "thank you, thank you, thank you." We know all things lose their impact with children if repeated too many times.

So what can you say? Here are some ideas:

- **I truly enjoy the smell of the cookies baking in the oven.**
- **I really appreciate the friendly cashier I had this morning.**
- **I'm so grateful our family has enough food to eat every day of the year.**
- **I notice how much your hugs in the morning make me happy.**

Okay parents, it's your turn. Please complete the following:

- **I truly enjoy** _____

    _____

    _____

- **I really appreciate** _____

    _____

    _____

- **I'm so grateful** _____

    _____

    _____

- **I notice** _____

    _____

    _____

GRATITUDE ACTION can be body language or facial expressions that show thankfulness that we as parents might feel. Parents, we need to be present. STOP doing whatever else you are doing and show your child, through your eye contact and body language, the pleasure and appreciation for what he or she has done.

Gratitude Talk for parents when coaching your children:

- When your child shows gratitude, you need to be able to recognize it and validate it.
- Coach them in a way that they will hear it.

What not to say:

- **"Why don't you say 'thank you' like the neighbor's child?"**
- **"I'm tired of having to ask you to say 'thank you'."**
- **"I'm tired of giving and you taking."**

What to say:

- **"That time you high-fived me really showed me your appreciation, buddy."**
- **"It would help motivate me to make those milkshakes in the morning if you showed me that you really appreciated them."**
- **"I will do my part once you do your part."**

If you like these how tos, there are more in Chapter 5 - What to Do About It.

What Is Entitlement?

Let's take a look at how entitlement is defined in modern culture:

- **The belief that one is inherently deserving of privileges or special treatment.**[13]

- **A belief a person is owed certain rights and benefits without further justification.**[14]

- **The right to receive something or to do something.**[15]

Entitlement is not about looking at the world from an optimistic "glass is half full" or a pessimistic "glass is half empty" perspective. It's more like: "I expect that glass to be full, and I want you to fill it!"

People describe entitlement as an ugly characteristic. Children we have spoken to say they do not like the feeling that comes with taking things for granted. It is frustrating for parents and unflattering when noticed by others in the community. The good thing is that feeling like you have a "right" to something is a learned behavior—which means it can be unlearned.

Common reactions to the word "NO":

If you think your child might have caught the **Entitlement Bug**, these will likely be their reactions to you saying "NO!"

1. **Disbelief:** *"You're kidding right?"*

2. **Confusion:** *"What do you mean, 'no'?"*

3. **Anger:** *"I hate you."*

4. **Pleading:** *"Pleeeease...I'll do dishes for a week."*

5. **Rejection of parent:** *"I wish Joey's parents were my parents."*

---

13. Oxford English Dictionary, www.oed.com
14. Dictionary.com, dictionary.reference.com
15. Merriam-Webster, www.merriam-webster.com

Entitlement Talk that further proves that your child has likely been infected with the Entitlement Bug:

- **All the other children have one.**
- **You never said NO before.**
- **It's so unfair.**
- **I deserve it.**
- **You owe me.**
- **Why are you so mean?**

Why Perspectives Need to Change

It is easy to not think about what you have, and who really means something to you, when you are a child. This is why children rarely discover gratitude on their own. Instead, they tend to focus on what they do not have and people they do not know. This can develop into a perspective that is overwhelmed with feelings of **sadness, deficiency,** or **inadequacy.**

Gratitude is not about appeasing the people that are giving. It is about introducing your children to a better way of living their lives, one that will bring them closer to other people, and make they themselves happier. Gratitude really can transform our lives, but only if we bring it out and dust it off regularly, instead of just once a year on Thanksgiving holidays.

We hope this book does enough to change your perspective on gratitude that you start to take it seriously as well. Young children will always respond if they see their parents engaging in a gratitude-based action. When you are grateful for what you have, you reach out to others to express your appreciation for them.

Words Versus Emotions: The Difference

Parents confuse words such as "thank you", with emotions such as gratitude. Whereas gratitude is a state of being, like happy or sad, a simple "thank you" does not have to have any gratitude tied to it at all. In children, most "thank you"s are said because they are expected, not because they mean anything.

How do you teach your children the difference between saying "thank you" and meaning thank you? Easy! Put them at the receiving end. When a child spends time working hard on something for you, all they want to hear is Mom or Dad's thanks.

Did your own parents ever try to get you to appreciate things by telling you about starving children in Africa, or people without fresh water in India? These anecdotes don't translate the meaning you intend. Children need more of an experiential understanding of what you're talking about. You may have briefly felt sad for those children, but your life circumstances wouldn't have allowed for you to fully understand their circumstances, so it likely shot out of your mind as quickly as it entered.

In this instance, it is always better to show your children what you mean. For example, imagine the situation where you are driving home with your child and you both comment on being hungry enough to eat a horse. You let your child know that there are no snacks in the car and that it will be half an hour until you get home. Take the **gratitude-boosting** opportunity to talk about how good the snack will be when you get home, and say, "Being hungry sometimes makes the snack taste better, doesn't it?"

Exercise: Gratitude with ATTITUDE—Not Words

Take the opportunity to grab some time with your child and throw down the **Gratitude with Attitude NOT Words Challenge:**

Imagine how you would show your gratitude to others if you had no voice. You may not use sign language or write. Remember: No speaking.

1. How would you express your gratitude if you could not say "thank you"?

- _____

- _____

- _____

2. Come up with three unique ways to say "thank you" without verbalizing it.

- _____

- _____

- _____

The next time you hear your child say "thank you" ask him/her: *"Why did you say 'thank you' for that cup of juice?"* It would be great if your child said something like, *"Because you got it for me specially after I said I was thirsty. I would have had to get it myself if you were busy."*

Or, next time you are cooking a special dinner, take 20 seconds[16] to express your own excitement about the love and attention that went in to preparing the family dinner and that you chose to make a special meal because you want them to be healthy and want them to feel cared for.

This will draw attention to the fact that gratitude is important in your household. It will also help demonstrate to your children a little bit more about your process behind the things you do for them. Children can tend to take being looked after for granted if they don't understand the depth and heart behind what we do for them.

By focusing on gratitude and a meaningful "thank you", you are making it clear that these acts are done out of love, but they should not be taken for granted. Food, washing, outings, treats, car rides, and clothing purchases are all opportunities for a meaningful "thank you".

If your child cannot tell you why they are saying "thank you", then you can work it out together. Eventually, they will begin to understand the gratitude loop and will begin to give back to you. As they get older, this will certainly make things like chore allocation easier.

Points to Remember, Actions to Take

- **Key 1: Gratitude has the power to heal, energize, and change your life.** It can turn contentious families around, stop constant fighting between siblings, and greatly improve the mindset of the child practicing gratitude.

- **Key 2: Appreciating something or someone almost always leads to closer relationships between people.** This is an essential part of forming and nurturing family and friendship-based relationships.

---

16. See our 20-Second Sound Bite in Chapter 5 (page 91).

- **Key 3: Affirmation strengthens relationships.** In human social dynamics, when you express gratitude, you are affirming the relationship between you and the person who has given you something of his or her own accord.

- **Key 4: How do you turn gratitude into action?** Again, the best way to teach children of any age is by example. When they see how you appreciate others, they will attempt to do the same. Whether it turns out to be less or more effort, they will finally understand WHY turning gratitude into action is important.

- **Key 5: What is entitlement?** Entitlement is a notion or belief that one is deserving of some particular reward or benefit. It is the belief that a person is owed certain rights and benefits without further justification, and has the right to receive something or to do something.

- **Key 6: Change your family's perspectives on gratitude.** Gratitude is not about appeasing the people who are giving. It is about introducing your children to a better way of living their lives that will bring them closer to others and make they themselves happier. Gratitude really can transform our lives, but only if we bring it out and dust it off regularly, instead of just once a year on Thanksgiving holidays.

TAKE ACTION Do the GRATITUDE with ATTITUDE NOT WORDS Challenge (page 37) with your children, and use it as a basis for helping them to understand why a meaningful "thank you" is very important. Whenever you get the chance, ask them "why?", or get them to tell you how they feel.

3

Where Does Entitlement Come From?

"So much has been given to me; I have no time to ponder over that which has been denied."

[HELEN KELLER]

Entitlement is a state that naturally develops when life's checks and balances are not in place. Children take when parents give.

It is what they do. When parents' giving has inadequate checks and balances, their kids become takers. It is not the fault of our children.

As resources become more plentiful, and our needs are met more easily, entitlement is becoming more common among children, teens and —yes–adults. When parents bend over backwards to keep their children in the latest clothes, shoes, electronics, and comforts...

- **to give them "what we never had"**
- **to make them happy**
- **to fit in with their friends**
- **"because we can afford it"**

...or any other reason that leads to the kids' taking being out of proportion to what they give, life's checks and balances are not even. This leads to entitlement.

Giving to, or making life easier for, our children is great. However, we cause damage when we do either to such an extent that our children **expect** and **demand** from us, or others. If a child or youth becomes entitled, it can make their entire life difficult. Once they begin to assume that they deserve advantages, they become easily disappointed, angry, feel hurt and frequently are resentful.

When they reach adulthood and have to struggle because life does not deliver them easy advantages, this is when that childhood entitlement will really work against them.

Notes from the Real Parenting Lab on Misguided Efforts

A couple that used to consult with us—the Smiths—had two teenage girls and a young son, about five-years-old. The couple was not financially secure, but they both had good jobs. They tended to prioritize their teens' unnecessary purchases because they felt guilty and inadequate if they said "no" due to financial strain, so they would overcompensate and say "yes" instead.

One daughter would say, *"I would have more friends and be more popular if I could go to the party—I only need $80." The other would say, "I'm depressed. I really want that new pair of boots we saw at the shop, Mom."* This kind of thing was going on constantly in their household—the unwelcome face of entitlement.

Nearly every time, the couple would accommodate the children. When they were younger, there were so many things they wanted that their own parents could not afford. That was the reason they worked so hard now. But this accommodation was also the very reason why their children were becoming so self-focused and demanding.

The parents shared the following incident, *"My daughter came home from school reporting that she had to stay in at recess because the teacher said she got out of her seat too many times. She said that the teacher was mean and punished her with no warning. I have to go down there and give that teacher a 'piece of my mind.' My daughter always follows the rules."*

- **We do encourage parents to hear their children and to support them when they need help. But in this example, we coached the parent to help the child to identify her own role in what happened first, so she could take responsibility for her part in the situation. Shielding children from the consequences of their actions further perpetuates the internalized view that the world revolves around ME.**

What Is A Misguided Effort?

A misguided effort, as we refer to in our psychology practice, refers to well-intentioned actions or statements to our children that backfire and end up with crummy results. A misguided effort in terms of entitlement, is an attempt to make your child's life easier, or better, by:

1. **Allowing them to do or have things just because you were not allowed to when growing up.**

2. **Making up for real or perceived shortcomings (your divorce, working overtime, their bad week with friends, being ill, etc.).**

3. **Giving them special advantages to reduce their stress or sadness. This, in many circumstances, is the right thing to do, but not if their sadness sprouts from their sense of entitlement, and most especially if giving to them is not warranted because:**

- **Their attitude is unwelcoming, unfriendly, uncooperative, or generally miserable.**

- **Their level of giving to the family is generally lacking.**

- **The reward, service, or benefit you give them is out of proportion (the checks and balances are significantly unbalanced: "Sure, we'll buy you a pony even though you punched your brother in the head today, Princess.").**

Remember how children learn. They learn by watching us, and less so by the words we speak. That means every time we reward them, they think they are acting in the correct way.

You can nearly always tell when a child is approaching a parent from an entitled perspective. When a child who has been touched relatively less by the entitlement epidemic asks for something and is turned down, he or she may be sad for some moments but then moves on. The entitled child does not. The entitled child does not accept "no" with grace.

Entitled children will continue to escalate the issue. They will register their displeasure and then repeatedly talk, plead, or whine about it, sometimes even berating, belittling, or comparing the parents to other, better, parents. Faced with this onslaught, it is easy to become angry or frustrated, and to feel like the situation is hopeless.

Just to be clear, our children, as a rule, do not have the right to demand anything from us. They are not privileged individuals and are not helped by being pampered, catered to, or overly indulged just because they live and breathe. As our children grow up, if they are too much the center of their parents' world, and are led to believe by our unintentional messages that they are the center of the known universe, they are at a disadvantage because, of course, that is not how human society works.

GRATITUDE TIP If you think your child is becoming entitled (or is already), it means that you have likely tried to make the world a satisfying, pleasant, fun, and happy place for them. You likely have protected them against consequences, and have taught them to expect the best in life.

However, we would like to ditch the "expect" the best in life and teach them to "work for" the best in life, instead.

If a child gets angry when their demands are not met, then subsequently receives what they were demanding, or when they are not put on a competitive sports team after tryouts, until their parent calls or emails and threatens the coach, this seriously damages the child's perspective on reality. He or she learns that benefits in life do not need to be earned. Instead, children learn that negative or aggressive behavior can be the key to what they want (or what they **think** they want), and that it pays to be unkind or a bully.

These kinds of misguided efforts by parents lead to children that put in little effort, have a tendency to be belligerent and angry, and who frequently fight with their parents. They also often end up with too much power and rule the home. Entitled children struggle to feel empathy for their parents (and others) and often lack the ability to appreciate that their parents are also real people with their own heartaches and joys, and do not exist simply to supply them with whatever they want.

The Haves vs. The Have Nots Rule

When we as parents attempt to help our children along in life by trying to make them happy by giving them every advantage and comfort we can afford, we are unwittingly making our children more fragile and unable to cope.

It's tempting for some to see a child who comes from a noticeably wealthy background and comment, "What a spoiled little rich kid."

The saying is universally acknowledged as a negative commentary on the over-indulged, "spoiled" child.

We are not fans of the word "spoiled". We still use it on occasion, because it is a word woven into the fabric of our society, with a universally understood meaning. But, the word remains negative. It implies that the child is "bad" or somehow at fault. This blaming of the indulged child is particularly odd when you hear a three-month-old infant being described as "spoiled"—as though it could possibly be the fault of the baby that their first party dress cost more than some people's first car.

So, how can a child possibly be "spoiled" if they do not come from a family of great financial advantage? Easily. We have access to a lot more today than did our parents, or their parents. Even if we are barely getting by financially, we can still afford to "spoil" our children through our actions, and the expectations those actions develop in our children.

When a child receives $100 for each A on a report card, a pony for their second birthday, and a new car when they turn 16, most of us would agree that this is too much—an overpayment. But what about those overpayments that are not so extravagant and expensive? Do they still qualify as "spoiling"?

Yes, if: a) the payment is out of balance with what is usually thought of as normal or typical and, b) this overpayment happens on a regular basis until a child comes to expect this as normal, expected, and deserved.

We would like to propose that it is really the attitude that counts here, not the amount of money that we have or spend. That there is no "haves vs. have nots", and socio economic status does little to prevent the creation of spoiled children.

The rule is that ANY parent ANYWHERE can spoil their child. But let's shift from the term "spoiled" to "entitled", because it is the expectation and demands of the child for the overpayment that is the additional troublesome part of the equation.

Giving favors, special advantages, or rewards—big or small—to children that are whiny, disrespectful or demanding, or take things for granted and do not consider the needs or feelings of others, teaches them that this is the right way to get results. (Passing a glass of water to a child that asks for it in a rude, belligerent manner, or hallowing the privilege to sit in the front seat after pushing their sibling out of the way are examples of this.) It doesn't have to cost any money at all to create opportunities for entitlement to grow in the lives of our children. Our children will never stop wanting things, advertisers have made sure of that. But this does not mean that we have to give in. Remember, our children learn more by actions than words. If we demand that they act, talk, and walk with gratitude and respect, they will do it because:

- **It is strongly modeled in our family and that modeling reinforces the family values.**

- **They understand that this is the way our family behaves and it will help them understand how to get what they need in a way that respects these family values.**

- **So, when we talk about entitlement, we aren't talking about the haves and have nots. Any child can be entitled if they adopt a certain attitude based on behavior they learned from us.**

Families with great financial wealth do have their own challenges with the overall entitlement concern. Families we have worked with that are very economically advantaged tell us that:

- **They have a challenging time with saying "no" to their children because they can afford any item or luxury. They want to make their child happy, and it is easier to say "yes".**

- **Sometimes they feel guilty and awkward about their money and can have a hard time instilling healthy values around giving and receiving—feeling like they need to "give, give, give" to their children because they can.**

In contrast, families that we have worked with who can barely afford rent or food tell us that:

- **They often will let their children disrespect the family rules to make up for the fact that they cannot provide the material comforts that others can.**

- **They will sometimes spend way too much money on coveted items that their children are asking for because they are feeling guilty about not having enough. This adds stress and anxiety when buying the designer jeans or concert tickets that "all the other kids have," leaves no money to pay essential bills.**

The haves and the have not families each have their own set of challenges when it comes to the issues of spoiling and entitlement, but the rule is that money does not matter:

Entitlement can occur no matter the financial situation of the family.

The Needs Trap: When Good Parenting Turns Bad

Now for a couple of tough questions. Are your child's needs almost always met? Do you work hard to anticipate your child's needs? Any good parent would—or so you would think. Perhaps one of the key reasons is because when we make sure our children are happy, it makes us happy.

But when our child's needs are constantly met, they are never allowed to need something—really need something—or feel what it feels like to go without, even for a small period, it makes them unable to deal with discomfort. This impedes their emotional development, as they never learn to cope with going without, or generate their own solutions to meet their needs.

If you are the kind of parent who:

- **Consistently gives your seven-year-old juice before he gets thirsty.**

- **Wraps your 11-year-old in warm sweaters before she gets cold.**

- **Intervenes in social issues too soon, before the 14-year-old experiences distress or has a chance to make sense of it on her own.**

GRATITUDE TIP Remember, when it comes to parenting, sometimes short-term advantage leads to long-term disadvantage. The repeated quick and easy "yes" to the chocolate bar request when our hands are full at the supermarket checkout, will lead to a lifetime of demands that grow faster than the weeds in your garden.

Then you are inadvertently raising a child who will be overly dependent and less able to cope with distress and discomfort as she gets older. Overindulging our children is destructive to their emotional strength, confidence, and ability to cope and bounce back from challenges.

When we constantly meet the wants of our children, they will be unable to determine what the difference is between *needs* and *wants*. "I'm your daughter," is not a good reason to buy something that your child wants. Nor is it okay for our kids to say something like: "I need those new sneakers."

If our kids say they "need" something, we have an opportunity to teach the difference between a *need* and a *want*. A questioning response, such as, "You *need* those new sneakers or you *want* them?", is a subtle cue to help our kids to understand the difference. That, and the reality that we need to make a commitment to ourselves to not meet our children's requests when they say they need something unless the something is food, shelter, or essential clothing.[17]

For now, remind yourself that we should allow our children to experience hunger, thirst, tiredness, and hurt feelings (within reason). This is part of the art of parenting: knowing when to protect and do for our children, versus when to stand back with love and encouragement and allow our children to do for themselves. As we explore these issues, we hope to help you find your own balance between the two. We want you to be confident that, more times than not, you are in order to allow your children to be their most emotionally strong, resilient selves.

---

17. We will talk more about this differentiation on page 136, where, as with all rules, there are exceptions. In this case, when our children's requests are more to do with love, connection, and attachment.

ENTITLEMENT CRUSHING ACTION The next time your child says, "I'm BORED!" and they look to you to solve the boredom problem, redirect them to find their own solutions even if it takes them the entire day to figure it out. It is not okay for your child to have this expectation of you to fix it for them. This is entitlement in the making.

The Praise Trap: Do You Do This?

Parents love to praise[18] their children—we are told that it is an essential part of support, love, and being a good parent. But did you know that many parents over praise their children? This misguided praise can cause serious issues in the lives of our children.

Misguided praise comes in a variety of different forms:

- **"Wow, this is the best picture in the world. You're a little Van Gogh!"**

  This praise is not valid because your daughter is four, and her art skills are age-appropriate, i.e. it looks like she drew it holding on to the crayon with her toes. You are missing the opportunity to value your daughter's effort and instead have mistakenly focused on the need to compare herself to others and be "the best."

- **"You are the best basketball player I've ever seen, and I watch NBA!"**

  This praise is not based in reality if your twelve-year-old son is not actually a child prodigy.

---

18. Just so you know—we are not the biggest fans of person-centred "praise". We talk in terms of process praise in our office.

- **"Your science project should have won. It destroys the other projects!"**

  This kind of praise is delivered quite independent of the merit of the project, and is focused on a "my child should win because he/she is my child" philosophy.

These types of praise teach our children that they are superior to others, and that they should be superior to others. It also teaches them:

- **That they need to be the best to get our love and attention.**

  Nothing he/she does will ever be good enough for us but perfection and first place.

- **That life will always be to their advantage, no matter what.**

  It does not matter whether they put in effort or not. Your child should win just because. This does not help our children focus on the positives of their effort or the fact that they are worthy of love and respect whether they win or not.

- **It negatively impacts their trust in you.**

  Real life is not stacked in their favor. Eventually our children will realize this, and they will be confused and blame us for teaching them otherwise.

There are definite dos and don'ts with regard to recognizing and encouraging our children. Praise does not exist as an emotional crutch; it is a legitimate way to express congratulations when they are due. But praise is always earned, and children that have become entitled do not tend to respond well to the concept of having to earn anything.

The best kind of praise involves recognition of the actions and intentions of your children that reflect the values, actions, and words that your family believes in *(reflect back to your answers on the Parenting Values Checklist in Chapter 1)*. Real praise should involve specifics and a true celebration of the child's achievement or effort.

- **Good Praise:** Nice helping with your brother, buddy!

- **Better Praise:** When I see you helping your little brother tie his shoes, I feel proud watching your kindness and leadership within the family. Awesome!

The Modeling Trap: The Grass Is Greener

One of the reasons a child develops entitled behavior is because they have modeled elements of their behavior on their parents' behavior and values. We have volumes of research on a child's tendency to learn by imitating their parents[19]. Interestingly, some demonstrated that children will follow *unnecessary* steps in a process (like stirring their juice with a spoon because they have seen their Dad stirring cream into his coffee) just to mimic their parents.

This is modeling at its best. As our children grow up and become pre-teens and teens, they will begin to model others' behavior in addition to the family's behavior. Friends, teachers, and other adults suddenly become influences. The child who has become entitled takes this a step further. They also want what these others have. If a child has internalized the belief that material possessions are necessary for comfort, that they indicate superior self-worth, or that they are owed things, they learn to envy and covet the possessions of others.

---

19. Nielson, M. & Tomaselli, K. (2010). Overimitation in kalahari bushman children and the origins of human cultural cognition. *Psychological Science, 21 (5)*, 729-736.

A child that has become entitled generally feels that they are not functioning at their best if they do not have everything—and more —than those they admire. It is the way they were raised, especially if parents wittingly or unwittingly spoke in front of them about:

- **What kind of a car, home, vacations, etc., they wish they had.**

- **What kinds of consumer brands they buy or wish to buy.**

- **How much money they wish they had, etc.**

The **entitlement bug** will leave anyone feeling unsatisfied with what one has (no matter what it is) and envious of others. This is one of the reasons why children who have become entitled get so upset if they are told that they cannot get the expensive new tablet computer because it costs too much money, or because they have not earned it. They are programmed to want more.

A child who has been bitten hard by the **entitlement bug** feels that they MUST have the new tablet computer in order to be seen as an equal by their peers. They have a tendency to believe that what others have (even models in commercials) is superior. They must have it in order to be acceptable, worthy and okay.

Of course, once they have the new computer, they will quickly move on to the next that makes them fit in better, or gives them status among their friends. Being unsatisfied with what one has, and always coveting the possessions of others, is a downward spiral toward life dissatisfaction. It's also a problem that tends to intensify with age.

GRATITUDE ACTION When an entitled child feels that their situation is inadequate, they will always look for a better situation, believing that one will come along. Teach your child how to be grateful for what they have and where they are, now.

In adulthood, those that were bitten by the **entitlement bug** as a child may skip from one job to the other — missing the opportunity to appreciate the experience while they have it. According to their belief system, there is always something better, they just have to wait until the world gives it to them. The trouble is, as we know, the world does not work that way.

The Truth about Entitlement

Where does entitlement come from? Surely there are many factors that affect how entitled a child feels? We ran a survey between 2012 and 2013 to find out exactly where adults believe entitlement in children comes from. The results were not what we expected.

Participants rated movies and TV as one of the leading causes, with 20 per cent of the blame, with peers at 14 per cent, teachers at 2 per cent, and "other" at 11 per cent, respectively. The main culprits, however, were PARENTS, who came in at a shocking 52 per cent. It seems that at some level, even we know how much we affect our children.

The truth is that YOU and I are the most likely cause of any of our children's entitlement issues. That is the truth, but it is not the end of the story. We can always change our children's behavior by adapting our own. (Sure, if your child is 17-and-a-half, you may have more limited success with beginning this program and having a huge impact. But you can certainly change how you act and react, relieving your strain and guilt, and provide the atmosphere for positive effects for your young adult—especially if they respect your judgment at some level.) It is never too late to stop, learn, and try something different.

Here is what you need to avoid in the coming days:

- **Your child is YOUR LIFE:** It is good to make your child a top priority, but you should never devote the majority of your time to meeting their every need and desire. The world does not revolve around them, and it is important that they understand this. It will benefit our kids if they realize that we are more than child-satisfaction delivery agents.

- **Not allowing your child to FEEL FRUSTRATED:** When your child feels frustration, it builds character and strength and shows them that they can be okay even when they do not have everything that they want, and when they are not as comfortable as they desire to be. Allow your child to feel bored, irritated, or dissatisfied—it will teach them how to cope with this state, to meet their own needs, or to make do with less.

GRATITUDE TIP Yes, we want your child to feel frustration, but we are not suggesting that you abandon your child. We are trusting that you have equipped him/her with fantastic coping skills to deal with frustration, but if you have not done so yet, now is the time. You are already taking steps by reading this book.

- **Being too involved with their EMOTIONS:** We all love our children, and it is difficult to know the difference between being empathic and tuned in to their moods and emotions, and being over-involved. We are all affected by their joy and pain, but when our ability to be okay is affected deeply by their moods each and every day, that is likely a sign that we are too involved.

- **Avoid OVERPROTECTING:** Parents that are overly involved with their child's feelings find it tough to tolerate the sound and words of their distressed or disappointed child. This incites those parents who tend to fuss over, and fix the problems of their children.

- **REWARDING certain behaviors:** Do not reinforce negative behaviors such as disrespectful voice tone, whining, complaining, or staged temper tantrums by attending to their discomforts.

We will go into more detail on how to shift your approach from an **entitlement–encouraging** family atmosphere to a **gratitude–encouraging** family atmosphere in the coming pages.

In the meantime, here's a quick **Entitlement-Crushing / Gratitude-Boosting** exercise to get your super-amazing, epically-fantastic parenting juices flowing (and so you know that we are most certainly in favor of attachment-oriented parenting, and we do not endorse chaining your children up outside in the winter to fend for themselves!):

Quickie Entitlement-Crushing/Gratitude-Boosting Exercise

How to Steps

Step 1:   **Meet your children's needs for love, connection, food, clothing, and shelter.**

Step 2:   **Teach / show your kids to communicate well:**

If your child says, "I'm thirsty," coach them to switch their words to something like: "I'd like a drink. May I have some orange juice, please?"

Step 3:   **Express empathy to your child:**
"I hear you that you're super-mad that I said you couldn't go over to your buddy's house."

Step 4:   **Teach them / show them how to take action:**
To meet their own needs and desires (whenever that is feasible): "If you'd like to invite your friend over, after you check with me about the dates, how would you like to contact her to see if she can come?"

To ask for help if they cannot / do not have the resources to do it on their own: "So you say that the bowl to put your cereal in is up too high for you to reach. Do you want to ask for help from someone taller to get it down, buddy?"

Step 5:   **Teach them / show them:**
To cope with any discomfort if they do not get satisfaction: "What do you want to think about that can help you feel a bit better about this, sweetie? Do you think it will help to think, 'This is so rotten! Why is my life horrible?' or something more along the lines of 'This is a huge disappointment, but I'm not going to let it ruin my day'?"

"What do you want to do that can help you feel a bit better about this, dude? Would you rather sit in your room and think about a bunch of bad stuff that has happened to you, or do you think it would help to play your favorite music playlist and read that joke book that always cracks you up?"

To be grateful / appreciative if they do get satisfaction: "Wow! I hope you really feel awesome that you figured out how to talk to your friend about the problem the two of you have been having. I think that was a creative solution. I'm hoping you're proud of how you said it."

ENTITLEMENT-CRUSHING ACTION Be extra aware that your child is always modeling and taking cues from your behavior. Giving in to their complaints will only fuel more complaints because you have taught the child that complaining leads to results.

Our Take on Generation ME

The media throws around the Generation ME term to describe the growing number of self-focused, low-empathy individuals who tend to value surface things, such as money, fame, and image. We want you to know that this is a trend that can be changed. Parents come into our office and raise their concerns about social media, wondering if there is a relationship between this self-focused behavior and their children's online presence. They feel that parenting is different now because of the impacts of social media. They can't fall back on parenting truths that their parents relied on. They are often fearful of the time and focus their children spend on themselves and expose or advertise themselves on their social media pages.

Parents see their children continually updating their status, following people they want to emulate, setting up profiles and photos that are all about themselves on various sites and social media apps. They observe that their children seem to be more easily prone to texting or messaging in insensitive ways and they wonder if their online behavior is bleeding through to real life behavior, further decreasing empathy with family and friends.

Parents are mindful of the barriers to empathy in many of our youth's modern social connections. Unfollowing and unfriending is easy online. The personal element can be removed so easily behind a screen. The awareness of how social media can impact empathy is one step in a movement towards buffering the negative elements that can come with its use. Children need us to be involved in their social media experience. It's parents' responsibility to educate ourselves because it is the first generation where children's knowledge frequently outpaces that of their parents. Remember parents, one way to increase our children's empathy is to utilize social media to help them to reach the masses for positive change. Many youth we see use social media to raise money for their sport teams, schools and causes that are dear to them. It can also be used as a platform to do good—and pay it forward.

Parents consistently write into our website **realparentinglab.com** asking if it is "normal" that their adolescent does not show any empathy on a day-to-day basis. The answer: of course it isn't.

Empathy —the ability to feel for and consider the experience of the other —is a vital component in social situations and a step up the **compassion ladder** that leads to a positive action for others. When children are low on empathy, they are self-centred—sometimes almost completely so. The risk of children lacking empathy is a factor in becoming an adult who rarely considers the needs or feelings of others.

Empathy is a very important social trait to nurture[20]:

- **It makes people kinder.**
- **It reduces prejudice and racism.**
- **It makes for better marriages and friendships.**
- **It reduces bullying.**
- **It is effective in the workplace.**

On every level, it is crucial that your child learns how to be empathic. Without empathy the connections in their lives will likely be fleeting and unsatisfying.

There are many empathy training programs available, but here are a couple of brief ideas to get you started:

You can promote empathy in your child by:

1. **Reading fiction and encouraging them to get into the mind or experiences of the characters.**

2. **Watching movies on mute and having each family member take turns guessing what a character is thinking or feeling.**

3. **Going out and about on field trip to watch people from a distance and guess their feelings and thoughts based on body language.**

4. **Doing service work together in which your children can see the difference they make (reading to under-privileged children, delivering food bank baskets to needy families, etc.) and then discussing the experiences.**

---

20. Wood, A. M, Froh, J. J., & Geraghty, A. (2010). Gratitude and well-being: A review and theoretical Integration [Special Issue]. *Clinical Psychology Review, 30,* 890-905.

5. **Sharing with your children the small and large things you do for those around you, and talking about how you feel about it.**

 ## Exercise: The Family Currency

Do you know what your **family currency** might be? This kind of currency generally does not have anything to do with money. It is simply the actions and efforts that have agreed-upon value within your family. Every family has some sort of currency, whether it is fairness, service, food, kindness for others, effort toward family values, or something else.

We would like you to think about what your family considers useful in trade with each other, and how valuable these things are in your family community:

- **Does saying "please" and "thank you" receive High (H), Medium (M), or Low (L) value rankings in your home?**
- **How about preparing a favorite snack for another?**
- **Or one person driving another to a special event, or to a required school event?**
- **How about tidying up common areas?**
- **Or being quiet while another rests?**

What about when one person gives as opposed to another? For example, is Mom cleaning up after her teenager given an (L) for Low value in our charting system below, but the teenager cleaning up after a family meal given an (H) for High value rating?

Does everyone in the family agree on the values of each activity? Does a hug from the gregarious, touchy-feely five-year-old hold less value than the hug of the withdrawn, slightly depressed 14-year-old?

Please know that there are usually a thousand different ways to view each family's **family currency**. Take a look at what you, as parents, value, and use it as a communication tool with your children. Many of the elements of currency will not be agreed upon between the adults and the children. This is normal, and your job is not to have the children see things the way you do.

This exercise is to further help you understand how your children value things and help you explain your own values to them. It should aid you in coming to a place of understanding, cooperation, and empathy, as well as expressing gratitude within the family.

Family Currency Log

Rating: High, Medium, or Low	Activity / Service / Statements	Who Gives?	Who Receives?
H/M/L			

- **Notice which elements of currency are easily agreed upon by different family members.**

- **Notice which cause the greatest number of discussions and disagreements.**

- **Notice what you may have misunderstood about the value that your children place on things.**

When you have a greater understanding of the various types of currencies in play in your home, you will be able to communicate your appreciation better to your family. You will also be able to provide your children with concrete examples about giving and receiving, making successful interactions more likely.

Points to Remember, Actions to Take

- **Key 1: Misguided Efforts:** A misguided effort is an attempt to make your child's life easier or better by, for example, allowing them to do or have things simply because you were not allowed to have them when growing up. Remember how children learn? They learn by watching you, not with words. That means every time you reward them (even when you do not think you are), they think they are acting in the correct way.

- **Key 2: Haves Vs. Have Nots:** The rule is that ANY parent ANYWHERE can spoil their child. Just because you do not hear the terms "spoiled little middle-class kid" or, "spoiled little under-privileged kid", it doesn't mean they can't be spoiled. It just means they cannot be given as expensive, or as many, advantages as those in higher income households.

- **Key 3: Needs:** When our child's needs are constantly met, they are never allowed to need something—really need something—and to experience what it feels like to go without, even for a small period. This impedes their emotional development, as they never learn to cope with going without, or to generate their own solutions to meet their needs.

- **Key 4: Praise:** Parents love to praise their children—we are told that it is an essential part of support, love, and being a good parent. But many parents over praise. Misguided praise comes in a variety of different forms.

- **Key 5: Modeling:** One of the reasons a child develops entitlement is because they have modeled their behavior on that of their parents'. Be careful of the behaviors you allow your child to view.

- **Key 6: YOU are responsible:** The truth is that YOU and I are the most likely cause of our child's entitlement issues. That is the truth, but it is not the end. We can always change our children's behavior by adapting our own. It is never too late to stop, learn, and try something different.

 GRATITUDE ACTION Create a list of your different family currencies to increase understanding, empathy, and gratitude in your home.

4

The Spoiled Child Syndrome: It is not the Child's Fault!

"What separates privilege from entitlement is gratitude."

[BRENE BROWN]

Pediatrician Bruce McIntosh coined the term "spoiled child syndrome." He viewed the term as poorly defined and derogatory, but avoiding the use of the expression "spoiled" can make it difficult when addressing parents' concerns about their child's behavior. Spoiling your child is not simply about overindulging them. In fact, McIntosh defined spoiled child syndrome[21] as characterized by excessive self-centered and immature behavior, resulting from the failure of parents to enforce consistent, age-appropriate limits.

We are seeing more permissive-indulgent parenting today than in the last two decades. We have found when working with parents in our psychology practice that they typically vacillate between a *boss-like parenting style* and a *buddy-like* parenting style.

---

21.   McIntosh, B., (1989) Spoiled child syndrome. *Pediatrics. (83)1*, 108-115.

These two styles of parenting are opposites. *Because I said so* parenting is more autocratic: "I'm the boss...children should be seen, not heard." Many parents that we have spoken to consistently reported that this was the parenting style their parents used when they were growing up. Parents described feeling devalued, controlled, and disrespected; and their parents' love felt conditional. The parents we work with consistently say, "I don't want to parent my child the way our parents parented us." So it is not shocking to see parents swing the other way towards a *buddy-like* style of parenting. These parents are very communicative and highly responsive to their child's individual needs and do not enforce many expectations or rules.

What we are shooting for is something in between: *fair-and-square* parenting. It is the style most likely to produce well-adjusted children. The parents serve as teacher or facilitator, with clear expectations and rules, working with the child to meet and follow them. Parenting decisions are based on mutually respectful forms of communication and limit-setting. This tends to have a win–win outcome: parents are able to set limits, and children experience a cooperative, supportive, and respectful interaction. It does take some work to get to this place, for sure, but it is worth it.

Notes from the Real Parenting Lab on Spoiled Children

We have found in our research, that often it is kind and well-intentioned parents that are unknowingly giving their children power that they cannot handle, even though the children think they can.

This will sound–all too familiar to those parents that just want to see their child happy. Here is an example from one of our parenting groups:

Shannon is a single parent in her mid-30s. She has a seven-year-old daughter.

Shannon: *"What do you want to wear to school today?"*

Daughter: *"My yellow t-shirt and red shorts."*

Shannon: *"It's too chilly to wear shorts today."*

Daughter: *"I WANT to wear my SHORTS to school!"*

Shannon backs off as her daughter's behavior and voice escalate. Shannon agrees to let her daughter wear shorts, even after she shared her concerns. On their way to school, her daughter says, "I'm too cold. This isn't a good idea. I want to go back home and get changed." Shannon is worried that her daughter is going to be too cold, so she turns the car around and takes her home to get changed.

What would you have done in this situation? Some of you may have made the same choices as Shannon. We find parents are also faced with a similar struggle when it comes to mealtimes: The child says what they want for dinner, and after it is made, they change their minds and then the parent will prepare them another meal option.

In both of these situations, the child is in control. Failure to provide age-appropriate limits will encourage acting-out behaviors. For instance, you will notice your child becoming easily frustrated when they cannot be the boss. This decreases your child's ability to be resilient in the face of challenge.

The risk of not setting limits with your child and facilitating spoiled-like behavior is very high. You may end up with emotional and behavioral problems in your child, such as oppositional behaviors, lying, aggression and impulsiveness. At the most extreme this may lead to conduct problems (stealing, breaking the law), getting in trouble at school or in the community, and the risk of substance use.

Age-Appropriate Limits (some examples):

	Ages 2-3	Ages 4-6	Ages 7-9	Ages 10-12	Ages 13-15	Ages 16-18
Chores*	• Unload dishwasher • Put away toys • Collect dirty clothes • Dust	• All chores previously mentioned • Make bed • Clear table • Load dishwasher • Take out recycling • Set table	• All chores previously mentioned • Vacuum • Fold laundry • Simple meal prep • Sweep • Get mail	• All chores previously mentioned • Clean toilets • Make simple meals • Wash/dry clothes • Feed pets	• All chores previously mentioned • Make full meals • Clean shower/tub	• All chores previously mentioned • Supervision of younger children's chores
Screen Time	Spending about two hours a day with screen media, the same amount of time they spend playing outside, and three times as much time as they spend reading books or being read to	Spending about two hours a day with screen media, the same amount of time they spend playing outside, and three times as much time as they spend reading books or being read to	• 1-2 hours per day • On average, kids are getting in 11 hours of screen time per day. • No cellphone	• 1-2 hours per day • On average, kids are getting in 11 hours of screen time per day. • No cellphone	• 2 hours per day • On average, kids are getting in 11 hours of screen time per day.	• 2 hours per day • On average, kids are getting in 11 hours of screen time per day.
Bedtime	7 p.m.	7:30 p.m.	8-8:30 p.m.	8:30-9 p.m.	9-9:30 p.m.	9-10 p.m.

*With young children, the chores do not need to be done perfectly. Just having the child involved in any way with contributing to the household helps them know they can have an important impact, and that their efforts are useful and valued. Even a two-year-old can bring one plastic cup out of the dishwasher as their chore.

We are not trying to cause undue parenting guilt or pandemonium here, but truly every parenting action (whether well-intentioned or not) that we apply when our children are even as young as one to two-years-of -age DOES affect:

- **How capable they are.**

- **How motivated they are.**

- **How responsible they are.**

- **How trustworthy they are.**

- **How kind they are.**

It also affects every other desirable or non-desirable characteristic about them when they are 12 years old, 22 years old, and beyond.

TIP 1 SPOIL-PROOFING YOUR CHILD Each time you find yourself thinking or saying to your spouse, *"We should deal with Junior's behavior / attitude before he's a teenager,"* that is an immediate signal to you to take action to deal with it NOW!

I'm SO Embarrassed By My Child's Tantrums

In the last decade, we have not met a parent who is not fully aware of the importance of consistency, structure, and limit setting. Parents do not need a PhD in parenting to figure this out.

However, even if you really are a rock star of a parent, it is hard to consistently have the stamina to go head-to-head with your child and assert your authority. Instead, parents will often spend valuable time and energy pleading, bargaining and, ultimately, giving in to their child.

Avoiding a scene in public is something that most parents try their hardest to do. Parents can be fearful of saying "no", especially in public. This fear and avoidance will create a situation where your child will learn that they are in control and you cannot handle them. (Eventually, they will believe this lack of control is true of all adults). The child concludes: "I can do as I please and demand to have my needs met at any given time."

- **Setting limits differently in public opens a gap in our consistency. Children will find any opportunity they can to hone in on our weak spots in parenting—when we are on the phone, when we have a friend over, when we are out for dinner, etc. These are the moments we must put in extra effort to fill any gaps in our consistency.**

Tantrum Tips

In very young children, consider these tantrum facts:

- **Tantrums appear around two or three and tend to vanish at four. There is a difference between a two- or three-year-old having a normal tantrum, and a five-year-old throwing a tantrum because she wants something you are not giving her.**

- **Parental response is critical during this time. You need to calm yourself, state clear rules, learn to vocally appreciate appropriate behavior, and teach empathy to the child when teaching opportunities arise.**

- **Giving in to the tantrum is the worst thing you can do. It will simply increase the frequency and severity of the tantrums the next time. These can be mild or shocking, depending on the child.**

Interestingly, many tantrums are directed towards an individual parent, proving that they are responding in an emotionally destructive way to get what they want with that individual.

TIP 2 SPOIL-PROOFING YOUR CHILD The next time your child begs for candy and you find yourself thinking that it is simply easier to give in than to hear the complaints and arguing, try saying "NO!" It may be exhausting and overwhelming and your child may be mad, but it will all make sense as you read what we have to say below.

Can Tantrums Be a Good Thing?

We have already established that in some cases, parents find giving in to their child's behavior is worth avoiding the embarrassment of a tantrum and/or the fear of losing their child's affection. What if we told you that tantrums are not so bad after all? Is it possible that your child's tantrums could mean what you are doing as a parent is ACTUALLY working?

Be prepared: should you decide to change your parenting approach from inconsistently reinforcing your child's misbehavior, you will need to power up your courage and dig in so you can deal with what comes next.

We are preparing you because, unless you are a behavioral psychologist, you may not fully grasp what is going to happen. We are sure you have all heard that it gets worse before it gets better, and in behavoural psychology, that process is called an "extinction burst."

Extinction not only applies to the poor dodo bird, it can also apply to human behavior. Extinction occurs when behavior that is typically reinforced or rewarded no longer receives rewards or reinforcement. This means that the undesirable behavior or target behavior will stop, or is extinguished.

What does this have to do with my child's misbehavior? Well, let us assume your child's reinforcements are co-sleeping, getting your attention (in a disruptive manner), or ice cream for breakfast. You have decided that you want this to stop. They are to move out of your bed, quit the attention-seeking behavior, and a healthy breakfast is a priority. This is where the mental control of the **ninja parent** is required—armor up and dig in! Up until now your child has been persistent in his/ her attempts to get these things from you. Your child has had more practice at winning the battle, and the new reality, or **extinction burst,** will result in them displaying more of the undesirable behavior you want to prevent. This escalation in behavior is happening because you have stopped reinforcing your child. Do not let your child beat you down.

When parents come to us and they have witnessed firsthand the extinction burst, they will say, "Dr. F, your suggestions are not working. In fact, my child's behavior is WORSE."

What parents are witnessing is:

- **Their child's behavior gets LOUDER and MORE persistent.**

- **Their child will work harder at pursuing them in order to break them down.**

If you remain courageous and consistent and dig in, your child will learn their poor behavior will no longer be rewarded. If you break down and reinforce your child's behavior during the extinction burst, the message you will be sending your child is,"I just have to get louder and push harder and my parent will back down, and then I will continue to get what I want".

The behavioral science behind extinction has been proven, both in the labs and real-life settings. When parents come to us and let us know that setting limits with their child to eliminate target behaviors does not work for them, what they are really telling us is that they were not ready to deal with the extinction burst and their child has broken them down.

They eventually reinforced the undesirable behavior by giving in. We understand that it is easier in the short term to stop the pestering and the tantrums by reverting back to reinforcing the inappropriate behavior. However, understand: you will be battling these behaviors long term. It is so important to stay the course and resist your child a bit longer. We assure you the extinction burst will end. We have science to back this up.[22, 23]

TIP 3   SPOIL-PROOFING YOUR CHILD Before changing your parenting style, make sure you are ready to walk your talk. Ninja parents, you will need to equip yourselves with the ENERGY, PATIENCE, and STRENGTH to make it through the extinction burst. You can do it!

Spoil-Proofing Your Child

With the upcoming arrival of the newest royal baby, sibling to Prince George of Cambridge, the question is raised, "How on earth do you spoil-proof a prince?" Well, the good news for Will and Kate is that it is possible. All the basic tenets on spoil-proofing your child are the same whether you are a prince or a commoner.

As we have mentioned, an overemphasis on trying to make your child happy all the time, and protecting them from disappointments, is one of the biggest parenting traps and usually results in short-term happiness and long-term problems.

Build your child's coping resources. Depriving children of the

22. Patterson, G.R., Littman, R.A. & Bricker, W. (1967). Assertive behavior in children: A step toward a theory of aggression, *Monographs for the Society for Research in Child Development, 32 (5)*, 1-43.

23. Drabman, R.S., & Jarvie, G. (1977). Counseling parents of children with behavior problems: the use of extinction and time-out techniques, *Pediatrics, 59 (1)*, 78-85.

opportunity to build their own internal coping resources to deal with disappointments is not what any parent intentionally sets out to do. Until you become a parent, you do not realize the emotional impact that seeing your child distressed can have on you. It can be quite emotional and overwhelming, further complicated with anxiety over what the outside world's perception is of your child as they tantrum, and the judgment you feel directed towards you. .

It is important to overcome concern around external criticism, and remember what your purpose is as a parent. Ask yourself a simple question: "Who is it that I want my child to be in the world?" *Go back to Chapter 1 and review the Parenting Values Checklist (p.19).*

- **Are your values consistent with your parenting approach?**
- **Will you be able to accomplish the task of shaping your child's life, values, and behavior, by your current parenting practices?**

Accept disappointment. Children need opportunities to learn to "do without" and to handle disappointment. Children will provide their parents with the opportunity to learn how to accept their child's emotions, and see that crying and yelling are not harmful to their child. If we give in to everything our child wants, it creates an unrealistic expectation of how the world will treat them.

Society will not tend to their every need. Parents have an opportunity to help their child learn by adapting their child-rearing practices, trying the strategies in this book, and understanding the full impact of their parenting.

Setting limits and validating your child's feelings. Children are entitled to have their parents accept the full range of their emotions, from the feel-good-happiness, excitement, and enthusiasm-to the

not-so-good-anger, frustration, and disgust. That's not to say, when a child chooses to do or say destructive things in reaction to their emotions, that they are entitled to do so. A very angry adolescent is allowed to say, "I'm so stinking angry with you, Mom," but is not entitled to throw a glass across the room and say "F#@% you, Mom."

Your child is not that special after all. We get it—all of us think our children are special. Have you asked yourself, *how healthy is it for my child to feel special?*

- **Being special means that they are not like other children, which introduces the idea that they are privileged in some way.**

- **If your child sees himself as special because he has been told he is, then he may find adapting in social situations at school or, later, at work, challenging. The outside world is not going to view your child as special. This may be hard for them to deal with.**

- **When children feel special, they often do not recognize the difference between asking for and demanding what they want. A child who believes they are special will demand, not ask.**

- **Do not confuse what we are trying to say. Yes, all children are special. But to treat children in a way that "special" translates to privileged does not help your child. We want children to feel valued and self-confident. Giving them positive attention and encouragement is worthwhile, but avoid overdoing it with praise.**

Spoil-Proofing Challenge

Choose an answer to this: Your child draws a picture. What should your response be?

1. **"You are an amazing artist!"**

2. **"What do YOU think of your creation?"**

3. **"We should tell your teacher how advanced your drawing is."**

4. **"It's great watching you do something you enjoy."**

Answers 1 and 3 are overdoing praise. Answers 2 and 4 are positive attention and encouraging.

Give your child real responsibility. We want to balance having too many expectations of our child with all the activities and schoolwork they are doing. However, protecting them from making a contribution at home and helping out, is not the path we want our children to be on. Helping our children gain a sense of accomplishment and competency in life instills a positive work ethic. It crushes privilege and entitlement, and it helps our children to solve their own problems, approaching life in a competent and self-sufficient manner.

Points to Remember, Actions to Take

- **Key 1: It is not the child's fault.** Spoiled child syndrome is the excessive self-centered and immature behavior that results from the parents' failure to enforce consistent, age-appropriate limits.

- **Key 2: Set age-appropriate limits.** Failure to provide age-appropriate limits will increase acting out behavior in your child. You will notice your child's behavior becoming disruptive and challenging when they cannot be the boss. Please remember it is temporary. Over time they will realize that they cannot win against your parental authority if you do not give in.

- **Key 3: There are risks to not setting limits.** The behavior you are unhappy about at 12-years-old will continue to be undesirable when your child is 21-years-old. The unfavorable outcomes of not setting limits with your child include lying, aggression, impulsiveness, and conduct problems.

- **Key 4: Tantrums are embarrassing.** Even though your child's tantrums are embarrassing, you must go head-to-head with them and assert your authority. Do not waste your time pleading, bargaining, and ultimately giving in: your child will see the gaps in your consistency and will push harder to have their demands met.

- **Key 5: Tantrums can be good in the short term.** When you stop rewarding your child's disruptive or undesirable behavior, they will tell you they are not happy with you by demonstrating even MORE undesirable behavior. If you consistently stop rewarding the undesirable behavior, your child's intense tantrums will decrease. Warning: tantrums will get worse when you first begin to change your parenting approach.

- **Key 6: Spoil-proof your child.** An over emphasis on trying to make your child happy all the time is a parenting trap that leads to spoiled child syndrome. Allow your child to build coping resources and accept disappointment while validating their feelings.

- **Key 7: My child is special.** If your child sees themselves as special, they may experience challenges adapting to social situations. If society does not view your child in the same way as you, it may be difficult for your child to deal with the real world.

- **Key 8: Give your child responsibility.** Real responsibility helps your child gain a sense of accomplishment and competency. It will crush privilege and entitlement. Your child will be better equipped to solve their own problems, and approach life in a self-sufficient manner.

5

What to Do About It

*"You cannot help people permanently by doing for them,
what they could and should do for themselves."*

[ABRAHAM LINCOLN]

Parents tell us that today's children have tons of material belongings, but do little to contribute around the house. They say the children assert that this is okay, normal in other homes and should be okay in their home. We've heard the term "Entitle-mania" batted around the community, and parents we work with say it is spreading like wildfire.

We know the problem exists, but now it is time to find practical solutions to challenge it. Society's focus today is on:

- **Avoidance of discomfort.**

- **Over emphasis on meeting your child's needs (Helicopter Parenting).**

- **Working only if there is payoff for the individual ("What's in it for me?").**

A cohesive family home, with children growing up resilient and filled with positive characteristics, is unlikely under these conditions.

We'd like to share reports from brave parents, willing to be open with us about their mistakes and challenges, as they seek a balance between caring, giving, and doing for their children. Then we will offer more hands-on, how tos.

Notes from the Real Parenting Lab: There Is No Easy Way Out

Gabby and Don were just like any other couple that walks through our office doors, adamant they want the best for their child. Unfortunately, because of their drive to give to their child "the life they never had," their son Miles is, as they say, "out of control."

Miles is not only an entitled child but, his parents say, he is also a "master emotional manipulator." At the tender age of eight, there are thousands of dollars' worth of gaming consoles, computer products, and hardware stacked in his room. He insists that he must have these things, and that he deserves these advantages.

In an attempt to keep Miles happy, mom Gabby, who works from home, admits to often giving him whatever he wants. "I know I'm not supposed to... and that I'm probably doing it all wrong, but I don't like to see him cry or get angry. It's easier to say 'yes'."

Like Gabby, many moms and dads often give in to their children because the repercussions seem too severe, bothersome, or time-consuming to deal with on a daily basis. And, the tantrums, anger, and acting out that can go on when a child does not get what he wants are very tiring—especially once an entitled attitude has begun to set in.

What Gabby and Don did not fully realize, is that they have unwittingly conditioned Miles to behave this way. They had an inkling that their behavior nurtured Miles' attitude, but did not know what to do about it. They continued to take the easy way out, giving in to their son to keep the peace. Miles learned that to get his way every time, all he needed to do was get upset.

The Overpaid, Ungracious Child

We recently conducted a survey that asked parents a number of questions based on their behavior with their children. The study revealed several very interesting things about the relationships between children who have become ungracious, and their parents.

Parents reported that they often overpay their children to perform a task. They also reported a desire to encourage characteristics such as entrepreneurial spirit and an understanding of the working concept of being compensated for providing a service. They emphasized the importance of increasing their child's positive emotional wellbeing by helping them to feel useful, and a contributing member of the household. To a busy parent, or to a parent that has not fully thought through the medium and long-term consequences of paying a child $50 to wash the family car, this may seem like a great way to motivate your child. But overpaying children is actually quite damaging to their ability to be strong and successful in the world.

Outcomes of Overpaying Our Children

Short-Term	Medium-Term	Long-Term
Happy child	Less likely to be thankful for the overpayment and more likely to demand/expect it	Adult who expects to make easy money
Initial enthusiasm to repeat the task again	Without overpayment, likely to avoid or be belligerent about contributing within the family	Adult who is less likely to work hard for a goal without immediate gratification
Thankful child	Less likely to think about how they could be of help to the family as a whole, or helpful to particular individuals in the family	Adult who is more focused on "What's in it for me?" than on the overall quality of the work or the enjoyment or pride in a job well done
Surprised child	Less thankfulness and gratitude	Self-centered adult who feels they deserve extra-special treatment and reward, independent of their effort

Overpaying our children has little to no positive medium-term or long-term effects and misrepresents real life. It makes for youths and adults who tend to work less and expect more, make unreasonable demands, and act selfishly.

Examples of Overpayment:

- **Paying a child for chores, such as making their bed, tidying their room, or helping with meals.**
  We recommend that families make it clear that Mom and Dad are not paid for cleaning out the dishwasher, so kids should not be paid either. Family and household chores are better presented as necessary family contributions. Period.

  If an allowance system is something that is important to your family to help a child understand money, and/or for them to save up for unnecessary items of indulgence (that ultra-cool skateboard or the latest sparkly sneakers), we recommend allotting a certain amount per week or month, independent of the required chores.

- **Paying above market value for services: a trip to the mall to buy $150 jeans in exchange for cleaning up the family room is not fair market value. (If you were paying a cleaning service to clean up your family room and you were paying $20 per hour, you would expect the cleaning service to complete the task in, for example, 30 minutes, making the fair market value $10, not $150.)**
  If you or another family member, a grandparent, say, decide to contract a child for help with something that you do not typically define as standard household contributions (such as reorganizing the storage unit, cleaning out the garage, etc.), ensure you are as specific as you would be with hiring any other service (time required to go a good job; completion time; clarity with what successful completion of the job entails; whether the payment is by the job, hour, or other unit of measurement; whether partial payment is allowable for partial completion, etc.).

- **Paying a child for good grades on their report card.**
  Although we do not see this as a pure overpayment situation,
  we do have thoughts on this. If we teach our children that high
  grades are anything but for their own benefit (current and
  future), we are missing excellent learning opportunities. We also
  know that a child taught to focus on grades fails to appreciate the
  most important parts of the school experience are:

  - **Ability to set and meet goals**

  - **Ability to study and learn**

  - **Ability to delay gratification and to work toward
    something in the future**

  - **Ability to motivate themselves when the going
    gets tough**

  - **Ability to work well with people—both agreeable and
    disagreeable**

    We see more children who are taught to overly focus on
    A's cheat on exams, plagiarize during their writing, purchase
    the previous year's exams (college level), copy homework
    from peers, or sweet talk parents into doing 90 per cent of
    their science project for them. Yes, the chances of achieving
    an A are increased, but at what cost to personal integrity and
    work ethic?

    We see, as with the difference between Process vs.
    Person praise later on in this chapter, that when we focus
    recognition ("I'm proud of what you did this semester")
    on the letter grade instead of the effort, work ethic, social
    adeptness in working with teachers/ peers, etc., a child's
    self-esteem is not well supported, and they are easily
    shattered if, for whatever reason, they don't attain A's.

GRATITUDE TIP Be careful not to confuse teaching your child the value of hard work, earning, and money, with bribing them to do chores. If they will not do it for the sake of contributing to the family, there is very little lesson involved.

Avoiding the Landmines of Bad Precedents

The same study that we conducted between 2012 and 2013 revealed a few other interesting facts about our survey group. There are bad precedents running rife in North American homes, contributing to the increasing number of entitled children:

- **Parents reported using rewards and bribes as a method of controlling their children, or making them do things that they did not want to do (homework, sports, piano practice, chores).**

- **Parents also reported that it is easier and quicker to just do something for their child instead of making the child do it for themselves. For instance, a parent said, "I'm not patient. I can't stand waiting five minutes for my six-year-old, who is struggling to tidy the covers on the bed. I'd rather just tidy it myself."**

- **Parents reported that they sometimes make parenting decisions according to whether their child will be happy with them or whether they will like or love them.**

- **Parents reported wanting to be the favorite parent, sometimes giving-in to demands or saying "yes" because of an unspoken competition with their spouse (or ex-spouse) to be their child's favorite.**

- **Parents reported that they often responded to guilt-inducing thoughts of their own making, for example, "If I say no, Junior may never get over it," or guilt-inducing comments from their children, such as, "Everyone else gets to go to the party, and now I'll be excluded forever because you won't let me go."**

What we know is that children who are parented according to the buddy-like style tend to be unhappy, with an inflated sense of self-importance. This is the opposite of good self-esteem. Parents seem to know that these precedents exist and, at some point, end up feeling powerless to change the negative patterns.

So the damage is done. These bad precedents result in selfish thinking, an inability to take personal responsibility, difficulty establishing personal identity, and incompetence in daily skills, as well as personal and self-care skills. In other words, these children become seriously disabled and they become unable adults.

It is time to draw the line. If your behavior is harming your child's future, you need to take responsibility now for the precedents in your home. There is always time to make a positive change.

Okay, so what is to be done to prevent and correct the entitle-mania? Let's take a look at solutions that will focus on **kindness boosters** and **gratitude boosters**.

REALITY BLAST Overindulged children with too many material items often fail to learn the skill of knowing what is enough. Because they always want, want, want, they are never fulfilled and are in a perpetual state of feeling empty and unsatisfied.

How to Foster Kindness and Gratitude: Part 1 – With a Focus on Appreciation

For the most part, parents do not enjoy cleaning the bathroom or cutting the lawn, and they do not get a monetary reward or special treat for doing it, either.

Communicating to our children why we do unexciting home maintenance—get up extra-early to drive them to hockey practice, or make them peanut butter sandwiches cut diagonally without crusts—helps them to learn to appreciate our efforts. This is the start of planting the seeds for our children being able to appreciate what not just us, but what others also do for them.

It is okay and, in fact, highly beneficial to make it clear that we sacrifice time, energy, money, and other resources:

- **To make a happy healthy environment for our family**
- **To demonstrate our love and caring**
- **To show appreciation for other family members**
- **Most of all, to show respect for each other**

Setting the tone and parameters around why you do what you do, and what is expected of all family members as a normal contribution to the family and home, and doing so without guilt, anger, or negative emotions attached is not easy. But it is a worthwhile and achievable goal.

Examples of acceptable sharing:

- **"I have decided to rearrange my golf game so I can come to watch your performance. I am excited to come watch you."**

- **"I could go for a pedicure today and would like to, but today it is more important to me to help you with your school project. Let's dig in and get it done."**

How often should we share with our children what we do for them?

This is a difficult one to define because it will be different in each family. The answer is, that it is beneficial to make regular statements, keeping in mind that over use will lead to our children tuning us out. We also want to avoid the risks of inducing unnecessary guilt.

When you share your efforts with your children, make sure your words are:

- **Free of complaint. Do not say: "I always cut my workout short so I can pick you up, and all I get from you is a bad attitude."**

- **Free of guilt. Do not say: "I never get to spend any time with my friends because I have to take care of you."**

- **Free of anger and frustration. Do not say: "I'm sick of making your lunches when you don't even thank me."**

- **Free of absolutes: I/you...never/always**

The 20-Second Sound Bite Rule

At all costs, avoid the mini-lecture: this is a recipe for a BIG power struggle. Children in our office tell us that lengthy verbal diatribes from their parents lead them to feel angry, and that they are less likely to listen to the message, more likely to do the opposite of what their parent wants. They are also more likely to feel guilty by the end of the lecture. Most of our appreciation-increasing thoughts can be shared in a **20 second sound bite.** Think about one idea at a time, and choose your words well so you talk less rather than more. After 20 seconds, stop speaking.

Also remember to practice what we call **mindful appreciation:** notice what your children do for you.

- **"You didn't have to bring me a clean towel when I asked for it, but I appreciate that you did."**

- **"You introduced me to your new friend, and I appreciate that. I want you to know that I noticed that you took the time to show respect by introducing me. Thanks, buddy."**

- **"Thanks for taking the time to add sparkles and all these details on the birthday card you made for me. I appreciate how much care you put into it for me."**

How to Foster Kindness and Gratitude: Part 2 – With a Focus on 'NO'

Say "no" to your children. It is hard, but remember, there is such a thing as a positive "no". You may avoid using it at times, associating the word "no" with anger, frustration, and guilt. Perhaps this is how it was used when you were a child. We know that you can say "no" in a supportive and loving way. Make sure your voice tone is even, your facial expression is calm, and anger is not in play when you say "no." It will help your children to listen and respect you better.

Say a **"modified no"** to your children. If you want to allow them a treat, let them know that they can have a small ice cream, but not a large, or one topping instead of two.

Say a **"yes/no" combo:** If they ask for two small toys from the dollar store (even though you can clearly afford the $2), you say, "Yes, you may have one but not two. You have the opportunity to make a decision about which toy is more important to you."

Say "yes" (well...it is actually a **"qualified no"**): "Yes you can go out once your room is clean." The no is implied: no clean room = no going out.

Teach your children how to deal with disappointment.*[24] When things do not go their way, cue your children to make a conscious decision of how to handle their anger, sadness, and resentment:

- **THINKING how bad it is that they have been disappointed, how unfair their life is, how much other people are unkind, etc., and...**

- **BEHAVING in an upset manner by crying excessively, slamming doors, using poor language, and stomping loudly or...**

- **BOUNCING back from the disappointment through thinking resilient thoughts, such as: "I don't like this, but I can handle it."or: "I'm mad that Mom said no, but I'm not going to let it ruin my day." And...**

- **DOING things that help them cope, like listening to music, reading, playing with the family pet, or engaging in other activities they find enjoyable.**

---

24. We help families to use thinking patterns and certain actions to help cope with all sorts of negative feelings at different ages and stages, and offer a short introduction to the idea here, as well as the concept of cueing our children to cope or not cope—as the child sees fit—giving the child control.

REALITY BLAST Our children do not have to like what we say or what our decisions are. They need some adversity and disappointment to thrive. We do not need to feel guilty about saying "no"or having rules. If our rules are fair, and we explain them beforehand, make sure our children understand them, and teach them the skills they need to follow the rules, we have done our job.

How to Foster Kindness and Gratitude: Part 3 – With a Focus on Empathy

Practice couch empathy: when sitting on the couch watching a movie with your child, ask them how the character in the movie may feel. Mute the sound and play a quick and fun game of "guess what the character is thinking"—this can help promote empathy in children.

Use photos of facial expressions and have your children guess the emotion depicted. There are many charts and images like this available for free online. Flashcard emotions for very young children (aged two to three) can go a long way in encouraging empathy, which we know ends up being both a **kindness booster** and a **gratitude booster**.

Kind children, rated as altruistic and empathic towards other children, usually have at least one parent who deliberately models helping others. The most crucial years are between the ages of two and four, when children are learning what is socially acceptable and what is not. Let your children know that the cookies your family is baking for their teachers represent a little extra effort to recognize and thank them for their staying up late to grade book reports and write up report cards. Make the efforts of others obvious through talking about them.

Wave a "thank you" to drivers that stop for you when you are walking at the crosswalk, or those who let you in to a lane of traffic, and say, "That driver didn't have to do that. She might have been in a hurry to get somewhere but did something nice for us by stopping/letting us in. Very cool."

How to Foster Kindness and Gratitude: Part 4 – With an Emphasis on Responsibility

We all want kind, capable, and responsible children. Here are some ideas on how to nurture responsibility:

- **If you want your children to understand the value of things, take them to work. Show your child what you have to do in an hour, then go to the grocery store with the amount of money you earned in that hour. Let them know that you worked hard to earn the money, so you choose to spend it wisely.**

- **Implement a system that allows your children to experience age-appropriate natural consequences of their actions. If there is dirty laundry on the floor of your 12-year-old's room and not in the wash basket, do not wash it. If your eight-year-old carelessly breaks something, she needs to replace it. If your 15-year-old loses a library book, he has to pay for it. These are real consequences.**

- **Teach your child that when we depend on others too much to have our needs or wants met, we are vulnerable to poor outcomes. Feelings such as helplessness, frustration, anger, and sadness kick in if others let us down. We can end up with thoughts such as, "Life is not fair." But if we can help ourselves and solve our own problems, asking for help only when we need it, we become empowered and are much more in control of our own happiness.**

- **Encourage recognizing others who might be part of your child's successes whenever it is appropriate to do so. If your child wins the spelling bee, help him identify and thank everyone that allowed him to experience this achievement. He can send gratitude notes to these people for added effect.**

How to Foster Kindness and Gratitude: Part 5 – With an Emphasis on Modeling

Again here are some thoughts we want to share with you about what you do rather than what you say.

- **Casually demonstrate to your child ways in which you are fulfilled and your needs are met. Show them that you have an abundance of greatness in your life. This may include existing activities, friends, community, comforts, and other things that give us pleasure.**

- Avoid talking about, or engaging in, activities that are focused on wants. For example, do not mention to your pre-teen that you cannot wait to go shopping at the mall to pass the time because you have been bored all day. Instead, frame the experience in a gracious, giving manner—I want to go shopping to get your father that steak he really enjoys.

- While you are shopping with your child, regularly purchase one extra can of soup for the food bank, one extra pair of socks for the homeless shelter, or one extra bag of dog food for the humane society, and have them help choose the items and drop them off with you.

- Try to avoid making "obtaining things I want" an activity or sport in front of your children. Try not to let them see you cruising online stores for objects of desire, and don't take them window shopping for material goods you'd like to own.

- Talk about occasional indulgences (purchasing that expensive pair of boots) by modeling your balanced thought process: "I am buying one pair of well-made boots instead of three lesser-quality boots so they will last me many years," or, "I have saved my money and have taken care of all the family's needs first, so I have made a decision to purchase these boots because I can afford it."

- Avoid acts of covetousness when your children are within earshot: "I would love to have their home"; "I wish we had a nicer car"; "Wouldn't it be nice to have that trip to Europe"; "I wish I had a nicer boss...".

GRATITUDE ACTION Teach your children the difference between a NEED (if I do not have it, I may die) and a WANT (if I do not have it, my life will keep going). A $100 designer t-shirt is a want; a piece of clothing to cover up a naked body in winter is a need.

Your Honorary PhD in Working with Appropriate Praise

As we have already mentioned, praise is one of those subjects that easily confuses parents. This is why so many of us get it wrong, and why we want to discuss it more thoroughly here. There is a big difference between, "I like your effort on the soccer field, Junior" and, "You're a great soccer player, Junior."

We would like to help you dig in to how we psychology types do our work and come to the conclusions we do. If you are game for some of the academic stuff, we invite you into our world in the next few pages.

Our colleagues, Mueller & Dweck[25] have spent years studying the effects of praise on students at a dozen New York schools. A specific study involving 400 fifth graders saw them individually completing a nonverbal IQ test that all children would do fairly well on. The researchers took care to praise each child, either by commenting on their **intelligence** ("Wow, you're really smart") or **effort** ("Wow, I see that you really tried hard on that question"). Then a second test option was introduced. At that point, the children had a chance to choose which one they wanted to complete.

25. Mueller, C.M. & Dweck, C.S. (1998). Intelligence praise can undermine motivation and performance. *Journal of Personality and Social Psychology, 75*, 33-52.

- **Option 1:** They were told that the test would be a lot more difficult than the first, but they would learn a lot from the puzzles.

- **Option 2:** They were told that the second test was easy, just like the first.

The results were startling: some 90 per cent of the children that were praised for effort volunteered to do the harder test. Nearly all the "clever" children chose to do the easy test.

What this shows us, is that if you praise intelligence without effort or hard work, children will get the message that it is better to play it safe and stick to easy things. As you can see, praise can backfire.

In general, further studies indicate that it is actually recognizing a child's process that produces a good result, while recognizing a trait has a negative effect. In other words, when we praise the EFFORT a child has put into something, she is more likely to be encouraged to seek out further knowledge and learn more, because she deems that her effort is something she can control.

In addition, if a child makes a mistake when they are focused on effort as a goal, they tend to not take it personally and instead seek out the right answer.

In contrast, person-centred praise, such as, "You are so clever," does not send the right message. A child starts to think about themselves as categorized or labeled "good" or "bad", "intelligent" or "unintelligent", "fast" or "slow." Children who are given PERSON-centred praise:

- Attempt to get more praise by choosing simple, easy tasks that are below their ability level.

- Will become anxious about letting you down.

- Will take fewer risks in academics, sports and other skill-based areas because they are afraid of failing.

Process vs. Person Praise: one more time

- Jane stacks blocks neatly for the teacher. The teacher comments on what a great effort Jane has put in.
  Result: Jane is motivated to do better with the next stack.

- John stacks blocks neatly for the teacher. The teacher comments on how intelligent John must be.
  Result: John experiences anxiety the next time the teacher asks him to stack the blocks. He wonders: What if she doesn't think I'm smart this time?

GRATITUDE TIP Always praise or encourage effort over ability. We are all born with abilities, and they are a natural part of who we are— but they do not make us better people. When you recognize your children's efforts, they will learn to work harder and reach further as they learn from you that it is a good thing to put in a strong effort.

Random, extra bonus information that you may be interested in: another unexpected result of studies on praising demonstrates that children who are rewarded for giving (volunteering, sharing) tend to not "give" for very long, they only do it when reinforced. This means that if you are bribing or rewarding your child to be giving, you are not teaching them anything other than they should wait for a reward before they give to others.

 ## Exercise: Process versus Person Praise

Now that you understand the difference between praising a child's personal traits and praising his/her process (effort, enthusiasm, consistency, determination), you can put it into practice at home. When parents do this for the first time with young children, they tell us they experience a very positive response.

As usual, if our children are going to experience any real, positive reinforcement from this new form of encouragement, the change must come from us, the parents. To begin, list three examples of both types of praise.

Process versus Person Praise Challenge

Action:	List three examples of statements you could make that are:	
	Process Praise	1.
		2.
		3.
Action:	List three examples of **Person Praise** statements that you want to **avoid**:	
	Person Praise	1.
		2.
		3.

Points to Remember, Actions to Take

- **Key 1: Do not overpay your child.** Helping your child to understand that their efforts are worth the same as others, and that their own efforts can bring rewards, will teach skills for long-term success and power up their ability to be strong and successful.

- **Key 2: Be mindful of bad precedents in your home.** If your behavior is harming your child's future, you want to take responsibility now. There is always time to make a positive change: no more bribery for doing chores; no more giving in because it is easy; no more trying to be the nice guy; no more being controlled by guilt.

- **Key 3: Foster kindness and gratitude.** Help your children to appreciate you, and show them how you appreciate them. Use the 20 Second Sound Bite rule to avoid lecturing.

- **Key 4: Foster kindness and gratitude.** Learn to say "no" in a supportive, loving way, and teach your children how to cope with disappointment.

- **Key 5: Foster kindness and gratitude.** Practice couch empathy, and point out others' good will and the good will of your children.

- **Key 6: Foster kindness and gratitude.** Focus on the opportunities your children have to take responsibility to affect others' lives, the family, and themselves. Allow them to experience the negative consequences of their actions.

- **Key 7: Model kindness and gratitude.** Avoid selfish statements and actions in front of the children. Avoid coveting and focusing on your wants. Teach the difference between WANTS and NEEDS.

- **Key 8: Practice process praise only.** Always praise effort over ability. We are all born with abilities, and they are a natural part of who we are, but they do not make us better people. When you praise your children's effort, they will learn to work harder and reach further— because they learn from you that it is a good thing to put in a strong effort.

GRATITUDE ACTION If you are prone to praising your child the "person" instead of the "process", then you need to switch it up right away! Changing to process praise will help your children learn that effort is required for success, and this makes them more likely to be kind, giving, and thankful people.

6

Gratitude Journaling

"Some of my greatest blessings call me Daddy."

[ANONYMOUS]

A gratitude journal is one of the linchpins of positive psychology, and an exciting way to teach your children how to appreciate their daily lives, feel happier, build up their immune systems, and sleep better.

The benefits of gratitude journaling are consistently emerging in research as having a powerful impact on the psychological, physical, and social experience of adults and children. Since we cannot deny the positive effects of using a gratitude journal, in our practice, we find ourselves recommending it, not only to children, but also to their parents as well as couples. We suggest doing the practice of Gratitude Journaling together, and individually.

Notes from the Real Parenting Lab on the Benefit of Journaling

Remember Miles, the child that got everything he wanted from his over-indulgent parents, Don and Gabby? We worked with their family over a few months, initially implementing small changes in family dynamics and, slowly but steadily, introducing the concept of appreciation and gratitude using **multisensory experiences.**

After just a few short months of gratitude journaling—an exercise we had the whole family engaged in—Miles started to pay more attention to what was occurring around him. He mentioned during one session that, "Every evening my family would speak about our gratitude journal after dinner." He would stay and participate instead of rushing off to play video games. Initially, he reported hating it, but when we followed up with him just a couple of weeks later, we could see a real change. Miles' mother also reported that his grandmother had been surprised one day, when asked by him what she was grateful for.

Now, don't get us wrong. Miles looked at us at first as if we were daft with our "notice the tiny details in life" stuff. At first he said that nothing much would impress him beyond his parents winning the lottery, or dinosaurs coming back to life. But we made a game of it, and we challenged him to find the tiny things that were worthwhile. It didn't take long to ignite his enthusiasm.

The journal entries began with just a single line focusing on his multisensory experience. Miles wrote:

"I appreciate my fluffy pillow when my heads touches it at night, it's soft."

"I appreciate the sound of rain because it helps me to feel relaxed when I'm nervous about going to school."

"I appreciate the taste and tingling of strawberry Pop Rocks candy exploding in my mouth."

Miles took to journaling extremely well and, by investigating his actions, thoughts, and experiences, he learned to have gratitude for both his parents. He wrote:

"I like my journal. It makes me think about stuff in different ways."

There are some kids that, without any prompting at all, will detail their sensory experiences when thinking about what they are grateful for. For instance, when we asked Madison, a 10-year-old girl we see, about any gratitude she might have for her favorite dinner, she described her mom's turkey feast:

"Your mouth is drooling, and your taste buds are tingling as your mind is transferred to happy land—a world full of pies, candies, unicorns, and rainbows. And your stomach is having a dance party of goodness. And everyone is screaming because it is so good."

Madison showed she understands the very essence of what we mean by **mindful appreciation**. And she is a natural at being attuned to the **multisensory experiences** that are worth paying attention to.

Why Should You Keep a Gratitude Journal?

Well, where should we start? By participating in the simple task of keeping a gratitude journal for as little as three weeks, researchers have found that participants reap many positive benefits. Actually, the results are quite overwhelming. More than one thousand people were studied, from school-aged children to seniors, and it was found that people who practice gratitude consistently reported the following benefits:

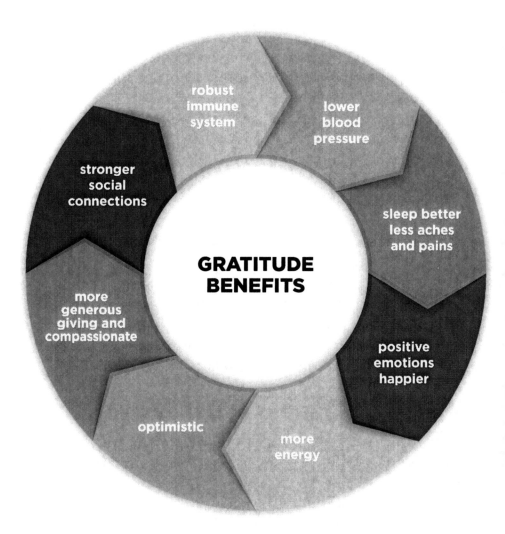

A gratitude journal is a great way to ensure that the members of your family are consistently refocusing their attention on the good things that happen in their lives.

There was a time when we were limited in what we knew about neuroscience. The research was narrow, and experts believed that once an adult brain matured, it was fixed—meaning that people's talents usually remained fixed over time.

Based on this old research, the "you can't teach an old dog new tricks" mantra was very relevant. However, new research on neuroplasticity indicates that the brain is far more complex than originally thought—with the ability to change rapidly under the right circumstances.

Simply put, if an adult loses the ability to see, their brain rewires itself, shrinking parts of the brain responsible for sight and creating new pathways to enhance other areas, such as smell, hearing. The plasticity of the brain can also be stimulated to grow and change if a person dedicates themselves to new experiences.

GRATITUDE TIP Dr. Dweck has contributed to research on fostering a "growth mindset" and has found that it is not what you know but how you grow. Open the door to continued learning via self-examination, to find new knowledge, skills, and behaviors to change the way you perceive the world. Gratitude journaling is a big part of this.

Aside from literally rewiring it, gratitude journaling is a positive way to influence your brain to develop an **attitude of gratitude.** Journaling draws attention to the good things in your life, which promotes awareness, abundance, and appreciation throughout the day. Not only do you attract more kindness and gratitude, but you give more of it as well.

If a basic formula for happiness existed, the attitude of gratitude would be the key ingredient.

Should Your Children Keep a Gratitude Journal?

Studies have indicated that there is an impressive range of benefits to helping your children keep a gratitude journal every day. Gratitude journaling is the way to go if you would like you and your children to be happier and experience the benefits researchers have been reporting:

- **Gratitude allows us to savor and acknowledge gifts that occur in the present.** Our gratitude practice through journaling can help to slow us down and participate in life in a more mindful way. Gratitude journaling will then help your child focus on positive emotions. Your child will likely become more aware of positive experiences in their daily lives. Being happier by celebrating goodness is a universal tool that parents can give their children.

- **Gratitude is a protective factor against negative emotions.** Journaling is the shift from passive participation in life to actively appreciating the gifts around us. As we savor these gifts daily or weekly, it can buffer any negative emotions that you or your child may feel.

- **Gratitude is a stress buffer.** Positive thoughts and focused attention on goodness are safeguards against daily stressors.

- **Gratitude increases your self-confidence.** When you journal about the goodness around you, you cannot help but feel good inside.

A basic gratitude journal does not have to be pages and pages long. It is essentially a chance to reflect on your day in a positive way. For children or adults, a single line for the small, medium, and large things in a day is enough to get them thinking along the right lines. Savoring the experience of gifts, large and small, helps us to achieve goodness in our daily lives.

 **Exercise: Gratitude Coaching**

Small (S), Medium (M), and Large (L) Gratitude

Please check which journal entries you consider to be

S   Appreciative but not essential, complements daily living

M   Valuable and adds meaning to daily living

L   Critical to daily living

	S	M	L
I'm grateful for my red barrette because it matches my red shoes			
I'm grateful for teachers that care about me			
I'm grateful for my courage when I was frightened going to high school			
I'm grateful for my strong heart and legs because without them I couldn't compete in track and field			
I'm grateful for the forts Dad and I build in the house			

When we recommend gratitude journaling to families, we emphasize that journaling is more effective once you are conscious of your decision to become more mindful of gratitude in your daily life. Make sure you talk to your child about it.

Depending on the child's age, it is more beneficial to start with a single line and build your way up to longer, more in-depth entries. Focusing on people is also important, as being grateful for things can be superficial and empty.

One gratitude—enhancing tool you may suggest to your children as they learn how to journal, is to suggest that they take a moment to imagine their life or day without the things they are grateful for. For example, try to dig deep and imagine what life would be like with no fingers, or no ability to smell, or to never again enjoy their favorite dessert. This tool can help a child put things into a meaningful perspective and boost their appreciation, rather than simply creating a list of good things that happened to them.

If daily journaling seems a daunting way to begin, research has also indicated that even short journal entries **once or twice a week** carry significant overall mood and health benefits.

Three Steps to Making It Stick

In Emmons & McCullough's 2003 study on gratitude, a group of young adults had been tasked with keeping daily journals of the things they were grateful for. The researchers assigned other young adult groups other topics to journal about, such as what annoyed them, or why they were better off than other people.

The results were quite significant over time. The young adults that kept gratitude journals showed greater increases in attention, enthusiasm, determination, and energy when compared with the control groups. Truly appreciating the positive aspects of our daily life has a powerful effect on the brain.

GRATITUDE TIP By following the three-step process to making the information stick in your child's mind, their brain will develop in positive ways. It opens them up to the good things in their lives and allows them to see the world from an entirely new perspective.

In our experience, we find that people absorb information best through a three-step process that allows us to remember or be mindful of the subject we are focusing on. By first *thinking it*, then *speaking it*, and then *writing it*, we can change our behavior and gradually fill our lives with a positive outlook.

Step 1: Thinking It

In positive psychology, behavior is influenced initially by the things we think about on a day-to-day basis. When your child begins a gratitude journal, they will start to think about the many things in their lives that they could be grateful for.

Eventually, this line of thought will allow them to appreciate things that they had previously taken for granted.

- **The first step to gratitude is thinking about it.**

GRATITUDE TIP **Thinking It** *should occur on a regular basis.* Try connecting your thoughts to a daily activity. SO if you are not a daily tooth-flosser, do not attach it to flossing. Instead, link thinking grateful thoughts to drinking water or getting dressed in the morning.

Gratitude is a practice, like any trait that you want to nurture. Just as intelligence is nothing without continuous learning, gratitude is nothing without daily application in your life.

A child who focuses on the positive is mentally strengthened: the simple act of thinking about all the things they are grateful for every day leads to a powerful cycle of positive thinking.

Conversely, you may want to counteract negative thinking in your child. If you find that they are preoccupied with pointless material wants and are weighed down by negative thoughts, practicing gratitude, with a bit of guidance from you, can change their mindset.

Thinking positive thoughts about what you are really grateful for in small, medium, and large ways always leads to greater understanding and a happier disposition. Children can be so easily bogged-down by material items which tend to distract them from the important things in life. These thankful thoughts help them rediscover what it really means to be happy and to feel better about themselves.

Step 2: Speaking It

If thinking about gratitude is the catalyst that opens you up to appreciating all the good things in your life, then speaking about it is the next logical step. When thoughts become ingrained in the human mind, they are spoken about more often.

You can always tell what a child is thinking because they will speak about it most often. It is a natural way to apply and explore what they have learned by realizing these thoughts through spoken words.

- **Speaking about gratitude is the next logical step.**

GRATITUDE TIP Speaking It* is best in a reciprocal fashion with others—at the dinner table, bedtime, or in the car. If you do not have anyone to Speak It to, then tell your cat. It is still spoken and communicated, which has the same positive impact.

Whereas thinking about gratitude is good, speaking about it is better. Research by Lyubormirsky and her colleagues[26] has shown that when we speak our gratitude aloud, we are more present in the moment, and that can be very valuable to children's emotional and psychological wellbeing.

See Appendix 3 in which we give you a template for Family Gratitude Dialogue to help with Speaking It.

---

26. Lyubomirshky, S. (2013). *The Myths of Happiness: What Should Make You Happy, but Doesn't, What Shouldn't Make You Happy.* Penguin Press

Verbalizing gratitude with others, teaches children to have an awareness of what goes on around them, including how people feel about them. When children speak about gratitude, they start to express it more effectively.

Studies by our colleague Sara Algoe[27] have also suggested that expression of this appreciation can repair damaged relationships within the family unit. As children grow, communication can become difficult, and the family can struggle when entitlement is constantly wearing down the bonds of love and kindness.

When a child speaks about gratitude, and begins to express it within their own lives, there will be a natural change in the family dynamics. Getting excited about good things that have happened to us is a lot healthier than the negative mindset of "want" that fosters selfish chatter and negative perspectives on life.

Step 3: Writing It

Without a doubt, the most effective method of actively increasing the levels of gratitude in your life is to keep a gratitude journal—every day or even once a week. For children that have experienced emotional periods of negativity, entitlement, and anger, there is simply no better remedy than writing down their feelings.

- **Fully appreciating gratitude comes when you write about it regularly.**

---

27. Algoe, S. B. (2012). Find, remind, and bind: The functions of gratitude in everyday relationships. *Social and Personality Psychology Compass, 6,* 455-469.

Algoe, S. B., Haidt, J., & Gable, S. L. (2008). Beyond reciprocity: Gratitude and relationships in everyday life. *Emotion, 8,* 425-429.

Algoe, S. B., Gable, S. L. & Maisel, N. C. (2010). It's the little things: Everyday gratitude as a booster shot for romantic relationships. *Personal Relationships, 17,* 217-233.

GRATITUDE TIP Research tells us **Writing It** once a week is enough to reap all the benefits.

As mentioned earlier, writing in a gratitude journal does not need to be overdone: a few single lines into a plain and simple journal is just as powerful as a jazzed-up notebook that your child has enthusiastically decorated with bling.

It shows that not only are children thinking about gratitude more often, but they are speaking about it more in an attempt to make it part of their lives. The writing stage is an explorative exercise in trying to gain a better understanding of how gratitude improves and enhances their own lives. Seeing a child change their perspective with a gratitude journal is incredible.

Writing down the things that they are grateful for is the easiest way to get children to take that in-depth step and further explore this fulfilling emotion.

Begin with bullet points if you have to. Many children will not like the idea of having this extra bit of homework to do all the time. But you will notice a change in attitude once the words sink in. That is because writing inspires new thought, which begins the learning cycle all over again. When children are thinking, they are learning and growing.

Get your child to write down their thoughts and chat about these thoughts afterwards during family time.

Eventually, the message will sink in. Children want to be happy, and you have to show them that the most direct route to happiness is by gaining adequate understanding of the things they could appreciate in their lives.

Learning from the Gratitude Journal

Children learn a lot from their gratitude journals. They become more self-aware as they are able to go back and see what they have been grateful for over the past few weeks. It really calls them into the moment, something many children struggle with in this busy modern age with all its distractions.

GRATITUDE TIP Begin by jotting down three to five things that you are grateful for every day. One line is enough. Ask your child questions like, "What rocked your world today?" and, "What positive learning experience did you have today?" to get the thoughts flowing.

Exercise: Try This Journal Exercise with Your Child

What if your child responds with an *"Umm...I don't know!"* to the question *"What rocked your world today?"*

Then you can cue your child.

- If you are stuck, met with resistance, and are looking for a few good ideas, then remember the multisensory experiences that we discussed earlier in this chapter, and try asking:

- **What's the yummiest TASTE that hit your tongue today?**

- **What did you HEAR that put a smile on lips?**

- **What did you TOUCH today that felt _____?**

- **What did you SEE today that helped you to be happy?**

- **What did you SMELL that was delicious for your nose?**

You need to guide your child on how to keep a gratitude journal so they can experience the personal gains and learn from it. When they are feeling down, it can be an exceptional tool for reminding them about the things in life that matter. Appreciation during the development years should never be underestimated—it is an essential part of being a happy child and teenager.

As we have said, we always recommend parents keep their own gratitude journals. Remember that our children learn more from what we do, than what we say. When they see our positive modeling of working to enhance our own gratitude, our children will notice. When we use a gratitude journal, it shows solidarity and is more likely to keep our child persisting at the exercise for longer. With the right motivation, eventually our children will begin to mentally store-up the good things that happen in their days in anticipation for the evening's journal entry.

After a few weeks of journaling and reflection, your child's perspective should begin to change. You can look forward to them sleeping better, interacting with you and others better, having higher energy levels, and beginning to foster a sense of empowerment— something entitlement tends to rob them of. When gratitude becomes action, lives change.

As your child notices and appreciates gratitude more often, they will become happier as people, and the "bad" things that happen to them in a day will not seem as bad.

Exercise: Your First Journal Entry

Parents can make the process of keeping a gratitude journal a very fun experience for children. Young children will love to spend a few hours decorating a special book with family photos, pictures, art, and stickers to personalize it. Older children will often enjoy doing the same thing, although they may like to do it on their own.

GRATITUDE JOURNAL ENTRY: February 19, 2013	
Small:	I'm thankful for the chunky peanut butter on my toast this morning.
Medium:	I'm thankful for my cat, Roger.
Large:	I'm grateful that I have all my fingers and toes.

It is your job to guide this process as best you can, encouraging the act of writing at a set time every evening, preferably after homework if the child is old enough. You should also pay attention to the way that your child learns. If they are more visual, then have them add a drawing to each entry.

Once you've chosen your gratitude book, you will need to create the first entry. Spend some time chatting to your child about gratitude and what it means in your life. Show them an entry from your own gratitude journal, and encourage them to take five minutes out of their day to consider the positive things that happened.

Then have your child write a simple line about their day, split into three sections—small, medium, and large. Small things will constitute the little things that your child was grateful for today, medium things will be something with more impact, and these will lead up to the large things, which can include anything more significant in their lives that they are happy to experience or appreciate.

Focus on being as specific as you can, and tell your child to do the same, to get the most out of the journaling experience. Be consistent, and make sure to encourage your child to write in their journal regularly.

Points to Remember, Actions to Take

- **Key 1: You should keep a gratitude journal.** Aside from literally rewiring your brain, gratitude journaling influences your brain to develop an **attitude of gratitude**, drawing attention to the good things in your life. This promotes awareness, abundance, and appreciation during the day. Not only do you attract more kindness and gratitude, but you give more of it as well.

- **Key 2: Your child will benefit from keeping a journal.** Depending on the child's age, it is more beneficial to start with a single line and build your way up to longer, more in-depth entries that involve significant detail. Focusing on *people* and *experiences* is also important, as being grateful for *things* can be superficial and empty.

- **Key 3: Use the three-step process.** We have found that we absorb information best through a three-step process, which allows us to remember and be mindful of the subject on which we are focusing. By first thinking it, then speaking it, and then writing it down, we can change our behavior and gradually fill our lives with a positive outlook.

- **Key 4: Think about gratitude.** Gratitude is a practice, like any trait that you want to nurture. Intelligence is nothing without constant learning, just like gratitude is nothing without daily application in your life. It is no secret that keeping a gratitude journal promotes positive thinking.

- **Key 5: Speak about gratitude.** Verbalizing gratitude with others teaches children to be conscious of what goes on around them, including how other people feel about them. When children speak about gratitude, they start to express it more effectively.

- **Key 6: Children should write down their feelings.** Writing down the things that children are grateful for is the easiest way to get them to take that in-depth step and further explore this fulfilling emotion. Researchers at the University of California, Berkeley, have already proven that gratitude journaling works.

- **Key 7: Learn from your gratitude journal.** After a few weeks of journaling and reflection, your child's perspective should begin to change. Your child should sleep better, interact with you and others better, have higher energy levels, and begin to foster a sense of empowerment—something entitlement tends to rob them of. When gratitude becomes action, lives change.

 GRATITUDE ACTION Use the natural process outlined in this chapter to get your child to focus on what he/she appreciates in his/her life. By thinking, speaking, and then writing about these things, they will soon invite gratitude into their daily actions. Get that gratitude journal started!

7

What if Entitle-mania has Already Hit Our Household?

"If there is anything that we wish to change in the child, we should first examine it and see whether it is not something that could better be changed in ourselves."

[CARL JUNG]

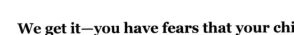

We get it—you have fears that your child is already entitled and that maybe it is too late. This is the reason we wrote the book. In this chapter, we are addressing children, teens, and young adults that have already had their behavior and attitude shaped by their environment. This is where ninja parenting comes into play. Armor up and keep reading: it is not too late.

Since instilling gratitude and kindness, and **busting entitlement**, is dependent on change on our part, we can have a positive effect on our children at any age, whether three or 23. Change is always possible, but of course, rarely easy. And your child may not welcome such change. We challenge you to do it anyway.

We have seen how the entitlement bug can infect your child, and spoken about how to crush it quickly. Now, let's look at the remedy when the **entitlement bug** has already taken hold.

Lasting, sustainable change, that allows your child to be resilient, independent, interpersonally connected, and successful, takes more than techniques or understanding. These are necessary, but not enough. If you think that your child is already infected by the **entitlement bug**, we first need to discuss what it will take to change your approach. Once you change, your child will follow.

Let's go over the necessary building blocks for the treatment of the **entitlement bug**. To build a remedy that lasts and provides protection from re-infection, you must:

- **Cultivate the belief that you can impact the entitlement that exists.**

- **Fully digest the knowledge and acceptance that entitlement is extremely negative and hurtful to your child—now and in the future.**

- **Focus on the long-term effects of the entitlement bug on your child, not on the short-term wants of your child, or the short-term comfort for yourself.**

- **Kick your own desires and wants to the extreme backburner (desire to be liked, desire to be the favorite, desire to be responsible for pleasing your child, desire to save or rescue your child from discomfort, etc.). This is not about judgment— we promise.**

- Have the ability to take some time to think about and to admit to yourself what you have done to unwittingly encourage entitlement. This will be the beginning of hatching a plan to bust the entitlement cycle.

- Build a tight plan to undo misguided efforts— reducing your child's upsets, protecting them from any uncomfortable experiences, etc. We have found that without a plan, we all tend to slide back easily into old patterns.

- Adjust your belief that emotional discomfort for your children is all bad. Without changing this belief, it will be very challenging for you to not step back in to rescue your child from their problems.

- Adjust any belief that you may be harboring that it is primarily your responsibility to make your child happy, comfortable, etc.

- Ask yourself whether life skills (cooking a meal, washing clothes, organizing belongings, changing their own light bulbs, managing their money, sewing on their own buttons, checking the oil in their car...) are in any way important to you. If so, now is the time to teach these things. These skills do not magically appear when a child turns 18.

- Determine if you have been over-prioritizing your child's studies, competitive dance, football, or any other single skill to the detriment of giving them the opportunity to develop responsibility socially within the family and for themselves (Junior does not do chores because he is working hard to get in to an Ivy League school...).

- **Be motivated to STOP MAKING EXCUSES for your child.**

  I know he's 15, but if I didn't tell him to brush his teeth, he wouldn't do it, and my dental bills are already too high.

  I'll help her with her project—just this one time—because if I don't, she will miss the deadline and she will lose marks.

  I guess I'll let him get away with yelling at me today— he's had a really hard day.

Notes from the Real Parenting Lab on the Ages and Stages of Entitlement Busting

It is not easy to know what to do to make changes, and what you might do varies according to how old your child is. Here are a few things to reflect on before we get down to the business of rehabilitating your environment and making a clean sweep of any **entitle-mania** that has taken hold in your family.

The Case of the Entitled Young Child (0–6)

If your child is four-and-a-half and is acting in ways that are lacking empathy, gratitude, and patience, you are fortunate—because at this age, kindness and gratitude are relatively easy to boost. With a well thought-out plan and consistency of approach among caregivers, entitlement busting is rapid and may be somewhat painful for parents but not as painful as it will be later on.

The Case of the Entitled Child (7–12)

This is the second most challenging age range to redirect entitlement that has already set in. It is not pretty to make changes with a child this age, but you want to make serious adjustments now. Once your children are teens and entitlement is a way of life, the blood, sweat, and tears involved in shifting are considerably greater.

At any of these ages, the key to success is choosing a path of action before you do or say anything new. With middle childhood—aged children, this is more crucial than with any other age, because their job at this developmental stage is to push back and gain independence, and their energy and egocentrism are both hitting new peaks naturally.

Before we show you how to construct a plan of **entitlement-busting** (*Appendix 2*), you must have the following:

1. **Backup: family or friends to support you.**

2. **Energy: do not take on entitlement-crushing with a feisty 11-year-old at the same time you start that huge new project at work.**

3. **Time: modeling, discussing, and being patient, are time-consuming and cannot be rushed.**

4. **Motivation, stubbornness, and a determination to stick to the plan, come what may.**

The Case of the Entitled Teen

You might want to sit down for this one. It should be no surprise that if you have an entitled teen whose behavior has been entrenched for over a decade, you are in for some trouble. Expect extreme pushback, anger, sullenness—maybe even some, *I hate yous*—and for things to get worse before they get better.

Start with small changes. Begin by targeting disrespectful tone, words, and body language. Firm limit setting might be called for—but we would like to see you take action without punishment if you can:

- **Look for natural consequences.** *I will not drive you to the concert, because I feel disrespected by the way I'm being treated. I don't believe that special privileges such as being driven to the concert today have been earned. You may walk or take transit if you would like.*

- **Look for special ways to occasionally recognize and encourage even the smallest act of kindness toward a family member.** *Hey, I really appreciate you tidying up the bathroom before your sister needs it to get ready for her dance recital. You know that's important to her. Can I take you out for a latte after your homework is done?*

The Case of the Entitled Young Adult

The English language is evolving in interesting ways to keep up with the concepts we are exploring in this book. *Helicopter Parenting, Hyper Parenting,* and *Invasive Parenting* did not exist in any dictionary anywhere 50 years ago. Nor did the terms that are now used to describe the young adult, and adult offspring, of this protective, entitlement-inducing parenting;

adultescent [ad-uhl-tes-uhnt]

noun combining "adult" and "adolescent"

- **Definition: a young adult or middle-aged person that has interests, traits, etc., that are usually associated with teenagers[28]**

Also sometimes called **kidult** [kid/adult] or **rejuvenile** [juvenile again], these fusions of the English language are generally used to describe the phenomenon of the entitled, child-like behavior of North America's teens and young adult offspring.

 REALITY BLAST Your adult child may not change for five years, 10 years, or ever—but YOU CAN.

No matter the age of your child, any positive change that you make is worth it. Even if your child is 32 and used to behaving in an entitled fashion within the family, when you stop your part of the cycle, the seeds of responsibility will be planted and may eventually grow. By the time your child has interacted with you and the universe in a negative pattern for decades, change is difficult. It's never impossible, but there is no quick fix.

---

28. Dictionary.com, dictionary.reference.com

What we hear about Entitled Adult Children

Frustrated parents come in to our office when they have not squashed entitlement early enough. The stories of a minor life setback (not getting a hoped-for job) resulting in an adult child moving back home, partying late at night, wandering around the house in pajamas, and living off their parents, are not infrequent.

Parents report paying off their adult children's credit cards after shopping sprees, paying for college tuition semester after semester for a child that fails class after class—even fighting battles with boyfriends or girlfriends on their behalf.

They generally recount these events with frustration, guilt, and—most noteworthy to us—presenting a version of reality where they had no choice but to rescue their child. They believe that their child could not handle the financial strain, emotional heartache, or other significant life challenges.

Of course, we all know there are choices—even the parents who face these situations know that they have a choice. Most of these parents have lost perspective and no longer trust themselves to make good decisions.

The Reality of the 'Adultescent' Phenomenon

There are a radically increasing number of young adults that still live at home. Modern polling trends measured by Harris Interactive and The National Endowment for Financial Education in conjunction with Forbes.com[29], revealed that some 23 per cent of non-student adults (aged 18–39) live with their parents, with males dominating this statistic.

---

29. Would-Be Empty Nesters Grapple With Adult Child at Home – Tips For Parents With Adult Children at Home, National Endowment For Financial Education, http://www.nefe.org/press-room/news/living-with-adult-children-at-home.aspx.

Although this is only a poll (not a peer reviewed study) if the results are representative, in the U.S. alone, close to 14 million adult children are struggling to leave their home of origin. We are no longer living with a minor problem when it comes to entitled adult children.

What about Us Parents?

If you have an adult child who is clearly behaving in entitled ways and has regularly sported a "me, me, me" attitude over the past 20 plus years, you have likely been giving way more than you received. You are probably weary of being underappreciated, treated poorly, and unvalued. And you are doubtlessly feeling ineffective. If any of this rings true for you, this entitlement cycle has been destructive for both your self-esteem and your **parent-esteem**[30].

Your emotional health at some point has likely taken a hit, expressed through unwanted anger attacks, spikes of worry, or deep sadness over the situation. And your relationships with your child(ren), your partner or spouse, and probably with your extended family and friends, have been negatively affected. If your child is in his/her 20s and still depending on you to save him or her financially, emotionally, or otherwise, it is high time to start thinking about **you**.

Quite aside from reading this book, it is time for some soul-searching. Be open to support from psychotherapy pep talks from no-nonsense friends — anything that will help you stay strong, assertive, and focused on standing up for yourself as you back away from entitlement-encouraging behavior.

---

30. We define parent-esteem as the sense or belief that our parenting effort and ability is adequate or good enough for our child(ren).

At the very least, you will be engaging in excellent self-care modeling for your child, even if they do not like or appreciate your changes or, worse, respond with angry threats to never call, visit, or talk to you again, if you cut him or her off.

Rehab for Entitlement-Enhancing Parents

Step I: The Issue of Expectations

Let's take a more specific look at what you *can* do.

Below is a rating scale asking you to think about the expectations you have coached, modeled, or encouraged in your children.

Expectations are different from hopes. Expectations are massive precursors for entitlement growth. When our child does not accept they might not get what they want, or that they might have to cope with disappointment, or use their resilience skills, this is a problem.

Throughout this next exercise, keep in mind to what degree you expect these things for yourself. Rate **yourself** to what degree you have coached your child—purposefully or accidentally—to expect:

Expectation-O-Meter

	Rarely	Frequently	Never
A "yes" in response to their requests			
To have their needs regularly met by others			
To receive what they want			
Immediate gratification			
Special or exceptional treatment			
To be entertained or stimulated at all times			
That life has to be happy or in their favor			

If you checked anything in the category of "rarely" or "frequently", it is time to rehabilitate your focus. Here's how:

- **Cue your children verbally:**

    "This may or may not work out..."

    "What's your plan to have a good day even if things don't work out?"

    "How are you going to be okay even if you have to wait for what you want?"

- **Positive modeling behavior:**

  Show that you never expect any of the above for yourself, and be very specific about the difference between having expectations and goals, wishes, and desires.

  Show that you can cope when any of the above does not work out for you, with calm facial expressions, relaxed body posture, resilient self-talk: "It'll be okay"; "I can handle this."

Step II: Taking One Last Look at Your Hesitance to Say "No"

We should all be able to say "no" within the context of a healthy relationship without any feelings of guilt, shame, remorse, or discomfort. Children who have become entitled are quick to key into these emotions to pressure their parents into giving them what they want.

To follow up on our earlier discussion, if your family is turning out children with entitled attitudes and behavior, we need to take a closer look at how you use — or do not use—the word "no".

There are a number of ways you should not use the word "no". From a young age, children can associate "no" with negative feelings, and many of them cannot stand to hear it, which is one of the reasons that it can invoke such negative behavior.

 GRATITUDE TIP Learn to say "no" with a caring demeanor (caring does not mean apologetic) so that your child learns it is okay to hear the word, and it is not the end of the world if they cannot have something.

NO Without the Anger

Certainly, disrespect from our children can be annoying. But while unreasonable demands, whining and lack of gratitude easily provoke irritation and anger, angry reactions from us do not help.

When we say "no" with anger, our children frequently react with anger back. And, if the same demands or behavior has been allowed unchecked in the past, they will also be confused about why you are angry. When they have previously had their needs met when acting in an entitled fashion, your unexpected anger and frustration could be interpreted as not being about their unacceptable demands, but about your anger management problem. This could make them:

- **Scared of you**
- **Back away from you emotionally**
- **Possibly angry enough to want to hit or hurt you in some way**

Remember: Anger never teaches gratitude and never teaches kindness.

- **Entitlement-Crushing Script #1:**

  "Do what you need to do first, and what you want to do, second."

- **Entitlement-Crushing Script #2:**

  "Talk with disrespect and the answer is NO."

- **Entitlement-Crushing Script #3:**

  "Ask me twice and the answer is NO. Ask me three times and the answer is NO for today, tomorrow, and the next day."

Step III: The Food, Shelter, Clothing Rule (FSCR)

You recognize that your family is affected by a cycle of entitlement, and now it's time to take a look at how your actions work to keep the cycle alive.

Parents need structure to help them make decisions about when to give and how much to assist, encourage, or provide support for their child. We find that during stressful times, when a parent is tired or otherwise not at their best, decisions that could reinforce entitlement tend to happen more frequently.

Entitled children will say nearly anything to get what they want—especially if they do not value compassion and appreciation.

Consider the following responses:

	Yes	No	Rarely
Comparitive: *But Johnny has this gaming system / gets to go to the sleepover...* Sound familiar? Of course it does. All children try this technique at some point. Does this argument influence you?			
Indebtedness: *But I cleaned my room and swept the yard! You owe me.* Are you influenced by this?			
Flattery: *You're so amazing, Mom. I drew you this awesome picture, and it took me three hours. Can I have X?* Oooh, this one is tempting—does it catch you?			
Empty promises: *I swear I will do better at school from now on if you get me X.* We have spoken about pre-payment to our kids in previous chapters. Are you vulnerable here?			

We are sure that you have heard variations of these negotiations while dealing with your own children—whether entitlement is a raging problem in your family or one that only occasionally raises its nasty head.

If you know that any or all of these situations influence your decision-making, it's okay, you're not alone. We suggest using strategies to buffer your vulnerability and help empower you to change. Use whatever reminder strategies that already work for you: Post-it notes on the side of your computer or on the bathroom mirror, setting a reminder on your phone, or anything else you know will prompt you to stand firm.

Also, consider adopting our *Food, Shelter, and Clothing Rule* (FSCR) to help you to stay aware of needs versus wants.

The FSCR states that parents are responsible for providing the necessities of life: food, a place to live, and clothing. Anything beyond these are unessential bonuses which, from a child's perspective, we could think about as a want, rather than a need.

It is a given that parents have a responsibility to provide the basics of the FSCR to their children, and that it is reasonable, that along with the expectation of giving to our children, to also expect appreciation from our children as they receive these basics. Any specific request, desire or demand, is technically outside the FSCR. Responding to our child's refusal to eat one brand of peanut butter over another is not following the FSCR. Considering a relocation of the family home because of a teen's assertion that the family needs to move closer to the beach is not following the FSCR. Shopping for a hard-to-find brand of sneaker for weeks because our child insists that Brand X is the only sneaker that is acceptable to wear, is not following the FSCR.

Consider whether the Food, Shelter, Clothing Rule makes sense for you. We are not suggesting you stick rigidly to it all days and in all ways. We fully support that the more a child or teen gives, the more they receive. The concept of the **Family Currency** is front and centre here. Mostly the FSCR can help you when you are feeling vulnerable, unsure, or when you find yourself waffling about your bottom line. Following the FSCR will give you a frame of reference to ensure that anything your child wants must be earned or requested in a kind and reasonable, non-manipulative way.

If you like the sound of the FSCR, feel free to talk to your children about it, but you do not need to tell them the rule. And remember: if you tell them you are going to institute the FSCR and you do not, it becomes an empty guideline which may backfire in terms of your overall gratitude/ kindness-boosting program.

If you do not want to get tangled up in empty promises, just use it as an internal mental filter through which you make decisions about what you will give and when, and as a discussion point with anyone you co-parent with (your nanny, your mother, your spouse).

FSCR Check In

For example:

- **SITUATION:** Your 14-year-old daughter Justine has asked to go to a sleepover at her friend's house.

  - **Filter 1:**

    Does her request meet the **FSCR**? No. This is a want, not a need.

  - **Filter 2:**

    Has she asked in a polite way? Yes, she asked in a very polite way.

  - **Filter 3:**

    Has she earned this privilege? Yes, she has been very diligent with keeping to the **Family Currency** *(see Chapter 3)* of keeping her room clean, helping out in the kitchen without being asked, and feeding the cat.

- **YOUR ANSWER: Yes**

GRATITUDE TIP Support your child to understand that hearing YES is a special treat with non-necessary advantages or privileges.

This practice works best when you start with your young child.

Step IV: The Issue of the Exception (which should not be an exception)

When do you give your child a free pass to ignore the kindness and gratitude rules in your family?

We work with many families whose children are facing chronic medical conditions (diabetes, renal disorder, Crohn's, chronic pain...), injury, or severe psychological symptoms (anxiety disorders, depression). Parents tell us that they have a very difficult time holding their children to the typical standards of behavior, attitude, and responsibility when their children are unwell.

When a child's medical or psychological condition is fragile for some time, it can be easy to unwittingly encourage entitlement. But, once the pattern is established, it is even more difficult to extinguish than it is for healthy children. We naturally tend to second guess ourselves about pushing sick children too much. Even after children recover, many families of previously sick children, keep reinforcing the overprotective precedent set when the child was unwell.

When our children are fragile, either physically or mentally, our normal reaction is to protect and rescue. That is fair and understandable. But, depending on the level of illness our child is facing, we still want to have a plan in place to keep at least a minimum level of respectful communication, expression of appreciation/gratitude, and contribution to the family. It is obviously not reasonable to have your child that just broke his leg clean out the dishwasher half-an-hour after his cast was set. It is reasonable to set the tone for him to express gratitude for a snack or a backrub however. It is also not reasonable to drop or flex your standards and family values for a child with a cold. Allowing a child to speak to you with a disrespectful or demanding tone is not reasonable in almost any circumstance. Even a child with laryngitis can use sign language to say "thank you."

It is important to adjust your expectations according to the level of your child's illness, but do not reduce your expectations to zero, or allow compassion to trigger excuses that feed the cycle of entitlement.

Take stock of the situations in which you have given your child—no matter what their age(s)—a free pass of some sort. Ask yourself whether you adjusted expectations to an acceptable level or to zero (or too low) using the following chart:

Parenting Exception-O-Meter

Situation	Acceptable Adjustment of Expectations	Expectations Too Low
Physical illness		
Emotional illness/ upset		
Failure at school		
Failure at extra-curriculars		
Social upsets		
Divorce		
Death in the family		
Other:		
Other:		

We invite you to reflect on any tendency to adjust expectations for your children too easily, and to notice when you tend to over-adjust or lower your standards. Text yourself a reminder, or use old school sticky notes to help you stay strong when faced with such a situation. **You can do this!**

Step V: Make a Plan

If you have made it this far, and you know you want to make a sustainable lasting change to your family environment, first of all: Great news!

Secondly, remember that one of the keys to success with changes of this magnitude is consistency. A consistent approach and plan is more effective and easier for parents and children alike. Hopefully, as you have been working your way through the book, you have had many ideas about how you could make a difference, and where you would like to make positive changes first.

We caution you to hold off on changes until you are truly ready—we will be going into this more in Chapter 8. If you begin **entitlement-crushing** without the following strategies in place, your success will be lower, and lasting change will be much more difficult to achieve:

- **A philosophical shift**
- **A clear vision of what you need to change about yourself**
- **Deciding on exactly what you are seeking to improve about your family culture in general, and your child's attitude and behavior**
- **All the techniques you are going to use to achieve your goals**

Use the template provided in Appendix 2 to construct your plan. Once you are happy with it, copy it, share it with your friends and family, and post it all around your home to help keep yourself on track. With a good solid plan, you can reach your goals.

Rehab for Entitlement-Enhancing Others

Once you have your plan ready, you may determine that you are not the only person who has unwittingly enhanced entitlement in your home. It is time to get serious with all your child's influential caregivers.

You may find your efforts undermined by your extended family, the babysitter/daycare/nanny, or your ex-wife or husband, but remember: the only person's behavior that you have full control over is your own. Keep to your plan and do everything you can on your own.

Hopefully, you have some degree of communication and cooperation with others who have influence with your child. Do what you can to share your plan: photocopy the pages from this book that inspire you the most, share the exercise pages you have completed, and demonstrate through positive modeling what you are trying to do to make the changes you feel are important.

Do your best to be firm, assertive, and share all that you know about the good that can come from maximizing gratitude and kindness. Hopefully, the care and compassion from the other adults in your child's life will shine through to inspire change that parallels your own.

It may be frustrating, but even if you slowly inch towards your goal, your children and family will be in better shape than they were before.

8

Believe in Gratitude and Your Kids Will Too

"When you believe in a thing, believe in it all the way, implicitly and unquestionable."

[WALT DISNEY]

These gratitude and kindness strategies come from years of extensive clinical research, and we have seen their success rates among parents that have approached us for help. We have found that, if you fully believe in gratitude, so will your children. A blast of daily gratitude by speaking it and doing it will combat any child's tendency to be entitled.

The good news is that entitlement is a learned behavior, which means that it can be unlearned and replaced by positive ways of behaving in a loving family and community.

Notes from the Real Parenting Lab on Changing Behaviors

One family we worked with really affirmed for us the power of practicing gratitude-boosting actions. They came to us reporting that their preteen children were acting out in disrespectful, self-centered ways. Once we began to understand the family dynamics, it became clear that the entitled behavior the children displayed mirrored the parents' behavior towards one another.

The parents admitted to screaming matches with verbal attacks, insults, constant belittling of each other. The children described feeling so angry about their parents' behavior that without realizing it, they would make hostile demands and talk and act in disrespectful ways themselves. It is no wonder the parents came to us so discouraged and saying their children would never back down.

Once we began to help them connect their thoughts, feelings, and behavior, the parents realized they were modeling the opposite of kindness, care, and empathy. They also became aware that their behavior towards each other was completely devoid of gratitude. At this point, we realized that movement toward change became a possibility.

We did many things with this family, from gratitude letters to intensive coaching on how to implement gratitude dialogue *(see Appendix 3 on page 181)* successfully. The gratitude dialogue was profound as they described their efforts toward mindful appreciation of each other. It took months of diligent daily action on everyone's part, but eventually the contempt began to melt away.

The children began to understand that the root of their demanding behavior was actually to have more family harmony. When we last met with the family, they reported more respectful interactions and that they were feeling more connected with each other.

Three Things We Know about Changing Behaviors

Before we can summarize and send you off, we need to put our academic hats back on to remind you of some of what we know about change. We psychologists have been in the business of change since the inception of our field, and we want to make sure that you make use of our colleagues' research, in addition to our own clinical experience, about how best to make sustainable changes.

ONE.

The first level of knowledge about change focuses on our thought process. Let's talk about the Einstellung Effect,[31] which looks at people's tendency to persist with the same approach to solving a problem whether or not the approach is effective. Yes: we all do this. The old adage of "try, try, try again" only succeeds if we do something different. Each time we say the same thing to our kids—"Stop whining to get me to say "yes","—and then we go ahead and give them what they want, we are repeating ourselves ineffectively, and causing no change in our behavior or that of our children.

The factors that help us to change our problem-solving strategy are two-fold[32]:

---

31. Luchins, A.S. (1940). Mechanization in problem solving: The effect of einstellung, *Psychological Monographs, 54,* 248.

32. Ericsson, K.A., Simon, H.A. (1984). *Protocol Analysis: Verbal Reports as Data.* Cambridge, MA: MIT.

1. **When we perceive that family dynamics are changing from an old way of being to a new way, a family might state:**

Old way of being	New way of being
Our home used to be an Entitlement-Encouraging home that functioned from the belief that: • more is always better, and • that if we could afford it, there was no reason to say "no" to our children.	Our home is a Gratitude-Encouraging home that functions from the belief that: • needs are differentiated from wants, and • that "no" (at the right times, with the right balance, and with love and support) is better for our children than saying "yes" too often.

2. **Additionally, we see the old problem itself from a new perspective, or see the challenge as a different or new challenge.**

   • **Example:** *Nicole finds her teen daughter is self-centred*

Old Perspective	New Perspective
• My child is selfish because she does not express gratitude when I do special favors for her and just demands more favors every day. • I need to make her less selfish. • I should ask her therapist to work on making her less selfish.	• My child needs structure, examples, and cues to show her gratitude appropriately. • I need to help my child to understand empathy for others and empathy for me. • I need to change my behavior so that I avoid rewarding or punishing demanding statements, and only reward a kind tone of voice and reasonable requests.

In the above example, the problem of the ungrateful, demanding child is the same, but under the Old Perspective it is expressed in a way that focuses on a negative label of the child. It does not appreciate the impact that the parent has on the child's behavior and seeks solutions which are not proven to work, such as "making a child be different", or looking to solutions outside the home as the primary agent of change.

In the New Perspective, we can see that the challenge is broken down into specific elements that are causing the demanding behavior and lack of appreciation in the child. We can see that when we look at all the elements of the problem (i.e., the lack of understanding of the child, the lack of modeling in the home, the behavior of the parent that keeps the problem going), the original problem is no longer so complex and is fixable.

What we know, is that we will tend to continue to parent in the same way that we always have, unless we make a conscious effort to do and see things differently.

Imagine a corporate executive looking at last year's company accounts and realizing that, in order to improve in the next fiscal year, some outdated operations must be rethought. Or a schoolteacher recognizing that this year's curriculum or class projects need to be adapted to a changing social environment to keep them relevant to the kids in the class.

Could your approach be reasonably conceptualized as an era that has passed, a parenting style that has become extinct, or a chapter that has ended? We encourage you to look at the current problems in your household environment —the challenges with your child's attitude, behavior, or emotions, and your own challenges—from a different perspective. Can you switch up what you do and create a new set of solutions that make more positive impact?

TWO.

The second level of knowledge about change focuses on the *emotional* variables that both get change going and maintain change. What we know is: both strong **negative emotion** and **optimism** are key emotional elements in successful change.

Whether you believe the popular sayings that sometimes people need to "hit rock bottom" or that there is "no pain, no gain" in relation to doing something new, we do know that more change happens when we experience strong negative emotion.[33]

Our behavior changes are more efficient when we experience a spike in upset, anger, distress, or another emotional state. In business, a team's productivity will increase before a deadline. A serious diagnosis (heart disease or Type II diabetes) can prompt radical, lifestyle changes.

For your family, we would like you to find motivation for change through picturing the happiness and peace you will experience once you have made all the switches and taken all the necessary actions to increase gratitude and kindness in your home. On the other hand, if your motivation is waning or your consistency is wobbly, consider what you may need to do to strengthen your determination to change. We do not want you to think about how angry you were the last time your 15-year-old showed you a sassy attitude, videotape your 8-year-old's temper tantrum to watch again and again, or to reread the self-centered birthday wish-list your 12-year-old wrote. We want you to take a look at the seeds that you have been planting that will grow into adult entitlement, or the weeds that are blocking out your child's ability to be kind, empathic adults. If nothing else will kick-start a change in your parenting and modeling, then envisage:

---

33. Isen, A. (1984). *Toward understanding the role of affect in cognition*. In P. Wyer & T. Srull (Eds.) Handbook of social cognition. Vol. 3. 179-236. Hillsdale, NJ.: Earlbaum.

- **The social problems**
- **The self-esteem problems**
- **The career problems**
- **The parenting problems when your children will face when they themselves become parents**

that will occur if your child grows up to be selfish and all about "me, me, me, more, more, more". We don't want you to worry yourself into a state of panic, but the reality is, everything you do now leads to the success or failure of your children. Kids do not just grow out of entitlement. They need our help, and they need it now.

Okay—enough doom and gloom: what about optimism? How many times during the reading of this book have you thought to yourself, "My kids will never go for that"; "I don't think I have the strength to do that", or, "This will never work"? Come on—be honest.

We know the techniques we talk about in this book work. If you need to read and reread it, look into the sources that we quote, make a PLAN, make a new PLAN, and then make another before your begin the change process, that is great: do it. You need to gather up an attitude and an approach that is filled with optimism. We know that change happens better when there is optimism for success[34]—and when the optimism is not blind. *Gee, if I just wish really hard for grateful kids, turn in a circle, and do a fancy dance, I bet my wish will come true!* Optimism should be based on good, solid evidence, planning, goal-setting, and a measured and consistent course of action and belief in change.

---

34. Tushman, M., & Romanelli, E. (1985). *Organizational evolution: A metamorphosis model of convergence and reorientation.* In L.L. Cummings and B. M. Straw (Eds). Research in organization behavior, Vol 7: 171-222 Geenwich, CT: JAI Press.

THREE.

The third level of understanding that we have about change has to do with *process*, or rather, *how* the change takes place. The elements of this section make good common sense, but we want you to know that there is also some solid research behind what we are saying as well.

Multi-level approaches to problems yield better long-term change[35]. Change of language, tone, AND parenting techniques—not just long-winded lectures on the topic of gratitude— and consistency of the interventions lead to long-term change[36] The following examples are a good place to begin:

- **Discussing gratitude every week over a number of years**

- **Living by the needs-over-wants philosophy through the developmental levels of your children**

- **Consistent engagement in community volunteer work**

A weekend-long extravaganza of action and communication—although a good start—is not going to do it.

A group of our colleagues grabbed our attention with their research on buy-in to change. Dodge[37] and colleagues have been working on how motivation, or buy-in to change differs for some—based on how much choice the individual has regarding what to change first. From our perspective, we have found this to be the case with many children.

---

35. Prochaska, J. O. and Velicer, W. F. (1997). The transtheoretical model of behavior change. *American Journal of Health Promotion, 12,* 38–48.

36. Ory, M.G., Jordan, P.J., & Bazzarre, T. (2002). The behavior change consortium: Setting the stage for a new century of health behavior-change research. *Health Education Research, 17,* 500-511.

37. Dodge, J. A., Janz, N. K. and Clark, N. M. (2002). The evolution of an innovative heart disease management program for older women: integrating quantitative and qualitative methods in practice. *Health Promotion Practice, 3,* 30–42.

Children seem to have a higher cooperation level with change (whether it is a family recycling program, exercise program, or clean-up schedule) when the parents set the goals and standards but the children have a choice in how or when the goals and standards are put in to play.

So, while working on our gratitude and kindness-boosting program, once you have decided what should be worked on first, be sure to include input from your children into your plan *(Appendix 2)*.

For example, if your plan were to encompass the following, ask your child(ren) to vote on where they would like the family's focus to begin:

- **Eye rolling**
- **Poor language**
- **Whining**
- **Begging after Mom/Dad has already said "no"**
- **Differentiating between wants and needs**

If you and your family are game to try this, depending on the age and enthusiasm of your child, go ahead and make up a contract that has all the bells and whistles: signatures, stamps, family coat of arms, etc., to make it official. Remember, though, parents hold the responsibility to monitor and follow through with consequences if the contract is broken.

A Model of Change

And finally, we need to make comment on our motivation for change for, of course, without motivation, nothing will change in any of our homes. Prochaska and colleagues[38] have researched and written extensively on health-encouraging behavior change. They began with positive change for addictive behaviors, before moving onto diet, exercise and other health and life-enhancing actions. We have adapted their model, called the Transtheoretical Model of Change, to create change-enhancing behaviors for the family. We will not spend a lot of time going through the details of our Family Change Model (FCM) here, but will rough in the concepts for you to consider. Then, if you like working with structure and would like to explore the model more, please do so in *Appendix 1 (page 165)* as you develop your plan.

There are generally five stages to change theories. In our experience, all five stages need to be worked through, with graduation to the next stage, only happening after successful completion of the previous stage.

The five stages are:

1. **The Unwilling** Where we sit when we have no conscious intention of change. Perhaps we are not aware of what it does to our children to say "yes" too often, for example. Or we have tried previously, failed, and are feeling defeated ("Entitlement is too ingrained in our family—I can't fight it"). We know we are towards the end of this stage when we begin to get a sense that our behavior is standing in the way of our goals—"Maybe the way I act could have something to do with the way with my children behave."

---

38. Prochaska, J.O., DiClemente, C.C., & Norcross, J.C. (1992). In search of how people change: Applications to addictive behaviors. *American Psychologist, 47*, 1102-14.

2. **The Waffler** We are becoming aware that our behavior is part of the problem, but still we have made no commitment to action. We suspect than anyone that picks up this book is at least at this stage. Possibly the length of time or effort required are standing in the way of commitment. One way to get past this lack of action is to do a pros/cons list and to work through whether the change is worth it to you. Months and months can be spent in this stage waffling back and forth, before readiness to move to stage three is attained.

3. **The Ignited** When we know change is necessary and we believe we can change. We have already made some initial changes: maybe we have said "no" a few more times recently and have observed our children's reactions; or we have not consented to a few requests that were delivered with poor attitude or disrespect. This is where you want to start anticipating obstacles and preparing for them: Great Aunt Ethel is arriving and always brings $80 worth of candy and a suitcase full of wants instead of needs. What to do to head off Ethel? The key to this stage is constructing a plan. Please take a look at *Appendix 2 (page 169)* for ideas on effectively building your plan.

4. **The Dynamo** Change is under way at this stage. Key success points are met when we stay clear about our motivation: Why is gratitude and kindness important to you? What are the values *(Chapter 1)* you are working on? Valuable actions at this point include:

   - **Reviewing motivation and goals on a daily basis.**
   - **Positive self-talk ("I can do this, I can do this…").**
   - **Support: hang out with other parents who believe boundaries are important.**

5. **The Curator** Usually considered to be achieved when positive change has been in play for approximately five to six months. The focus is on planning for pitfalls and weak spots, such as:

   - **Christmas/holiday gift-giving, birthdays, high school graduation, etc.**
   - **When there are friendships or other social situations that might stand in the way of your goals—play dates with extremely entitled children or those with indulgent parents.**

Keeping the Cycle Going
– Even When No One Is Looking

Gratitude and kindness come from time investment and sincerity. You cannot pretend to adopt an attitude of gratitude and then behave in a contradictory way when your children are not around. True change is required, and that starts from within you.

This is a message to communicate to your children as well. In the beginning, they will be "going along" with gratitude journals and letters and chores—but most will expect the change to end at some point and to revert back to old entitlement patterns.

You cannot allow this to happen. There are two main assets that you have to invest in if you want the gratitude cycle to really take hold in your home:

1. **Action/Participation** You and your other parenting teammate(s) —spouse, mother-in-law, nanny—must **sincerely participate** in this (it does not work if only one care-giver does so).

2. **Time / Effort** As a parenting team, you must be willing to **dedicate time and effort** to helping your children in a nurturing way.

GRATITUDE TIP It is never too late to raise your children as grateful and kind individuals. Evidence suggests that these individuals will be the vessels for social change in the future.

9 Fun Ways to Teach Empathy

There are so many great ways to inspire your children to cultivate empathy. We suggest trying one of these exercises every day.

1. **Teach them to be curious about other children.** Very empathetic people are naturally curious about other people. Your child can cultivate empathy by asking meaningful questions. Provide your child with a repertoire of questions that they could ask someone that they are getting to know, such as: "What parts of your vacation did you enjoy the most?" "Why?" or, "How would your friends describe you when you're on the playground?"

2. **Teach children to challenge what they know.** Assumptions about other people are just assumptions—they have no basis in fact. Inspire your children to learn about others using facts and personal experience to make better judgments.

3. **Wear someone else's shoes.** Young children will love the literal translation of this one! Simply give them a pair of mom or dad's shoes to wear and ask them to perform a task that mom or dad does every evening. It will not be easy, and the lesson is clear.

4. **Listen with your ears, eyes, and body.** When your children share something that is important to them, make sure you take some time to drop everything, give direct eye contact, and show through your body language that you really care about what they are saying.

5. **Volunteer.** It can help to have a real volunteer experience. For example, go down to the local park or beach and clean up trash while discussing how you will help save the birds in the area from eating unsafe things.

6. **Encourage the imagination.** When reading your children a book, stop and ask them to talk about the characters, describing how they could be feeling about their situation.

7. **Do a fun run.** A charity fun run is a great experience for young children looking to learn empathy. Learn about the cause, and talk about the people or animals they will be helping. Help them collect donations for every mile they run. This is how they can actively contribute to a worthy cause.

8. **Switch sides.** When siblings get in an argument, play a game called "switch sides", where they each have to take on the other's argument and role play it.

9. **Play "I Spy Emotions".** When you are taking a leisurely drive somewhere, point out different things along the way and ask your children to describe the emotions generated by what they see.

The Wisdom of Age: Growing Up Thankful

With age comes wisdom is an old saying that still rings true for parents, especially when they recognize the long-term benefits of daily gratitude in their children. Scientific research has also shown us that there are dozens of benefits that you will begin to experience once gratitude becomes a daily habit in your family's life.

- **Emotional needs:** being more relaxed, feeling good, more resilient, less envious, and able to recall happy memories.

- **Social needs:** having more real friends, healthier marriages, deeper relationships, and being kinder to others.

- **Career needs:** better management, goal achievement, improved networking, improved decision-making, and increased productivity.

- **Health needs:** improved sleep, less illness, more exercise, increased energy, and longevity.

- **Personality needs:** less materialistic, less self-obsessed, increased self-esteem, more spiritual, and more optimism all lead to one thing, happiness!

Points to Remember, Actions to Take

- **Key 1: Believe in gratitude.** We have found if you fully believe in gratitude, so will your children. A blast of daily gratitude by *speaking it* and *doing it* will combat any child's tendency to be entitled.

- **Key 2: Dedicate yourself to real change.** Lasting change happens when we shift our thoughts and involve our emotions, and when our actions involve multiple levels of change

- **Key 3: Follow the Family Change Model.** Our FCM leads you through how to assess your readiness for change, and then teaches you how to move forward towards actions that bring about sustainable change.

- **Key 4: Teaching empathy can be fun!** The process can be pleasurable, and is most powerful when all family members experience the exercises.

- **Key 5: Practice gratitude every day.** Even in small acts of kindness, there are big rewards. Kindness activates the seed of gratitude, and gratitude nurtures acts of kindness.

- **Key 6: Raise your children to be grateful.** The daily practice of gratitude is a way to focus on what we give rather than what we receive. We hope that after you have read this book, you will implement these very real changes by taking action in your life towards more grateful living. Your children will follow your lead.

TAKE ACTION! Make some time in the evening when your whole family is home to create a gratitude chart. This chart will help you stick to the routines and rules that you need to put in place in order to make gratitude a daily family habit.

Conclusion

*"Kindness is a language which the deaf can hear
and the blind can see."*

[MARK TWAIN]

We are always advising parents to pick their battles. Yet **entitlement-busting** and **gratitude-enhancing** are battles we hope you are compelled to pick now that you have read our book.

Some would say **ninja parenting** is required to prevent the **entitlement bug** from spreading any further. But parents: this battle is worthwhile!

Kindness and gratitude can be powerful allies in life to form strong social connections and to feel happier and physically healthier. As a parent, it is your responsibility to be the spark that lights the fires of change in your home. With a proper understanding of gratitude comes a happier, healthier outlook on life.

We have helped children of all ages open their hearts to kindness and gratitude with the essential tips inside this book. In order to feel good, you must be able to connect it to outward actions.

So we hope that when you put this book down, you will implement these very real changes.

The daily practice of gratitude is a way to focus on what we give, rather than what we receive. This helps us to experience life more fully. This is truly a gift that we can provide to our children, families, and communities.

Appendix 1 - How Ready Am I to Change?

Family Change Model

What I do to encourage kindness and gratitude and crush entitlement in my home.

Circle the statements that are true for you and your family

UNWILLING STAGE	What I can do:
• I feel confident that entitlement is not a problem for us • There are few parent behaviors that I think I should or could change to encourage kindness/gratitude with my child(ren)	• Review the Family Values Checklist (p. 19), and speak with family/friends about whether your parenting lines up with your values **Other ideas to keep me moving forward:**

WAFFLER STAGE	What I can do:
• I am beginning to see that there are things I have done that may have encouraged my child(ren) to act selfishly or to believe that they are deserving of things that they do not earn	Make a pros/cons list about: • keeping your behavior the same versus changing it to be even more actively encouraging of kindness and gratitude • your child(ren)'s level of entitlement staying the same, versus a reduction in entitlement (short and long term) **Other ideas to keep me moving forward:**
IGNITED STAGE	**What I can do:**
• I am working on some TO DO lists for myself to help keep me on track with following through on rules with my children • I have been making notes in this book and for myself with each situation that I notice my child(ren) acting entitled • I have been noticing the situations where it is hard for me to say NO	• Compete the PLAN in Appendix 2 (p. 169). • Speak with family members about their involvement in the PLAN • Look out for potential obstacles to following through on the PLAN • Help yourself to successfully implement the PLAN through reminders on your phones, sticky notes, visual charts in the kitchen, on your computer, in your car, etc. **Other ideas to keep me moving forward:**

DYNAMO STAGE	What I can do:
• We have had some family discussions and have made some changes with rules ("ask twice and the answer is no"; "requests made with whining or disrespect always receive a no") • We have a commitment to do some family volunteer work at the homeless shelter over the holidays	• Post and regularly review your Family Values Checklist to stay focused on your goals. • Engage in positive stress management for yourself • Surround yourself with family and friends that can support you when follow-through with your PLAN becomes difficult **Other ideas to keep me moving forward:**
CURATOR STAGE	**What I can do:**
• For the past six months or more we have been quite consistent with weekly gratitude sharing before bed • We have done a better job with all showing our appreciation for each other— at least every second day for the past six months	• Regularly noticing the positive steps forward with your behavior • Regularly noticing the increases in gratitude and kindness of your children, however small • Continuing to make plans that can be practiced on a long-term basis • Adjusting the PLAN as your child(ren) get older and their needs change **Other ideas to keep me moving forward:**

Appendix 2 - The PLAN

To Enhance Gratitude and Kindness and Crush Entitlement

Please take a look at all your notes in the margins and your answers in Chapters 1–8, and take your time, over a number of days or weeks, to fill in the details of your PLAN.

Part I: Pre-planning the PLAN

Here are the **Top Six Family Values** that are important to me/us right now:

1.	
2.	
3.	
4.	
5.	
6.	

Here are the **Top Six Gratitude Benefits** that are important to me/us right now:

1.	
2.	
3.	
4.	
5.	
6.	

Here are the **Top Six Misguided Efforts** that are important to me/us to change right now:

1.	
2.	
3.	
4.	
5.	
6.	

Here are the **Top Six Entitlement Qualities** I see in my home that I/we want to focus on crushing:

1.	
2.	
3.	
4.	
5.	
6.	

Part II: Planning the PLAN

Considering your answers to all your Top Sixes and considering all you have read in Chapters 1–8, let's problem solve step-by-step how you want to implement your goals and knowledge into positive action:

Entitled behavior / attitude to crush	
1.	
2.	
3.	
4.	
5.	
6.	

Grateful/Kind goal behavior/attitude to replace entitled behavior/attitude	
1.	
2.	
3.	
4.	
5.	
6.	
Actions I can take to model positive behavior/attitude	
1.	
2.	
3.	
4.	
5.	
6.	

Words I can speak to encourage positive behavior/attitude (why it is important to our family, etc.)	
1.	
2.	
3.	
4.	
5.	
6.	
Rules or structure I can put in place to further encourage positive behavior /attitude	
1.	
2.	
3.	
4.	
5.	
6.	

	How I can give recognition and encouraging feedback for small, positive steps toward the goal
1.	
2.	
3.	
4.	
5.	
6.	

Part III: Troubleshooting the PLAN

A. **Securing backup:** List the family members / caregivers with whom you would like to share your gratitude and kindness goals and visions. Choose parts of your PLAN and passages from Chapters 1–8 that you think will help your support team to understand where you're coming from, and then talk about it. Here is my backup:

1.	
2.	
3.	
4.	

B. Predicting roadblocks: Things **within myself** that I will have to be aware of in order to successfully implement the PLAN (my old habits, my busy schedule; my tendency to feel guilty when I say no, etc.), and solutions for each potential roadblock:

1.	Roadblock	
	Solution	
2.	Roadblock	
	Solution	
3.	Roadblock	
	Solution	
4.	Roadblock	
	Solution	

C. **Predicting roadblocks:** Those **within our family** environment that I will have to be aware of in order to successfully implement the PLAN (family members who will not actively cooperate in the PLAN; family traditions that do not support the PLAN; special events that may not support the PLAN, etc.), and solutions for each potential roadblock:

1.	Roadblock	
	Solution	
2.	Roadblock	
	Solution	
3.	Roadblock	
	Solution	
4.	Roadblock	
	Solution	

D. How I will stay on track: Structural aides that will help keep me focused on the PLAN (where I will post the Family Values; where I will place reminders to myself about doing my positive modeling behavior; when I will structure the family's gratitude meetings or gratitude journaling; when we will negotiate and discuss the Family Currency, etc.).

1.	
2.	
3.	
4.	
5.	
6.	

E. Who to call / what do to for support: This is for me/us when beginning the changes or maintaining the changes becomes challenging (keeping up my personal stress management plan of exercising through the week; journaling; speaking with members of my parenting group; having like-minded family and friends on speed dial to call for encouragement if I run out of steam, etc.).

1.	
2.	
3.	
4.	
5.	
6.	

Appendix 3 - Family Gratitude Dialogue

Expressing gratitude and appreciation for family members will help to strengthen family bonds and ward off feelings of entitlement. As we have said all along, we need to express gratitude by doing it (physical action), writing it (gratitude journaling), and speaking it (gratitude dialogue). A gratitude dialogue can be a powerful way of creating a family atmosphere where parents can model their gratitude and appreciation for each other.

Try this Gratitude Dialogue SCRIPT with your children or spouse:

Three Steps:

1.	**I am grateful to you for... (when I saw/heard)**	
	telling the children to keep their voices down because mom needs some extra rest	
2.	**I felt... (grateful, cared for, loved, etc.)**	
	so thankful to you	
3.	**because ...**	
	I feel so supported and cared for by you. It's another reminder of the nice things you do for me.	

Practice Gratitude Dialogue Exercise:

	I am grateful to you for... (when I saw/heard)
1.	
	I felt (grateful, cared for, loved, etc.)
2.	
	because ...
3.	

Appendix 4 - The True Meaning of 'Yes'

Read this every time your gut tells you that "yes" might not be the answer you want to give.

What damage is really caused when we give in to our children's whining, negotiating, flattery, demands, or anger? Entitlement is fostered when we allow emotional manipulation—whether it be demands, threats, misbehavior, or "buttering up"—to trigger our emotional underbellies.

If a child has become entitled, the child only ever wants—in a seemingly never-ending fashion. There is always something new, something better...and the emotional (not to mention financial) cost of having an entitled child or teen is astronomical.

When you say "yes" (when you want to say "no"), a couple of things happen:

- **Your child is manipulating you to get what they want, and while the power of persuasion is useful in adult business relationships, effective adult persuasion has rational thought and good information as fuel—not whining.**

- **Rewarding inappropriate persuasion techniques sets our children up for failure in the world outside of your family. A child that will not accept a "no" for an answer is asserting his or her right to have whatever they want. This makes it clear that they can get away with anything and have anything—which is destructive for a child or teen.**

When you say "yes" to your child without a solid framework about why they have earned the "yes"—how it makes sense in the family currency—you are giving him or her permission to be entitled. You are letting them know that it is okay to believe that "yes" is the rule, their right, and what they should expect. When our children reach adulthood, if someone else has not enlightened them to the fact that "yes" needs to be earned, the rest of the world will not find their expectations as charming. Our children will struggle on every level—at college, with relationships, and at work.

We know that when a child hears a "yes" when they have not earned it, or when they have cheated or manipulated a "yes" out of us in a fashion that does not make sense in terms of our family values, they feel less happy, proud, and fulfilled, on average, with the "yes." Think of how much better an A used to feel in school when we worked our butts off for it than when we gave a half-hearted effort and seemed to luck into high marks. When we work for something, and when our payoff feels valid and fair and right, it feels better. We feel better about ourselves, and better about our environment.

This is the true meaning of saying "yes" too often. The more we say "yes" to buying them candy, toys, clothes, or other items they covet every time we are at the market, the more they will believe that it is normal. They will expect it each and every time, growing in entitlement and feeling worse about themselves (maybe even feeling like a cheater) and worse about us (maybe that we are weak or easily foiled) on each occasion. When a child that has become used to an entitled way of life does not get what they want, they are confused, upset, and unable to cope.

Let's work to make "yes" an obtainable goal for our children to reach, give them clarity regarding what it takes to receive a "yes," and help them to feel proud and worthy when they hear one.

Appendix 5 - Crush Entitlement—20 Random Acts of Kindness

You Can Do These as a Family

Ideas:

1. Make a care pack for the homeless. Simple toiletries can be very helpful—shampoo, soap, deodorant—AND add an inspirational note or a poem to the package.

2. Donate used books to the library.

3. Pay for the meal or coffee for the person behind you in line.

4. Do a household chore for someone.

5. Adopt a family at your child's school to help with school supplies, food, and warm clothing.

6. Prepare a box lunch for your child's teacher.

7. Write a "thank you" note to your mail carrier.

8. Volunteer at the food bank.

9. Buy dessert for a stranger.

10. Return grocery carts.

11. Write a "thank you" note to your police or fire department.

12. Share inspirational quotes with friends and family members once a week.

13. Let someone go in front of you in line.

14. Share a snack with classmates or co-workers.

15. Say "good morning" to people.

16. Say "I love you" to someone.

17. Put a coin in an expired meter.

18. Offer to babysit for a new mom or a single mother.

19. Give up complaining for 21 days.

20. Sincerely compliment someone every day.

References

Algoe, S. B. (2012). Find, remind, and bind: The functions of gratitude in everyday relationships. *Social and Personality Psychology Compass, 6,* 455-469.

Algoe, S. B., Haidt, J., & Gable, S. L. (2008). Beyond reciprocity: Gratitude and relationships in everyday life. *Emotion, 8,* 425-429.

Algoe, S. B., Gable, S. L. & Maisel, N. C. (2010). It's the Little Things: Everyday Gratitude as a Booster Shot for Romantic Relationships. *Personal Relationships, 17,* 217–233.

Baumgarten-Tramer, F. (1938). Gratefulness in children and young people. *Journal of Genetic Psychology, 53,* 53-66.

Drabman, R.S., & Jarvie, G. (1977). Counseling parents of children with behavior problems: The use of extinction and time-out techniques, *Pediatrics, 59,* 78-85.

Dodge, J. A., Janz, N. K. & Clark, N. M. (2002). The evolution of an innovative heart disease management program for older women: Integrating quantitative and qualitative methods in practice. *Health Promotion Practice, 3,* 30–42.

Dunn, E., & Norton, M. (2013). *Happy Money: The Science of Smarter Spending.* New York: Free Press Simon & Schuster.

Ericsson, K.A., & Simon, H.A. (1984). *Protocol Analysis:* Verbal Reports as Data. Cambridge, MA: MIT.

Emmons, R.A. (2007). *Thanks! How the Science of Gratitude Can Make You Happier.* Boston, MA: Houghton Mifflin Company.

Emmons, R.A., & McCullough, M.E. (2003). Counting blessings versus burdens: An experimental investigation of gratitude and subjective well-being in daily life. *Journal of Personality and Social Psychology, 54,* 377-389.

Falk, A., & Fischbacher, U. (2006). A theory of reciprocity. *Games and Economic Behavior, 54,* 293-315.

Isen, A. (1984). *Toward understanding the role of affect in cognition.* In P. Wyer & T. Srull (Eds.) Handbook of Social Cognition. Vol. 3. 179-236. Hillsdale, NJ.: Earlbaum.

Luchins, A.S. (1940). Mechanization in problem solving: The effect of Eistelling, *Psychological Monographs, 54,* 248.

Lyubomirsky, S. (2013). *The Myths of Happiness: What Should Make You Happy, but Doesn't, What Shouldn't Make You Happy.* Penguin Press.

McCullough, M. E., Tsang, J. A., & Emmons, R. A. (2004). Gratitude in intermediate affective terrain: Links of grateful moods to individual differences and daily emotional experience. *Journal of Personality and Social Psychology, 86,* 295–309.

McIntosh, B., (1989). Spoiled child syndrome. *Pediatrics. 83*, 108-115.

McCullough, M., Emmons, R.A., & Tsang, J. (2002). The grateful disposition: A conceptual and empirical topography. *Journal of Personality and Social Psychology, 82*, 112-127.

Mueller, C.M. & Dweck, C.S. (1998). Intelligence praise can undermine motivation and performance. *Journal of Personality and Social Psychology, 75*, 33-52.

Nielson, M. & Tomaselli, K. (2010). Overimitation in kalahari bushman children and the origins of human cultural cognition. *Psychological Science, 21*, 729-736

Ory, M. G., Jordan, P. J., & Bazzarre, T. (2002). The behavior change consortium: Setting the stage for a new century of health behavior-change research. *Health Education Research, 17*, 500-511.

Patterson, G.R., Littman, R.A. & Bricker, W. (1967). Assertive Behavior In Children: A Step Toward a Theory of Aggression. *Monographs for the Society for Research in Child Development, 32*, 1-43.

Piaget, J. (1952). *The Origins of Intelligence in Children.* International Universities Press Inc.

Prochaska, J.O., DiClemente, C.C., & Norcross, J.C. (1992). In search of how people change: Applications to addictive behaviors. *American Psychologist, 47*, 1102-14.

Prochaska, J. O., & Velicer, W. F. (1997). The transtheoretical model of behavior change. *American Journal of Health Promotion, 12*, 38–48.

Seligman, M.E.P. (2002). *Authentic Happiness: Using the New Positive Psychology to Realize Your Potential for Lasting Fulfillment.* New York: Free Press Simon & Schuster.

Seligman, M.E.P., Steen, T.A., Park, N., & Peterson, C. (2005). Positive psychology progress: Empirical validation of interventions. *American Psychologist, 60*, 410.

Tushman, M., & Romanelli, E. (1985). *Organizational evolution: A metamorphosis model of convergence and reorientation.* In L.L. Cummings and B. M. Straw (Eds). Research in Organization Behavior, 7, 171-222 Geenwich, CT: JAI Press.

Wood, A. M, Froh, J. J., & Geraghty, A. (2010). Gratitude and well-being: A review and theoretical Integration [Special Issue]. *Clinical Psychology Review, 30*, 890-905.

Online Resources:

Dictionary.com, dictionary.reference.com

Merriam-Webster, www.merriam-webster.com

Oxford English Dictionary, www.oed.com

Would-Be Empty Nesters Grapple With Adult Child at Home – Tips For Parents With Adult Children at Home, National Endowment For Financial Education, http://www.nefe.org/press-room/news/living-with-adult-children-at-home.aspx.

Positive Psychology: Harnessing the power of happiness, mindfulness, and personal strength, Harvard Health Publications. (2013)

About the Authors

Carla Fry, Psy.D.,
Registered Psychologist

Dr. Carla Fry was born in Western Canada and grew up appreciating the clean air and great outdoors of the Rocky Mountains, Pacific Ocean, and wide-open prairies. She was inspired by many strong family members, a number of whom were women of atypical character.

Dr. Fry spent more time in figure skating rinks than in shoes as a youth. Her career working with children began with her first job as a teen teaching young hockey players and figure skaters.

She was fortunate enough to be exposed to the field of psychology at the tender age of 13 by an innovative grade school teacher. Since that time, Dr. Fry has been an avid people watcher, and has had the privilege as a psychologist, to help thousands of children, youth, and adults to "maximize their happy" (a Dr. Carla-ism).

Positive Psychology's research and applications are woven in to her writing, speaking, consulting, and treatment. She lives thankfulness as much as she spreads it, and is grateful—in no particular order—for the smell of fresh cut grass, her kids, popcorn, and warm tropical trade winds in the evening.

Lisa Ferrari, Psy.D.,
Registered Psychologist

A life-long Vancouverite, Dr. Lisa Ferrari loves the city in which she lives and works.

Dr. Ferrari comes from a large, close-knit family that spans the globe. It was this family that planted the seeds for growing her passion to help children and parents strengthen their family bonds.

Balancing her thriving psychology practice with teaching as a professor in graduate counseling psychology programs, Dr. Ferrari also enjoys sharing her expertise when called upon by television media, professional groups, and local organizations.

Dr. Ferrari delights in the beaches, cuisine, and traditions of her Mediterranean roots. She loves to travel and spend time with her large family and vast network of childhood friends. Gratitude runs deep in her veins, whether the topic of conversation is black tea, her daughter's daily antics, her adopted rescue dog, or projects that foster resilience in children and families.

For more information on Dr. Carla Fry and Dr. Lisa Ferrari visit www.realparentinglab.com

CPSIA information can be obtained at www.ICGtesting.com
Printed in the USA
LVOW07s1216080116

469678LV00025B/832/P